MARKETING INFORMATION SYSTEMS

Marketing Information Systems

DESIGN AND APPLICATIONS FOR MARKETERS

VAN MAYROS AND
D. MICHAEL WERNER

CHILTON BOOK COMPANY · RADNOR, PENNSYLVANIA

Published in Radnor, Pennsylvania 19089, by Chilton Book Company
and simultaneously in Scarborough, Ontario, Canada,
by Nelson Canada Limited
Library of Congress Catalog Card No. 81-69051
ISBN 0-8019-7133-0
Designed by Jean Callan King/Visuality
Manufactured in the United States of America

1 2 3 4 5 6 7 8 9 0 1 0 9 8 7 6 5 4 3 2

CONTENTS

PREFACE

This book is about the identification, retrieval, and use of marketing information. We have taken a "how-to" approach, working from the viewpoint of a marketing manager, who today requires MKIS guidelines for determining (1) what information is needed, (2) where it can be obtained, and (3) how it can be reported and used. You do not have to be a computer programmer to use our applications. You do have to be a marketing practitioner (manager, planner, or analyst) who needs answers to questions that require the gathering and use of information.

The Marketing Information System guidelines presented here can be used as a model in any business organization. They are general enough to allow sections to be removed and used independently of the others. Yet the segments of our MKIS model are linked to one another. In other words, when designing your own MKIS, the model can be adopted in part or as a whole.

Our MKIS design, development, applications, and enhancement are an outgrowth of years of study and corporate applications work in Marketing. Because we have found that most of the current literature surrounding MKIS is short, theoretical, and vague, we have tried in our approach to be less theoretical and more explicit, and to give real-world applications.

While we are solely responsible for the final product, we would like to express our sincere appreciation to several individuals: To Jean Jones, who was responsible for our preliminary drafts and designs; to Ann Van De Water for her extreme dedication and exceptional abilities; to Roxann Mayros for her insight and assistance from conception to completion; and to Mariana Werner for her understanding and good humor.

SECTION I

DESIGN

Introduction to Marketing Information Systems

The Role of the MKIS in the Corporate Environment

Managing Marketing Information

CHAPTER 1

Introduction to Marketing Information Systems

Scope of the Book

Marketing Information Systems, written for the marketing practitioner, concentrates on the applications that the marketing manager, systems analyst, or general business manager will encounter in his daily work activities when dealing with an MKIS, or Marketing Information System. Our major emphasis will be on MKIS applications that help solve marketing problems and answer fundamental marketing questions. As such, the book goes beyond the technical level of just designing and implementing a marketing system.

While the framework of this or any other MKIS lends itself to computer use for data storage and reporting, this is not a book about computers or about the methods of computer programming. If your job requires making marketing decisions, our goal is to acquaint you with the systems tools that are available for your daily analyses and planning. If, on the other hand, you are a computer programmer or systems analyst who must deal with the marketing-management team, our goal is to acquaint you with the unique needs of the people you must deal with.

Not everything in this book will be or should be computerized. The principles we advocate of applying a systems approach to organizing marketing information can also be used in manual operations. Although you will probably rely on computer support for much of your system, we emphasize information needs and applications first, and then the use of a computer. The computer is a tool, to be used by the MKIS manager in association with the Data Processing manager. Our object here is to show how a specific, useful system can be designed and maintained—most likely with the help of an Electronic Data Processing department.

Applying the MKIS in the Corporate Environment

A systems approach to organizing marketing information is dramatically different from systems used for other business disciplines, such as accounting or payroll. Most business systems handle transactions between parties and deal largely with routine day-to-day operations within a particular functional area. Furthermore, other systems usually are not unique to a given organization.

A payroll system, for example, may be similar in Company A and Company B. Both companies must withhold income taxes from their employees. Both companies also produce the same standard reports detailing who got paid what and when. But although marketing systems from one organization to the next do have some common ground, and although standard detailed sales reports may be similar from Company A to Company B, the applications for specialized information reporting may be radically different.[1] These differences are brought about by the very nature of the marketing discipline itself and the answers it requires of its information system.

Most marketing questions revolve around one of four major areas: sales force, product, customer or market. Many of the questions may not be unique to your organization, but the applications will be. What do sales and marketing managers want to know from their information system?

Sales-Force Questions

1. Who are the best performers and why?
2. Who are the worst performers and why?
3. What attributes are associated with these performers?
4. How many sales representatives do we need?
5. How many sales calls per market segment should we make?
6. What is the optimal compensation plan that will reward good sales performance and also maximize corporate objectives?
7. How are we affected by lost sales representatives?
8. In which territories can we expect the greatest sales improvements?

1. For this reason, we try to be as non-industry-specific as possible. Obviously there will be a great degree of difference between a bank's MKIS and that of an electronics manufacturer. Using our examples as a guide, you should apply your own solutions to your particular problems.

Product Questions

1. How well is each of our products doing?
2. What is the sales history of each product?
3. What is the life cycle of each product?
4. What is the actual and intended return on investment (ROI) of each product?
5. What makes a "good seller?" What are the key determinants?
6. What is the competition doing with similar products?
7. Do we have the "right" products matched to the "right" markets?
8. Where are the potential sales improvements by product line?

Customer Questions

1. Who are our best customers?
2. Who are our worst customers?
3. How many customers have we lost and why?
4. Why did they become dissatisfied?
5. How and why have we gained new customers?
6. Who are our potential customers?
7. How can we reach them?
8. Where are the potential sales improvements by customer?

Market Questions

1. Who are our strongest competitors?
2. What are their strengths and weaknesses?
3. What are their marketing strategies?
4. What resources do they have at their disposal?
5. Which market segment(s) should we target?
6. Where are our new markets located?
7. Where are we making/losing profits?
8. Where are the potential sales improvements by market?

These questions are the most common ones asked by most managers. Yet, depending upon the particulars of your organization, you should be able to come up with many more. As we will show, the first role of the MKIS designer will be to uncover the most relevant questions for his organization. Building a Marketing Information System is an art as well as a technology. To apply systems technology effectively to an MKIS, you must be able to apply a logic to the framework of your organization's key questions.

Beyond the Traditional Marketing Information System

Traditionally, most marketing departments have had to rely on other departments in the company for their information. For example, the accounting department is generally responsible for the periodic reporting of sales activity, and the production department is responsible for reporting product inventory status. We do not approach the MKIS as a way to change the functional reporting responsibilities of these marketing-support departments. Rather, we want to expand Marketing's role in the generation of all marketing-related information. We want to place the responsibility for marketing information clearly in the hands of the marketing manager. For instance, if you need to know how many customers purchased your new product last month and the total amount each customer purchased, it is not enough for the controller of your company to inform you only of the number of units sold. Granted, that is information, but it is not the information you need for intelligent decision-making. Of course, you may still have to go to the accounting, production, and research departments for much of your information, but if you know what you need beforehand, you can approach these marketing supporters with a master plan of your data needs.

The MKIS at its most basic level is created by the other functional areas of your company and by any external information that happens to trickle in. In the basic system (Figure 1.1), note that the arrows go only one way—toward Marketing. The information you get, perhaps randomly and sporadically, is defined for you by other areas of the company and by the external environment. There is little or no interaction between you and

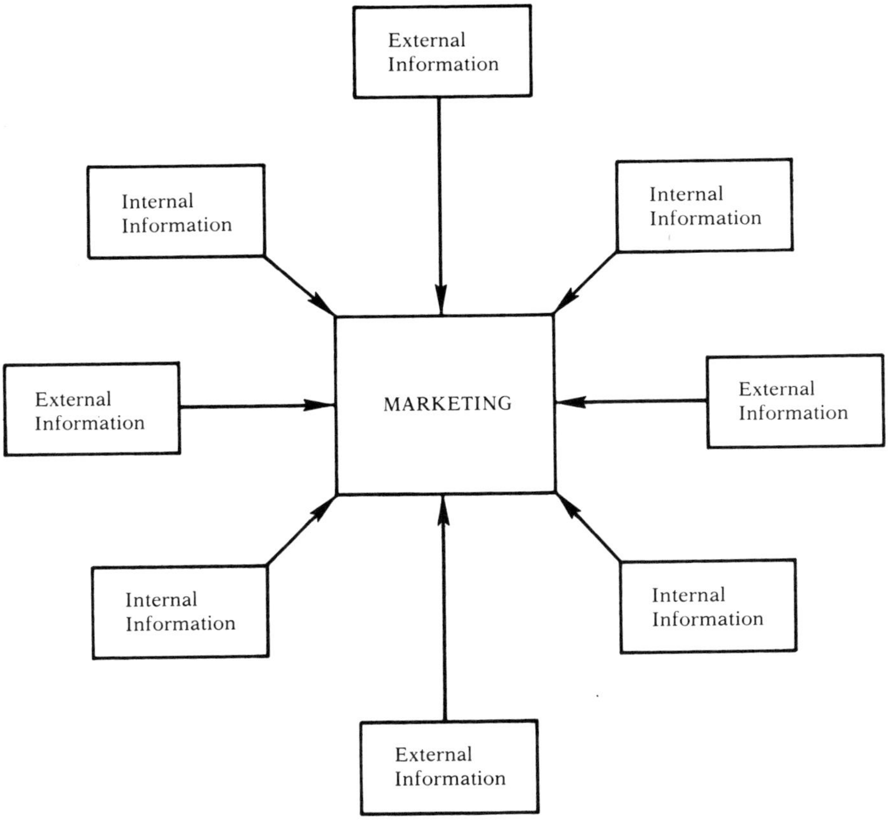

Figure 1.1 The traditional Marketing Information System

your counterparts in other departments. They supply you with information, and you use it *if you can*. There is no policy description for needs from external sources. Unfortunately, this kind of system is the most prevalent one in the business world today. Usually it is developed by a data processing group that fits your requirements around the marketing information supplied to the computer from other departments. Your goal, and ours, will be to change this basic process into one that encourages the flow of information *both* ways, and puts the marketing information you need into a package that you can use.

Regardless of whether you are in marketing or systems, two things are certain:

1. The Marketing Information System sits squarely in the middle of the marketing department's relationship with both other major functional areas of the organization and with sources external to the organization
2. The marketing manager sits squarely in the middle of the MKIS

Figure 1.2 highlights the relationships of the MKIS to the major departments of the company. These relationships represent the process of internal information exchange. Note that the arrows flow both to and from the core of the MKIS. Obviously, for the MKIS to function properly and to

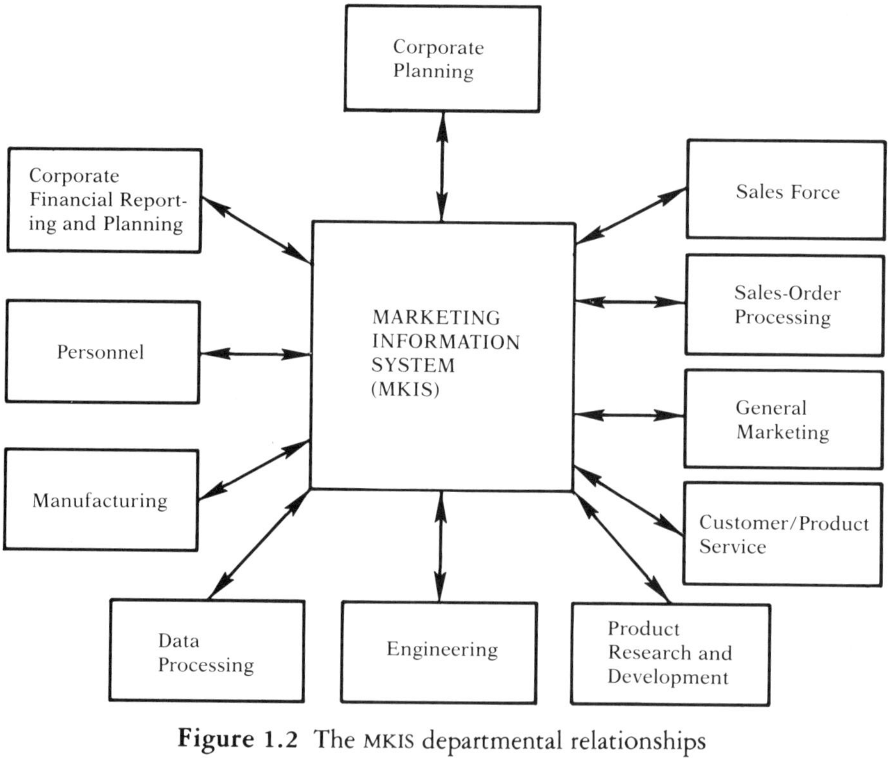

Figure 1.2 The MKIS departmental relationships

be a dynamic system, it has to provide information as well as gather and integrate the responses and needs of its principal partners.

Table 1.1 illustrates the nature of the interplay that should exist between the MKIS and these other departments. It shows the functional inputs that come from the company's major departments and flow into the MKIS. It also shows some of the items (outputs) that might be provided by the MKIS to these related departments. Obviously you may spot one or more areas of input or output that are not included in Table 1.1. We cover input/output topics in much greater detail in the later chapters that deal directly with the MKIS application (Chapters 4 and 6 through 9). Here we want to keep the discussion general and simply restate that the MKIS can and should be the cornerstone around which all marketing-related decisions are made.

Marketing information also comes from sources external to the organization. Marketing management does not exist in a vacuum, immune to outside forces. To answer the key marketing questions and to develop strategic plans, management must be open to what is occurring outside of those relationships that take place between the functional areas within the organization.

Figure 1.3 displays the external side of the relationship fundamental to the Marketing Information System. Again, as with internal sources, the arrows flow both to and from the MKIS. The MKIS requires information that will provide additional insight to enable the user to use external sources for greater strategic applications. Table 1.2 highlights the forms that the external information can take and the ways it can be used by your MKIS.

Figure 1.4 depicts the role of the marketing manager, the major decision-maker, in the Marketing Information System scheme. He is the principal user of the MKIS and the person upon whom the responsibility for effective marketing decision-making and planning lies. By utilizing the statistical models and reports provided by the MKIS, the manager makes policies and recommendations based on a defined process. He is not a "guesstimator" making seat-of-the-pants decisions; rather, he is truly a manager of his department's actions.

TABLE 1.1
Internal Functional Area Inputs to Outputs from the MKIS

FUNCTIONAL AREA	INPUTS TO THE MKIS	PROVIDED BY THE MKIS (OUTPUTS)
• Corporate Planning	• Corporate objectives • Expansion plans	• Measurement of Marketing's progress toward goal attainment • Data for market analyses of new products or new markets
• Sales Force	• Sales • Feedback from the field	• Sales analysis by sales rep
• Sales-Order Processing	• Invoices and shipments • Back-order status	• Sales analysis of product/service lines • Equivalent replacement products; communication to the sales force
• General Marketing: Marketing Research, Planning, Promotion, and Administration	• Types of new products/services with market possibilities • Consumer response to existing products/services • Planning and promotional campaigns	• Data for market analyses of potential new products and customers • Sales analysis of current products/services to current customers • Media and lead analysis
• Customer/Product Service	• Feedback from customers and sales force on product reliability and performance	• Storage media for complaint file and new product ideas
• Product Research and Development	• New-product development schedules	• Proper timing for new-product release and phase-in
• Engineering	• Engineering schedules for products	• Proper timing for new-product release and phase-in
• Data Processing	• System for organizing data files and reporting operating results	• Details of what the marketing group needs in computerized reports
• Manufacturing	• Inventory status	• Forecasts: production and inventory updates
• Personnel	• Background on sales and marketing employees • Salary/performance review data	• Effects of a learning curve for sales force • Determinants for future employee selection
• Corporate Financial Reporting and Planning	• Product pricing and costing • Marketing/sales expenses	• Profitability by product or sales rep

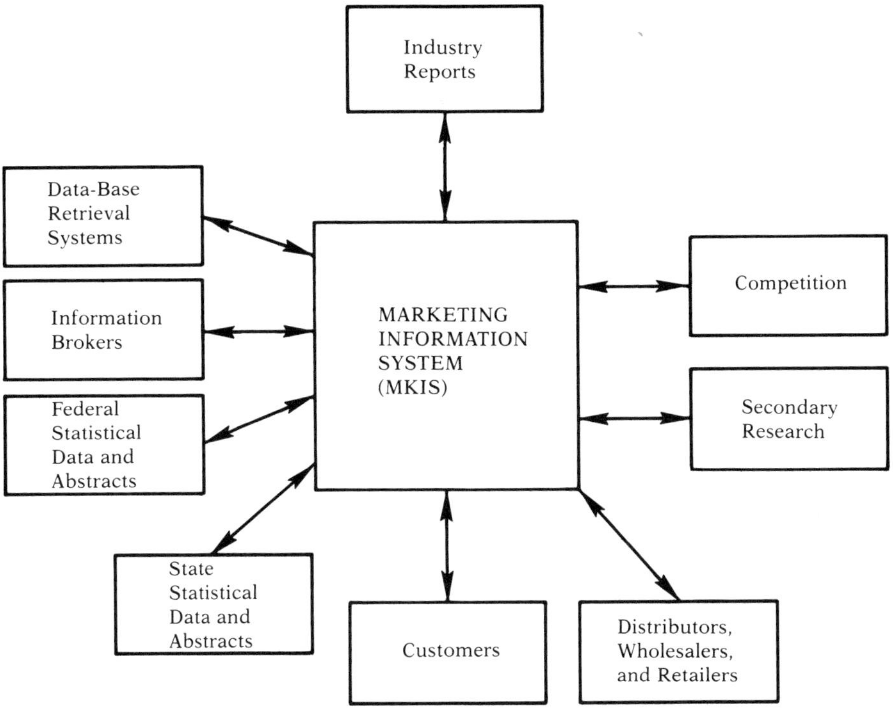

Figure 1.3 MKIS external source relationships

Definition of a Marketing Information System

The MKIS revolves around the decision-making needs of the marketing manager. But just exactly what is a Marketing Information System? Stated most simply, it is an organized set of data that is analyzed through reports or statistical routines (models). The data are transformed from raw numbers into information to help the marketing manager substantiate his general assumptions or to help him provide answers to questions that he may not be sure about (see Figure 1.5).

MARKETING

The marketing manager faces a daily barrage of problems and questions that require him to make decisions about the company's product, custom-

TABLE 1.2
External Functional Area Inputs to Outputs from the MKIS

FUNCTIONAL AREA	INPUTS TO THE MKIS	PROVIDED BY THE MKIS (OUTPUTS)
• Industry Reports	• Corporate data and analysis • Industry news	• Industry growth and trend statistics • New technology and products
• Competition	• Products and product literature • Other corporate literature	• Technology comparisons • Financial comparisons • Capitalization analysis
• Secondary Research	• Special market facts	• Market segmentation and profile
• Distributors, Wholesalers, and Retailers	• Market conditions • Consumer analysis	• Special sales programs • Sales analysis • Pricing policy input • Market segmentation
• Customers	• Profile data • Sales data	• Customer segmentation • Profile analysis • Product history
• State Statistical Data and Abstracts	• Corporate, competitor, and state statistical comparisons • Economic/financial data	• Competitive analysis • Corporate profile • Market-segment analysis
• Federal Statistical Data and Abstracts	• Securities and Exchange Commission data • Department of Commerce Bureau of Census	• Corporate financial profiles • Market potential profile and analyses
• Information Brokers	• Special studies • Market news	• Special customer-segment identification
• Data-Base Retrieval Systems	• News abstracts • Product, market, and industry news and analysis • Economic news	• Changes in product positions, markets, industries • Economic influences on sales potential • News influences on market

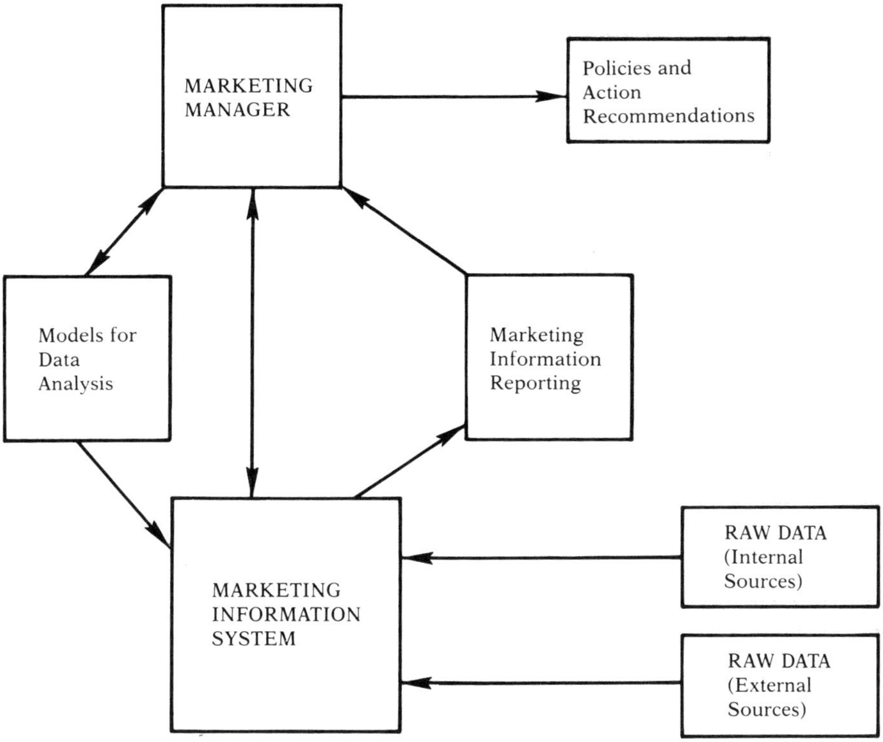

Figure 1.4 The marketing manager and the MKIS

ers, sales force, and markets. In order to answer these marketing questions or to solve these problems, the manager will rely upon his experience and intuition to give him a general "feel" for what the solution should be. But he can make an effective decision only after he has studied information related to the problem or question. This information is generated by the system.

INFORMATION

Information should be distinguished from data. Data are raw numbers. Information is "processed" data that provide more than just a number. If we know that the Flashbright Camera Company sold 15,000 cameras last month, we have raw data. But we do not know if Flashbright had a good sales month or if it is on the verge of losing its market. If we know that the 15,000 units of sales were Flashbright's biggest month of the year, up from 7,000 units in the same month a year ago, then we have information. Now we can use the data, which has been transformed into information, to answer questions or make decisions.

THE SYSTEM

The system is what holds the framework together. It is a unified scheme that brings together all of the components being used (raw data, information, reports, and models) in order to meet your marketing objectives. The

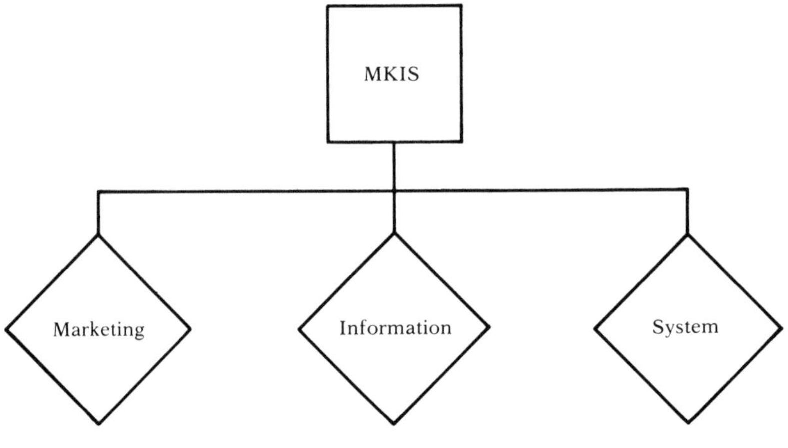

Figure 1.5 The Marketing Information System: A definition

system is the process whereby raw data is extracted from its source (a sales order or an expense report, for example), analyzed through a report or model, and turned into information that can be used to make a decision.

A Note on Organization and Contents

This book is divided into four sections: Section I, *Design* (Chapters 1 through 3), introduces the MKIS and discusses what information is needed to support the marketing function. It includes the Marketing Information Questionnaire and shows how to begin your MKIS design. Section II, *Development* (Chapters 4 and 5), shows you how to define your needs, how to get the information where you want it, and how to put it all together. You will be asked to review the input-output relationships that exist within your organization's departments and to define an MKIS framework that ties your system together. Section III, *Application* (Chapters 6 through 9), applies the framework built in Sections I and II and shows how to use your data to make decisions. Section IV, *Enhancement* (Chapters 10 through 12), deals with the management of the MKIS team and reviews several system alternatives. Chapter 12 provides a step-by-step guide for designing and implementing your Marketing Information System.

At the end of each chapter, we include an Action Plan. If you take your own specific applications, apply them to the concepts contained in each chapter, and follow the guidelines provided in the Action Plans, you will in fact be building your own MKIS. Every MKIS is unique, and no book or manual can build a system for you. But if you take a step-by-step approach and follow the Action Plans, by the time you have finished this book, you will have designed your own Marketing Information System.

How you use this book depends upon your needs. If your interests are primarily in marketing and sales analysis, and if you are not actively designing and/or implementing an MKIS but want to review applications of marketing information, we suggest that you review Chapters 1 (Introduction) and 2 (The Role of the MKIS in the Corporate Environment). Then proceed directly to Section III, *Application*. However, to use the book as a guide to MKIS development and implementation, proceed as follows:

1. Review Chapter 1 (Introduction)
2. Read Chapter 12 (The MKIS Action Plan Checklist)
3. Proceed sequentially from Chapters 2 through 11.

However you use the book, we hope that you will benefit from it. Marketing is the last business discipline to have received attention from computer and information technology. In a very real sense, we are just at the edge of a marketing information frontier. We hope that you will find as much enjoyment exploring the applications along this frontier as we did in writing about them.

Action Plan

1. Make a list of the departments or subdepartments in your organization that interrelate with Marketing. What kinds of general data or information do they provide you? What kinds do you provide them? How does the information exchange take place (meetings, written reports, computer printouts)? Diagram this information exchange process. Also begin to organize your needs for external information.
2. Who is responsible in your company for providing information to the upper levels of marketing management? (Review Figure 1.4).
3. How would you categorize the stage of MKIS development in your organization? Make a tentative schedule of how you would take it from its present stage to the level you view as optimal.
4. Begin an ongoing relationship with your Data Processing and marketing-support departments. Perhaps you can develop a weekly or monthly work session to discuss your information needs. Make sure that you establish objectives for fulfilling your department's needs.

CHAPTER 2

The Role of the MKIS in the Corporate Environment

Knowing Where You Want to Go: The Marketing Information Questionnaire

Before you can define the scope of your MKIS system, you must evaluate your information needs. It is important at this early stage to know what the principal users of your system will expect to obtain from it. If you don't know where your organization is and where it wants to go, it will be difficult to pinpoint your information needs. If you confuse "nice to have" information with "must have" information, you will probably end up with a system that only partially fulfills your requirements.

The Marketing Information Questionnaire (Tables 2.1 A–J) is divided into ten areas: sales, product, consumer, market, marketing planning, market research, promotion, distribution and logistics, lead handling and control, and information access. Of course, you can modify the questions to meet your particular requirements.

The questionnaire contains a total of 116 questions. To evaluate your particular organization's marketing information needs, answer each question in two parts. For the first answer (A), evaluate your organization on a scale of 1 to 10, where 10 is equal to a strong *yes* and 1 is equal to a definite *no*. For the second answer (B), rate the importance of the question to your organization. For example, look at the first question (1A) in the Sales Analysis Questionnaire (Table 2.1A): "Can you currently identify geographical sales by sales representative?" For answer A, you might scale it at 5. In other words, on a scale of 1 to 10, your organization does an average job of measuring/tracking sales by individual sales representative. For answer B, you might scale your response at 10, which means that you feel that it is extremely important for your organization to have accurate and quality sales data by sales representative.

The Marketing Information Questionnaire should be approached honestly and objectively. By doing so, you will have laid a great deal of the preliminary MKIS groundwork. What you should look for are trends in your responses. As in the example above, a 10 response in Column B with only a 5 response in Column A would show that you need to dramatically

(Text continues on page 29)

TABLE 2.1
Marketing Information Questionnaire
Table 2.1A Sales Analysis

	A Performance 1 ( ) 10	*B* Importance 1 ( ) 10
1. Can you identify geographical sales by:		
a. sales representative?	( )	( )
b. distributor?	( )	( )
c. customer type?	( )	( )
d. account type?	( )	( )
e. product type?	( )	( )
f. geographical location?	( )	( )
2. Can you successfully measure cost of sales?	( )	( )
By product line?	( )	( )
3. Can you measure sales by consumer-profile	( )	( )
distinctions? Classifications?	( )	( )
4. Can you measure sales by product line or product class?	( )	( )
5. Can you measure sales (units and dollars) by day, week, month, quarter, and/or year?	( )	( )
6. Can you measure annual gross and net contribution by:		
a. product line?	( )	( )
b. geographical location?	( )	( )
c. consumer type?	( )	( )
7. Can you measure your direct cost of sales?	( )	( )
8. Can you identify any seasonal or cyclical sales variations?	( )	( )
9. Can you measure the average order size by account?	( )	( )
10. Do you know who your "lost" customers are?	( )	( )
11. Do you know who your "inactive" customers are?	( )	( )

Table 2.1B Product Analysis

	A Performance 1 ( ) 10	*B* Importance 1 ( ) 10
1. Does your existing product line(s) satisfy consumer needs and expectations?	( )	( )
2. Do you know why a particular product(s) has a larger volume base than other product(s)?	( )	( )
3. Does your existing and/or proposed product line offer competitive differentiation?	( )	( )
4. Do you know what your competitors' product lines will look like in the future?	( )	( )
5. Can you calculate an expense (fixed, variable, overhead) breakout for each product?	( )	( )
6. Can you identify specific life-cycle stages for each product?	( )	( )
7. Can you identify the status of each product within the product-development life cycle?	( )	( )
8. Can you track (sales by customer) new-product introductions?	( )	( )
9. Are your existing product forecasts accurate?	( )	( )
10. Is your existing pricing policy effective with regard to expenses, competition, and inflation?	( )	( )

Table 2.1C Consumer Analysis

	A Performance 1 ( ) 10	*B* Importance 1 ( ) 10
1. Do you know who your consumers are?	( )	( )
2. Do you know where your consumers are located?	( )	( )
3. Do you know at what point you obtain your consumers?	( )	( )
4. Do you know why your consumers buy from you?	( )	( )
5. Do you know how you obtain your consumers?	( )	( )
6. Have you profiled your total consumer base?	( )	( )
7. Have you identified specific consumer attributes particular to a given product class or product line?	( )	( )
8. Do you know which consumers purchase the largest majority of products?	( )	( )
9. Can you identify and locate your potential consumers?	( )	( )
10. Are you using the most effective means possible to reach your consumer base?	( )	( )

Table 2.1D Market Analysis

	A Performance 1 ( ) 10	B Importance 1 ( ) 10
1. Which geographical area has the greatest capacity (potential) for:		
a. unit sales growth?	( )	( )
b. dollar sales growth?	( )	( )
2. Does your existing sales network (direct or indirect) cover your sales areas adequately?	( )	( )
3. Can you specify why some market areas are better performers than others?	( )	( )
4. Can you identify the characteristics of a successful market area?	( )	( )
5. Do you currently attempt to use answers to Question 3 to direct unique promotional strategies to separate geographical regions?	( )	( )
6. Does your current market information provide sufficient data to measure market growth, decline, trend, change, potential, and/or performance?	( )	( )
7. Do you establish sales quotas based on your knowledge of geographical areas?	( )	( )
8. Do you have a detailed demographic profile for each market segment?	( )	( )
9. Do you know which market segments your products fall into?	( )	( )

Table 2.1E Marketing Planning

	A Performance 1 ( ) 10	*B* Importance 1 ( ) 10
1. Can you identify and measure specific organizational objectives as they relate to Marketing?	( )	( )
2. Can you identify new-product requirements through your consumers?	( )	( )
3. Can you identify specific territories or geographical splits and product introductions or test-market programs?	( )	( )
4. Can you identify which geographical regions have and/or will offer the best return and contribution margin?	( )	( )
5. Can you identify effective and ineffective sales or promotion methods?	( )	( )
6. Do you know where your organization stands with respect to:		
a. organizational identity?	( )	( )
b. marketing identity?	( )	( )
c. market?	( )	( )
d. industry?	( )	( )
e. sales?	( )	( )
f. product?	( )	( )
g. consumer?	( )	( )
7. Have you ever conducted an extensive situational analysis?	( )	( )
8. Do you currently have a formal marketing plan or program?	( )	( )

Table 2.1F Market Research

	A Performance 1 ( ) 10	*B* Importance 1 ( ) 10
1. To what extent are you capable of analyzing particular product-line profitability?	( )	( )
2. Do you know your current market share in units and dollars?	( )	( )
3. Can you calculate (in part or whole) the impact of a competitive new product?	( )	( )
4. Have your past promotion efforts been cost-effective (costs compared to increased sales)?	( )	( )
5. Do you understand your existing/proposed product differentiation picture?	( )	( )
6. Do you know the current product mix of competitors A, B, and C?	( )	( )
7. Do you know the current promotion mix of competitors A, B, and C?	( )	( )
8. Have you tracked your market and/or consumer profile over the last five years?	( )	( )
9. To what extent do you currently engage in either primary or secondary market research?	( )	( )

Table 2.1G Promotion Analysis

	A Performance 1 ( ) 10	*B* Importance 1 ( ) 10
1. To what extent do you know to whom to direct specific methods of promotion?	( )	( )
2. To what extent are you achieving maximum promotional efficiency?	( )	( )
3. How well can you measure the results of each promotion strategy?	( )	( )
4. Can you track whether your existing or past promotion activity has had any impact on sales volume?	( )	( )
5. How well can you control the direction or pace of your products' life cycles through promotion?	( )	( )
6. Can you calculate promotion from a cost-benefit analysis?	( )	( )
7. Can you identify which past promotion programs were better than current programs?	( )	( )

Table 2.1H Distribution and Logistics

	A Performance 1 ( ) 10	*B* Importance 1 ( ) 10
1. Does the nature of your product line dictate special or unique distribution channels?	( )	( )
2. Can you identify your distribution costs?	( )	( )
3. Does your distribution network foster Marketing's effectiveness?	( )	( )
4. Can you respond to different consumer concerns, needs, and expectations through your distribution network?	( )	( )
5. Can you identify the cost of an average service or sales call?	( )	( )
6. Can you calculate and analyze:		
a. inventory control costs?	( )	( )
b. actual shipping costs?	( )	( )
c. carrying costs?	( )	( )
d. service or follow-up costs?	( )	( )
e. physical location costs?	( )	( )
7. Can you prepare and analyze which distribution method or network is most effective?	( )	( )
8. Does your distribution network promote effective two-way communication between your company and your consumers?	( )	( )
9. Does your distribution network lend itself to promotion, consumer cultivation, and/or competitive data and information?	( )	( )

Table 2.1I Lead Handling and Control

	A Performance 1 ( ) 10	*B* Importance 1 ( ) 10
1. How well do you currently develop potential customer lists from one or more types of inquiries?	( )	( )
2. How well do you identify the location and the actual number of leads you receive?	( )	( )
3. How well do you answer all leads?	( )	( )
4. Can you consistently prioritize your leads?	( )	( )
5. How well do you work with your distribution network to take advantage of leads?	( )	( )
6. How well can you measure the actual sales volume resulting from lead inquiries?	( )	( )

Table 2.1J Information Access

	A Performance 1 ( ) 10	*B* Importance 1 ( ) 10
1. Does your organization require additional data or informational sources for market research, promotion plans, marketing strategies?	( )	( )
2. Do you currently have effective external data source lists?	( )	( )
3. Do you routinely structure and use external information?	( )	( )
4. Does your existing information system provide sufficient informational support to conduct:		
a. situational analysis?	( )	( )
b. consumer profiles?	( )	( )
c. consumer segmentation?	( )	( )
d. market segmentation?	( )	( )
e. sales analysis?	( )	( )
f. product analysis?	( )	( )
g. marketing planning?	( )	( )
h. market research?	( )	( )
5. Do you have ongoing access to:		
a. an in-house computer?	( )	( )
b. timesharing?	( )	( )
c. mini-micro computer?	( )	( )
d. computer graphics?	( )	( )
e. computerized statistical models?	( )	( )

improve your sales reporting system, at least at the level of the sales representative. If you want to compare your current effectiveness across the ten areas covered in the questionnaire, complete the following steps:

1. For each Table, sum up your answers for Column A
2. Sum up your answers for Column B
3. Subtract your Column A total from your Column B total

4. Divide the difference obtained in step 3 by the number of responses in that Table

The results can be used to compare one section of the questionnaire with another. The higher the average difference between B and A answers, the higher the relative importance of that section of questions. In fact, you may want to rank the B-A average for each Table in order to provide an initial priority list in designing your MKIS. Of course, keep in mind that only you can evaluate whether going from a 4 to an 8 is more important than going from a 7 to a 10.

Understanding Your Corporate and Marketing Environment

As you use the Marketing Information Questionnaire, you will begin to see how your organization regards information and its uses. But you will still have to go beyond this before you can begin to design your MKIS. Every organization must understand what needs its product or service satisfies within the consumer environment. Every organization must also identify its purpose and goals. In other words, the organization must define what it is, where it has been, and where it is going so that it can better evaluate new opportunities as they arise. For example, if your company is heavily involved in acquisitions as a means of increasing growth, you will want your MKIS to provide data/information for adequately handling requests with respect to the market aspects of new ventures. Or, if your company views increased sales as coming from existing product lines, for your MKIS to be an effective tool, you will have to provide a solid information base for analyzing product sales trends, target marketing, and customer and field product-line feedback. The goal at this point is straightforward: You must grasp the essentials of your organization's information needs. Of course, you cannot anticipate all future needs, but by understanding where your organization seems to be heading, you will be better equipped to build an effective MKIS that can handle future requests.

As you begin to take an overall look at the corporate environment that influences information needs, you will have to narrow your focus and look at the marketing unit as a separate entity. In many instances, your corporate goals and your marketing goals will be identical. However, as you explore the marketing environment, you may begin to notice several subtle differences. One of those differences is in the thinking of a sales executive and that of the marketing executive.

In his article "From Sales Obsession to Marketing Effectiveness,"[1] Philip Kotler contrasts the ways in which these two executives think about their corporate goals. Table 2.2 highlights the key distinctions that Kotler has observed.

Without question, each component in Table 2.2 has direct implications for every MKIS. Although we are not trying to argue for the "right" way of thinking, a great deal of evidence supports the trend away from "sales thinking" toward "marketing thinking." Yet, if you are involved in MKIS design or implementation, you will have to be aware of both ways of thinking. To provide access to the data, your MKIS will have to address the requirements of both sales and marketing.

The MKIS implications of the sales executives' way of thinking include:

1. A focus on sales numbers, both units and dollars. The sales executive will want to know who the best product and field performers are (distributor, sales representative), based on sales volume alone. He will tend to shy away from performance measurements based on profitability or profit contribution. The sales executive will also be very comfortable with reporting applications that record sales and sales performance by sales volume.
2. A tendency to "fight fires" rather than concentrating on future planning. The sales executive will require straightforward report applications: Who is buying what and in what quantities? The focus is usually on time periods (month, quarter, and fiscal year).

1. Philip Kotler, "From Sales Obsession to Marketing Effectiveness," *Harvard Business Review*, November-December 1977, pp. 67-75.

TABLE 2.2
The Differences in the Way Sales Executives and Marketing Executives Think

SALES EXECUTIVES	MARKETING EXECUTIVES
1. *Sales Volume Rather than Profits* Sales executives aim to increase current sales to meet quota commitments and to achieve good commissions and bonuses. They are usually not attentive to profit differences among different products or customer classes unless these are reflected in compensation.	1. *Profit Planning* Marketing executives plan sales volume around profits. Their aim is to plan product mixes, customer mixes, and marketing mixes to achieve profitable volume and market shares at acceptable levels of risk.
2. *Short-Run Rather than Long-Run Terms* Sales executives are oriented toward today's products, markets, customers, and strategies. They tend not to think about product/market expansion strategies over the next five years.	2. *Long-Run Trends, Threats, and Opportunities* Marketing executives study how the company can translate these into new products, markets, and marketing strategies that will assure long-term growth.
3. *Individual Customers Rather than Market-Segment Classes* Sales executives are knowledgeable about individual accounts and the factors bearing on a specific sales transaction. They are less interested in developing strategies for market segments.	3. *Customer Types and Segment Differences* Marketing executives try to figure out how to offer superior value to the most profitable segments.
4. *Field Work Rather than Desk Work* Sales executives try to sell to customers instead of developing plans and strategies and working out methods of implementation.	4. *Good Systems for Market Analysis, Planning, and Control* Marketing executives are comfortable with numbers and with working out the financial implications of marketing plans.

Source: Reprinted by permission of the Harvard Business Review. Excerpt from "From Sales Obsession to Marketing Effectiveness" by Philip Kotler.

3. A micro view of the organization's customers. The sales executive will probably know a great deal about certain customers (particularly those he dealt with when he was a sales representative), but he will not be able to classify them into market or consumer segments. As a consequence, the sales executive will want to see sales reports by individual customer.

If your MKIS design is to be slanted toward the needs of the sales executive, you will want to focus on the report applications found in Chapters 6 and 7 (*Sales Management Report Applications* and *Product Data Bank Report Applications*), and use chapters 8 and 9 for background information.

The MKIS implications of the marketing executives' way of thinking include:

1. A desire to review product and sales profitability and to go beyond "just sales numbers." The marketing executive usually measures product and field performance from a P&L standpoint. Therefore, he will require report applications that provide this emphasis.
2. An inclination to look for trends. The marketing executive will require more information than the sales executive in an effort to uncover where the organization's product and field performances have been and where they are going. He will also look more at customers' (aggregated into segments) buying habits. The marketing executive usually requires report applications that group products, customers, and sales representatives into common categories.

If your organizational requirements necessitate an MKIS that is oriented toward the "marketing way of thinking," you will probably want to focus your report applications on those found in Chapters 8 and 9 (*Consumer Data Bank Report Applications* and *Market Data Bank Report Applications*), and deal more generally with Chapters 6 and 7.

Of course, there is often a very fine line between the sales and marketing mentality, so you will want to consider both when designing your MKIS. If your organization is moving from a sales to marketing orientation, you will have to capture adequate amounts of sales data as well as plan to include marketing-oriented applications.

Tying Together Corporate and Marketing Needs and Objectives

A Marketing Information System has one purpose: to provide accurate and timely data and/or information to management decision-makers. Thus, the designer of the system must know what their most frequent requests are likely to be. A good way of doing this is to take a look at how corporate and marketing objectives filter down through the organization. Figure 2.1 illustrates a general schematic of this top-down direction.

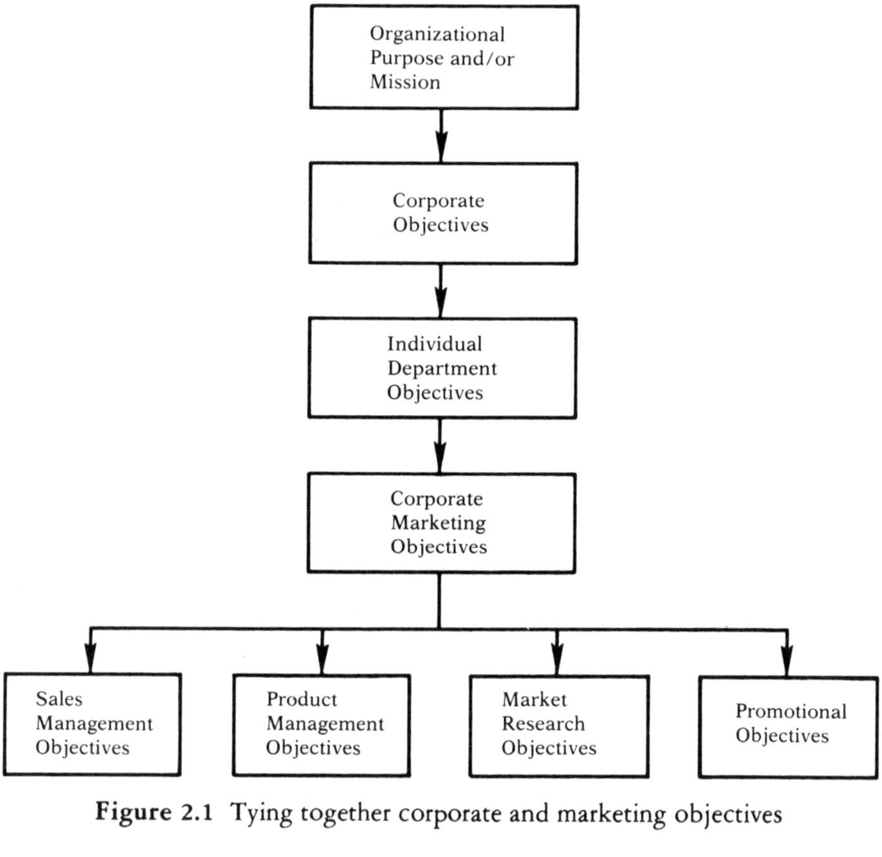

Figure 2.1 Tying together corporate and marketing objectives

To illustrate further how objectives filter down and ultimately tie to an organization's plans for designing an MKIS, let's consider what might happen in a hypothetical company, the Baker Brewing Company, a producer and distributor of beer and ale.

Phase 1: Baker's Board of Directors has determined that the company's effort during the next five years should be geared toward increasing Earnings per Share (EPS) at an average yearly rate of at least 20 percent. Further, because of various restrictions, they have also decreed that this growth must come from existing product lines or those already in internal development, because no further acquisitions can occur.

Phase 2: Given the broad outline provided from the Board, the upper levels of Baker's management team have devised a set of three corporate objectives for the upcoming fiscal year:

a. Increase unit sales in each of its product lines by at least 20 percent

b. Decrease production costs on a per-unit basis by 8 percent.

c. Maintain distribution costs on a per-unit basis at levels equal to or lower than current costs.

Phase 3: With the three corporate objectives in place, the Board then set up secondary goals for each functional area within the company. If each subgoal can be met, the three corporate objectives can be achieved. One of the goals of Research and Development, for example, might be to develop two new products for the highly profitable malt-liquor market. The Personnel Department might be asked to institute training programs to help increase production efficiency. Similar goals could be set in place for all areas of the company.

As the goals for corporate marketing become established, the implications for the Marketing Information System become more direct. Table 2.3 provides a view of the link that exists between several of Marketing's objectives and the MKIS. As you review the objectives in the Table, note that virtually every marketing objective and most corporate objectives

TABLE 2.3
Marketing Objectives–MKIS Implications, Baker Brewing Company, Fiscal Year 1983

OBJECTIVE	MKIS IMPLICATIONS
1. Increase Misty Malt unit sales by 35 percent or more	1a. Be able to monitor past sales by distributor in order to set quotas 1b. Be able to forecast and track sales by distributor 1c. Identify target consumer segments
2. Maintain Light Bake beer at its current 18-percent market share	2a. and 2b. Same as 1a. and 1b. 2c. Be able to monitor competitive sales by geographic area
3. Complete a market segmentation analysis for all market segments in which Baker is involved	3a. Segment definition 3b. Portfolio Analysis of each segment: Baker product positioning versus the competition
4. Develop consumer profiles for all of Baker's segments	4a. Be able to store and retrieve primary and secondary market-research data 4b. Develop the capability to link 4a. to actual consumer purchases
5. Maintain distribution costs at current levels	5a. Be able to track per-unit expenses through a distributor profit-and-loss system.
6. Expand promotional mix on all Baker's Ale products	6a. Be able to correlate promotional expenses to sales activity

have a link to the MKIS. What this means is that you will have to track all objectives, both explicit and implicit, on a regular basis in order to ensure that they are covered by the MKIS.

Establishing Communication Between Marketing (User) and Data Processing Management

Once you have uncovered the corporate and marketing objectives that will have an impact on your MKIS design, you will be ready to pursue a system's work relationship with your Data Processing Department. One approach that you could take might include the following four steps:

1. Analyze all of the components of the current sales and marketing report system. You should be able to document who is using which report (or on-line screen) to obtain what data.
2. Document the relationship between the corporate and marketing objectives and strategies and your present information system. As you prepare a list of objectives to MKIS linkages, as shown in Table 2.3, you should list those information needs that are currently not being fulfilled by the present system.
3. Begin a "planned interface" with Data Processing management. Establish a formal informational exchange session between Marketing and DP and include such topics as contents and structure of files, the sources of file and report contents, data-access methods, current edit and maintenance procedures, and proposed DP changes. The goal of this interface is to enable each side to evaluate the current system. This interchange will allow Marketing and Data Processing to develop an expanded MKIS framework. (The "how-to" of this framework development will be addressed in Chapters 3 and 4).
4. Provide a documented outline of how the marketing/sales objectives will affect the need for broader informational support, expanding on Step 2.

In order to foster an effective relationship between Marketing and Data Processing, three basic attitudes are necessary for early success.

1. System involvement must be initiated by Marketing, the user department. Faced with constant machine, system, and personnel problems, Data Processing in most cases will not seek out more work from Marketing. The saying that "no news is good news" is certainly valid from the systems analyst's viewpoint concerning his user relationships.
2. The Marketing Information System is an ongoing system and as such will require discipline and organization from start to finish. One

person should be given the overall responsibility of designing the system and spearheading its implementation.

3. The system should be managed all the way through to the upper levels of management. All decision-makers must be involved for the system to be a success. Because so much of a good MKIS will be future oriented, it will take strong management involvement to keep it moving, particularly when day-to-day DP crises begin to infringe upon DP support time. In addition, involvement at all levels will provide a greater degree of synergy.

In short, the Marketing–Data Processing commitment to open, effective communication will lead ultimately to an accurate assessment of what your organization's marketing data needs are.

How Data Processing and Marketing Management View One Another

The Data Processing manager's concept of Marketing is often a limited one, due to the problems and pressures he faces within his own department. First, there are never enough people. Second, there is never enough machine time. Problems occur because of these two shortages, and they are compounded by the fact that DP generally receives many more user requests than it can process. Most DP people are technicians with little, if any, business or marketing background. The result is that the "pushy" users tend to get most of the attention and service.

The Data Processing manager tends to view Marketing as:

1. The taking and filling of orders
2. Market and consumer analyses are "extras" that can be tacked on to existing sales-order entry systems
3. Always wanting to have more data than can possibly be used

The consequences of these attitudes are:

1. The existing Marketing Information System becomes heavily sales-reporting based

2. The system becomes bogged down with too much data (sales orders) and not enough information
3. Because marketing may be looking for more from its system than Data Processing knows how to provide, the potential for communication problems arises

On the other hand, the marketing manager's view of his Data Processing Department is clouded by misconceptions about the true nature of computers. Like most of us, the marketing manager tends to shy away from computers and systems technology. Yet he also expects them to be able to perform miracles in data manipulation. To say "we'll just let the computer do it" is much easier said than done. Very few non-DP management people can appreciate the complexities of designing and implementing a computer system.

The marketing manager tends to view Data Processing as:

1. A group of people with a sophisticated machine who cannot make it work effectively
2. Prone to be more involved in financial and manufacturing applications than in marketing
3. Unable to fulfill "simple" requests

Many of these attitudes, on both sides, have evolved over the years because there was actually very little use of the computer for marketing applications. As this changes, and as Marketing Information Systems become a force in every organization, many of the communication problems will naturally disappear. Until that time, though, those of us involved in MKIS design must encourage marketing people to take the initial step at bridging the gap.

Action Plan

STEP 1: UNDERSTANDING THE CORPORATE AND MARKETING ENVIRONMENT

1. What are the distinctions between sales and marketing in your organization? Make a two-column list of the differences.
2. How do marketing/sales objectives relate to your corporate-management objectives?
3. How are corporate goals and objectives translated into marketing plans? Can you re-create the relationship in Table 2.3?

STEP 2: DATA PROCESSING-MARKETING COMMUNICATION

1. How is communication between the two departments now handled?
2. Who sets the priorities? Who *should* set the priorities?
3. What procedures should you establish to make the Data Processing-Marketing communication process run more smoothly? Try to define frequently used Marketing and DP terminology in order to avoid ambiguities.
4. Identify initial MKIS objectives as they relate to DP management and corporate objectives.

CHAPTER 3

Managing Marketing Information

Managing Management

Managing practices vary from one organization to another. However, some basic premises exist upon which all managers manage. Most managers establish objectives to help them measure success or failure. The tasks set up to meet these objectives generally are consistent with a plan or a planning process. Controlling and overseeing the tasks to achieve the objectives are a manager's prerequisite for success. Thus, the manager who is most effective is the one who provides sufficient communication across all organizational lines in order to accomplish a particular goal. The core of this activity or process is decision-making. In today's society, decision-making is almost synonymous with the manager and the management function.

We define the managerial process here to emphasize a valuable point. It is never enough as a manager to realize that you need additional informational support to manage effectively. System development will require significant assistance among many specific groups within the organization. Managers realize the need for additional informational support but are often wary of computers, statistical modeling, and research techniques. The MKIS development manager or team must demonstrate to management that the MKIS offers a means of significant support and not a replacement of management's job functions. In many cases, all the processes involved in effective management will be required to persuade top-level management of the need for that additional informational support. Of course, this support should help facilitate the core of all the management processes—decision-making.

To document effectively your informational support requirements, use the following "managing management" checklist as a guide:

1. Establish firm objectives that an MKIS will pursue
2. Design the tasks to achieve your objectives
3. Establish control procedures to influence the direction and pace of the tasks
4. Organize whatever resources are necessary to achieve your objectives

5. Make sure that all employees involved in helping to achieve the objectives know what their roles are and what is required of them and by what date
6. Most important, let top-level management know which decisions you currently cannot accurately analyze and act upon because you have insufficient data.

By following these six steps, you will be prepared to justify the resources necessary for the MKIS, and thus you will in fact be managing management.

Several examples of effective communications tools are presented in Tables 3.1 and 3.2 to help you visualize this process. Table 3.1, a memorandum intended to be presented to the organizational decision-makers, serves as formal notice to top-level management not only of the need for an MKIS but also as a statement of objectives. It should outline the objectives that the organizational decision-makers recognize as the most important and, in many cases, essential. The memo should also stress the additional informational requirements that are necessary to satisfy your objectives.

To support your statement of objectives, you will need further documentation. You must present management with a systematic procedure for outlining the approach you will use to develop, apply, and

(Text continues on page 48)

TABLE 3.1
Statement of Objectives for a Marketing Information System

Memorandum

Date:
To:
From:
Subject: Marketing Information System Objectives

John Smith and I have detailed several additional informational objectives that would improve our sales information system. We feel it is imperative to develop a sales/marketing information system capable of accomplishing the following:

TABLE 3.1, ***continued***

1. Identify "target" accounts in each territory
2. Determine which accounts provide the greatest return in the shortest amount of time
3. Identify parameters of target accounts, i.e., existing sales, sales potential, competitive influences, purchase history, etc.
4. Identify the most efficient and profitable territories
5. Enhance the territory profit-and-loss report with (a) comparative reporting, (b) trend analyses, and (c) profitability analysis
6. Define market potential and penetration by territory
7. Identify noncontributing products
8. Identify highly profitable products
9. Create meaningful sales forecasting, by territory, using historical trends, market-potential parameters, industry growth data, and demographic and psychographic support data.

We have addressed several approaches for the development of this Marketing Information System and recommend the following objectives and informational improvements:

1. To establish a marketing information data base capable of providing a new series of marketing-related reports.
   A. Territory Account Master
   B. Customer Summary Statistics
   C. Territory Summary Statistics
   D. Market Parameter Summary by Division
   E. Market Parameter Summary by Territory
   F. Industry Competition Summary by Territory
   (Includes advertising and marketing strategies of all competitors, market analysis, and promotional effectiveness).
   G. International Competition Summary
   H. Territory Support Summary
   Outline documenting support variables, i.e., newsletter distribution, introductory letters, specification-sheet distribution, select brochure distribution. Distribution to all potential accounts, all target accounts, all active accounts, and a percentage of inactive accounts based on priority potential.

2. To administer the complete implementation, organization, and maintenance of an ongoing Marketing Information System.

TABLE 3.2
Marketing Benefits Package, XYZ Corporation
MKIS Control and Planning Outline (Presystem Planning)

I. MKIS Planning (understanding the intricacies of XYZ marketing)

A. Coordinate internal marketing efforts with overall corporate planning.

B. Establish data base for corporate and marketing strategy.

C. Analyze how we can satisfy the needs of the marketplace *and* improve our performance in the marketplace.

D. Define the direction of XYZ marketing based on our distinctive competence.

E. Understand and evaluate the market opportunities available to XYZ.

F. Focus all efforts toward the satisfaction of consumer needs.

G. Evaluate potential strategic alternatives (contribution, growth, profitability).

H. Provide functional support to other XYZ departments.

I. Establish XYZ goodwill and communication.

II. Analysis of Marketing Planning: Situational Analysis

A. The market: Define significant variables that relate market potential within each territory.

1. The nature of contribution analysis, projected growth, our competition, identification of potential new accounts, inactive account identification, sales trend analysis, sales summaries and potential, consumer characteristics profile, facilities identification, consumer breakdown by territory, market statistics, demographics relative to XYZ, and governmental influences

B. The company: Seek communication improvements with support and other functional XYZ departments.

1. Product-line analysis and new-product-introduction control
2. Manufacturing cooperation through improved forecasts
3. Engineering efficiency through a better understanding of the market and consumer needs
4. Top management support of marketing strategies based on statistical support data
5. Improved communication and coordination among all departments
6. Better identification of major strengths and weaknesses
7. Better understanding of marketing opportunities
8. Identifying specific needs of market(ing) research

C. The environment: Variables that stimulate sales potential through marketing and promotional diversification.

1. Media distribution (television, radio, newspaper, magazines)
2. Trade journal and specialty distribution
3. Newsletter distribution (outlines new company developments)
4. Introductory letters (direct mail)

TABLE 3.2, *continued*

5. Bulletin or specification-sheet distribution (reveals significant independent appraisals of company products)
6. Select brochure distribution
7. Distribution to all potential accounts, all target accounts, all potential new accounts, all active accounts, and a percentage of inactive accounts based on priority potential

III. Marketing Research and Analysis

A. Sales forecasting: Based on historical trends, market potential influence, personal/psychological influences, industry growth statistics, demographics and model simulations.

B. Sales evaluation: Based on net sales divided by total expenses (efficiency index), net contribution totals, net sales, sales experience, territory history, territory potential, historical sales trends by product

C. Consumer profile: An analysis of consumer, XYZ, and competitor attributes important in the sales decision process. Opportunity analysis is a branch of the consumer profile. A detailed examination of who Carl Consumer is should be presented.

D. New-product introduction: Evaluated with respect to existing product lines and market opportunities by territory and geographical area.

1. Product quality/breadth
2. Pricing
3. Marketing communications
4. Distribution
5. Selling methods
6. Market-share potential
7. Net contribution potential (return on investment)

IV. Establishment of Objectives

A. Evaluation of major opportunities.

1. Potential new accounts
2. Contribution analysis
3. Relating market parameters to priority-potential ranking
4. Sales forecasts
5. Sales analysis

V. Strategy Selection: MIS Functional Support

A. Evaluation.

1. Market identification: Needs, potential, and opportunities. Where we (XYZ) have been, where we are now, and where we are going
2. Market-share analysis, i.e., product positioning, sales analysis, product-line analysis, etc.
3. Purchase-decision mechanics: How does Carl Consumer come to purchase or select XYZ rather than our competitors' products?

TABLE 3.2, *continued*

4. Competitive product-line differentiation

B. Operational.

1. Product-line quality: Acceptance of the correct product with respect to timing (life cycle), product-mix acceptance and diversification, market-acceptance potential, competitiveness, return on start-up costs, price, selling efficiency, and advertising

C. Development of composite marketing strategy–marketing communications.

1. XYZ marketing objectives
2. Major objective(s)
3. Potential market analysis
4. Consumer characteristics (analysis)
5. Product characteristics (analysis)
6. Jobs to be accomplished
7. Cost-benefit analysis
8. Alternatives and resources available
9. Recommendation(s)

VI. Development of Action Plans: Based on composite strategy selected (what, when, why, where, who?)

VII. Budgets and Controls

A. Budgets: Based on objectives and return-on-investment analysis.

B. Control: Calendar-based objectives.

VIII. Coordination: Everyone who is instrumental in program implementation should influence the development of system variables, its applications, and the management of information processing—an information system.

construct the proposed Marketing Information System.[1] Table 3.2 shows the marketing benefits that are to be derived from an effective MKIS. Too often managers find the intricacies of the Marketing Benefits Package difficult to understand. Thus your documentation for marketing control and planning functions should be as simple as possible if you are to be ultimately successful.

Note that Sections V–VIII of Table 3.2 deal with the operational aspects of the MKIS. The operational aspects include cost expenditures, return on investment (ROI), action-plan statements, budget guidelines, and a management-by-objectives participation proposal. Detailing these elements as you present your MKIS proposal, as well as elucidating your

1. See numbers 3 through 6 of the "managing management" checklist.

marketing philosophy (see Table 3.3), should give management enough information to appraise the MKIS proposal fairly. Remember that management must be able to see exactly why and how an MKIS will be bottom-line effective. The information in Table 3.1, when detailed and presented to management, should answer the most important questions and concerns. By elaborating on each point in the control outline, you will have designed effective planning documents and tools.

Data Needs Assessment and the Marketing Philosophy

The manager in today's demanding, competitive, cost-conscious environment will find information provided by the MKIS a valuable asset. One of the major attributes of a successful manager is decisiveness. To be decisive, you must be totally informed. How does a marketing manager determine his data and information requirements? There are certain standards, goals, and objectives that represent a yardstick by which managers are measured. Many organizations establish formal, agreed-to operating objectives for a period of time. Each manager, of course, is responsible for attaining measurable results. It is essential that the manager understand what will be required of him, and he must know what additional informational support he needs to achieve his objectives.

The recommended approach for determining your data requirements is twofold:

1. Control the input of subsystem requirements
2. Determine the extent of your marketing-data requirements through the use of the Marketing Information Questionnaire (Tables 2.1 A-J) in Chapter 2.

Figure 3.1 provides an overview of the typical subsystem requirements in many organizations today.[2] Specifically, you want to uncover how market-

2. General departmental interface relationships were discussed briefly in Chapter 1 (Figure 1.2) and will be detailed in Chapter 4.

ing informational needs relate to each department. By structuring the various interface relationships in your organization, as shown in Figure 3.1, you will have a better organizational awareness.

The structure illustrated in Figure 3.1 depicts a typical organization's information flow. Each input flow is initiated at the department level and is ultimately processed utilizing specific file transformations and, of course, the central processing unit (CPU). The bottom left-hand corner of the flow overview provides a system summary of the organization's informational processing. When you understand this, you will be able to determine if your present informational support system (total marketing reports) is providing you with the kind of interdepartmental information you require to make marketing-related decisions.[3]

Of course, your major goal is to determine the total informational requirements from a marketing perspective. Every marketing organization operates around a customized marketing philosophy that is developed through years of experience and operation. Each philosophy is unique to each organization. The philosophy revolves around organizational attitudes, perceptions, approaches, and strategies. Use Part B of the Marketing Information Questionnaire in Chapter 2 (Tables 2.1 A–J) to determine your own Marketing Philosophy. The Questionnaire acts as a bridge for identifying marketing information requirements. Each response is measured as to how well the organization is currently implementing a specific marketing discipline, and it shows how important this discipline may be within the marketing department. The higher the response, the greater the perceived need for that specific piece of information. By reviewing Part B (Questionnaire) responses and identifying the questions with high values (greater than 5), your marketing department's profile or philosophy will begin to emerge. Once you have established your Marketing Philosophy, you can assign priorities for your data needs assessment.

The Marketing Philosophy, presented in Table 3.3, provides an example of how to structure the prioritized marketing information needs

3. Chapter 4 details the data elements associated with Interdepartmental Interfaces. Only a general introduction is needed here.

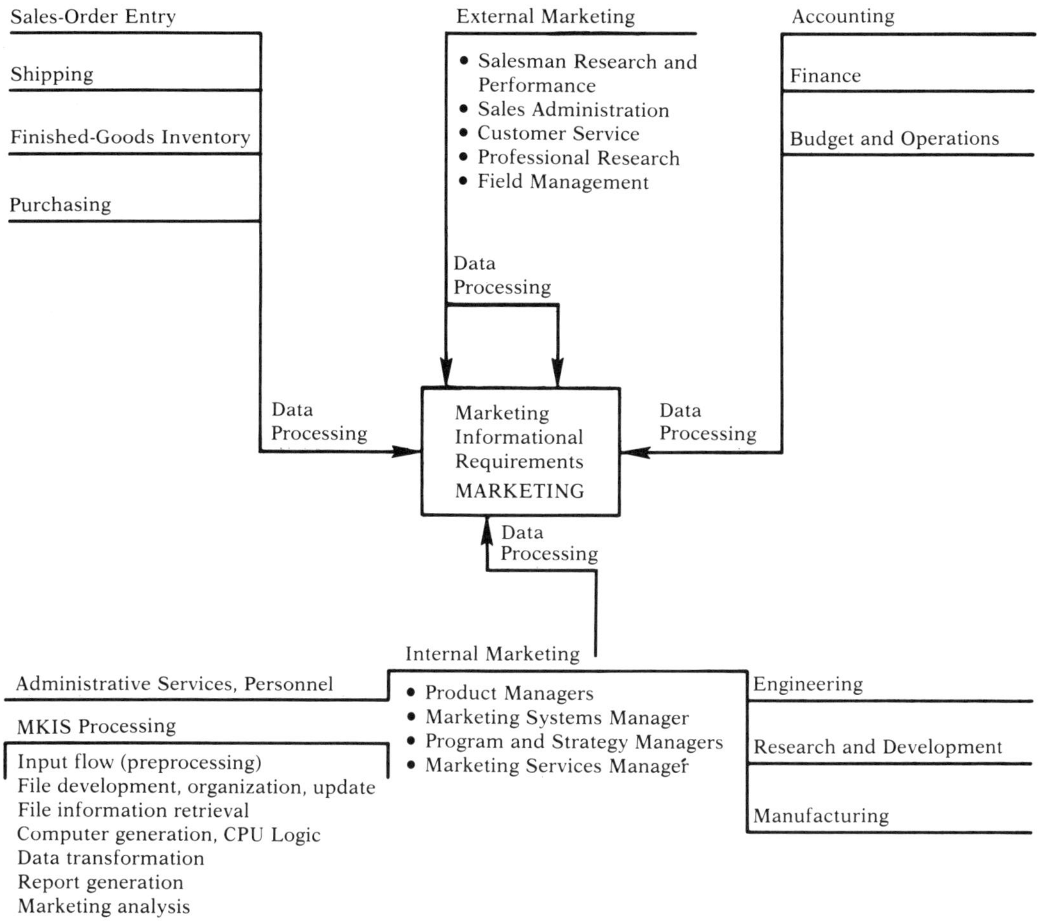

Figure 3.1 Marketing interdepartmental information flow: general overview

t you identify from the Questionnaire. The intent is to provide an example of how to determine your data requirements by using the marketing-philosophy approach. The Marketing Philosophy differs from the Marketing Information Questionnaire. The Questionnaire identifies specific information needs for MKIS support and is used more to identify specific marketing applications. The Philosophy, on the other hand, attempts to identify the broader perspective. As a reflection of the Questionnaire, it attempts to match these applications within the larger scope to generate data requirements. The Marketing Philosophy in Table 3.3 is consistent with the Marketing Information System Framework presented in Chapter 4.

TABLE 3.3
The Marketing Philosophy

Use in conjunction with the Marketing Information Questionnaire (Table 2.1 A-J)

SALES ANALYSIS (2.1A)

- The identification of geographical sales distinctions by sales representative, customer type, and account type
- The calculation of cost of sales by product line
- The measurement of net contribution by product line and geographical location
- The identification of lost and inactive customers

PRODUCT ANALYSIS (2.1B)

- The examination of product differentiation by competitor
- The calculation of expense type for each product line
- The measurement of new-product sales by customer
- The measurement of the effect of product-pricing policies on sales

CONSUMER ANALYSIS (2.1C)

- The identification of the who, where, when, and how of the consumer base
- The creation of a consumer profile
- The identification of specific consumer selection attributes
- The identification of consumer segmentation by contribution and geographical area

TABLE 3.3, *continued*

MARKET ANALYSIS (2.1D)

- The determination of a geographical area's sales potential
- The identification of a successful market area
- The examination of market changes, trends, declines, growth, and performance
- The creation of a detailed demographic profile by market segment

MARKETING PLANNING (2.1E)

- The forecast of new-product requirements by consumer
- The isolation of the geographical areas that provide the largest returns and profit margins
- The measurement of promotional effectiveness by specific technique
- The identification and collection of data for an extensive situational analysis

MARKET RESEARCH (2.1F)

- The identification of product and geographical-area market share
- The examination of new competitive product impact in the market
- The identification of competitive product technology
- The identification of secondary research techniques

PROMOTION ANALYSIS (2.1G)

- The identification of promotional effectiveness
- The measurement of the effect of promotional activity on sales
- The calculation of promotional cost benefits

LEAD HANDLING AND CONTROL ANALYSIS (2.1I)

- The identification of potential customer lists
- The creation of a lead-priority system
- The measurement of the effect of leads on sales volume

INFORMATION ACCESS ANALYSIS (2.1J)

- The identification of secondary information sources
- The identification of external data for situational analysis, consumer profiles, segmentation, market analysis, market planning, and market segmentation
- The examination of the uses of microcomputers, timesharing, and graphics for data presentations

Do You Need an MKIS?

A sound Marketing Philosophy allows you to keep in perspective your total marketing effort. Each manager is faced daily with similar types of information needs, and all too often the data support is lacking or is just not available. This situation can lead to a "seat-of-the-pants" decision, which often is devastating if you are then asked for supportive evidence of how you came to that decision. Before you establish your Marketing Philosophy, ask yourself whether or not the information generated by your system is capable of answering or supporting the data requirements of your current marketing philosophy. If you decide that it is not, you must then determine the costs (opportunity costs) of not having the information available. If the benefits outweigh the costs, you need a Marketing Information System.

Begin to outline your Marketing Philosophy by listing systematically all data elements contained in your present marketing-report system. Then list the data elements necessary to support your "marketing-philosophy" data base. An objective comparison should support your intuitive observations, and it is also helpful in determining the data-file elements. Table 3.4 and Table 3.5 A–D illustrate an objective comparison. By comparison, the current or existing marketing-report data base looks like an exaggeration. Table 3.4 is an example of a simple marketing data base. From this data base, several similar sales reports might be generated. But because the reports might seem to be routinely familiar, many managers will look only at one or two of them. The prospect of all reports containing exactly the same information is unlikely, but to the busy manager who has time only to read each report superficially, there are few differences. Thus, because of a limited data base and similar report outputs, many managers fail to utilize even a limited marketing information system.

The data base presented in Table 3.5 A–D expands the type and level of informational support, and it increases the likelihood that you will respond to the new and different marketing reports that result from the

(Text continues on page 66)

TABLE 3.4
Current Marketing Report Data-Base
Sales Reporting System
XYZ Corporation

Catalog Number	Date of Purchase	Customer Name
Product Class	Invoice Number	Customer Address
Product Description	Order Number	Number of Back Orders
Product Code	Ship Date	Customer P.O.
Sales	Order Quantity	Active Date
Credits	Ship Quantity	Inactive Date
Net Sales	Model Number	Freight Amount
Quantity	Serial Number	State Tax
Unit Price	Standard Cost	City Tax
Customer Number	Department	County Tax

TABLE 3.5A
Data Elements for Sales-Management Report Applications

RAW DATA ELEMENTS	CALCULATED DATA ELEMENTS
Order Date	Order Quantity (units): Day, week, month, quarter, year
Ship Date	Ship Quantity (units): Day, week, month, quarter, year
Product Name	Sales Amount (dollars): Day, week, month, quarter, year
Product Model/Serial Number	Unit Sales Trend*: Percentage change in the current two-quarter average vs. the previous four-quarter average
Order Quantity (units)	Incentive Amount: Incentive rate × sales amount
Ship Quantity (units)	Net Units Sold: Ship quantity less return quantity
Sale Amount (dollars)	Net Dollars Sold: Net units sold × sale amount per unit
Invoice Number	Percentage Change from Last Month (units and dollars): [(This month—last month) ÷ (last month)] × 100
Purchase Order Number	Percentage Change from Last Year (units and dollars): [(This YTD − Last YTD) ÷ (last YTD)] × 100
Customer Number	Percentage Achievement: [(Actual ÷ Forecast) × 100
Territory Number	Gross Profits: Net sales less manufacturing costs
District Number	Total Controllable Expenses: Travel and entertainment + telephone + samples + supplies + literature + shows + exhibits
Region Number	Total Noncontrollable Expenses: Subtotal of all expenses not included in controllable
Customer Name	Total Expenses: Total controllable expenses + total noncontrollable expenses
Customer Address	
Incentive Rate	
Return Quantity (units)	
Forecast (units)	
Manufacturing Costs	
Travel and Entertainment Expense	
Telephone Expense	
Sample Expense	
Supplies Expense	
Literature Expense	
Trade Shows Expense	
Exhibits Expense	
Auto Lease Expense	
Auto Maintenance Expense	
Customer Service Expense	
Salary Cost	
Incentive Cost	
Building (office expense)	
Insurance Expense	
Fee Expense	
Sales Representative Name	

*Includes "Percentage Down Trend," "Territory Trend," and "Account trends."

TABLE 3.5A, *continued*

RAW DATA ELEMENTS	CALCULATED DATA ELEMENTS
Sales Representative Address	Profit Contribution: Gross profits less total expenses
Sales Manager Name	Percentage of Net Sales: Any P & L line item (either raw or derived data element) as a percentage of net sales
Sales Manager Address	Standard Commission: Sum of all incentive amounts for a given period
Premium Adjustments	New-Account Bonus: New-account units × dollar award
Employee Hire Date	Total Commissions Payable: Standard commission + premium adjustment + new-account bonus
Employee Current Status Data	Efficiency Index: An expense-to-sales ratio
Current Annual Salary	Last Four-Quarter Units
Employee File Comments	Quarterly Average Prior to "Lost"
	Rank
	Sales $÷ Sample $
	Sales $÷ Total expense $
	Profit Contribution $÷ Sales $
	Total Customers: All and by product line
	Average Dollar Customer: Total $ sales ÷ Number of customers
	Number of Customers Buying Only 1 or Only 2 Products
	Active/Mature: Customer who buys on a regular basis
	Inactive/Lost: Customer was active but stopped buying
	New: First-time customers
	Reactivated: Were inactive but initiated new purchases

TABLE 3.5B
Data Elements for Product Data-Bank Report Applications

RAW DATA ELEMENTS*	CALCULATED DATA ELEMENTS
New-Product Rating	New-Product Value: Product rating × relative-importance weight
New-Product-Idea Generation Date	Product Segment Sales: Sum of all products within a common product class
New-Product-Idea Screening Date	Total Market Estimate: Sum of all products within a common product class for all companies in the industry
New-Product Feasibility Research Date	Market Share: (Product segment sales ÷ Total market estimate) × 100
New-Product Business Analysis Date	Percentage Change in Market Share: [(Current Period Market Share − Last Period) ÷ Last Period] × 100
New-Product Prototype Testing Date	Sale (units) by Consumer Segment: Sum of all products sold to customers in a common class
New-Product Test-Marketing Date	Unit Growth Rate/Year: [(Current Year Sales − Last Year's Sales) ÷ Last Year's Sales] × 100
New-Product Full Release Date	Average Sale per Sales Representative: Total $ sales ÷ Number of accounts
Product Price Ranges	
Consumer Segment Targets	
Product Name	
Product Specifications	

*Can also include any or all data elements from the Sales Management Data Bank. Only unique elements are included here.

TABLE 3.5C
Data Elements for Consumer Data-Bank Report Applications

RAW DATA ELEMENTS	CALCULATED DATA ELEMENTS
Consumer Name (direct)	*PRODUCT-LINE PERCENTAGES*
Consumer Address	Percentage of product line by segment
Consumer City	
Consumer State	*PROFILE DISTRIBUTION PERCENT*
Consumer Zip Code	Percentage of each profile code by segment
Consumer Name (indirect)	
Consumer Address	
Consumer City	*PRODUCT SEGMENT PERCENT*
Consumer State	Percentage of each product by segment
Consumer Zip Code	
Phone (1)	
Phone (2)	
Primary Contact Location	
Profile Status	
Occupational Status	
Title/Distribution	
Education	
Age	
Sex	
Marital Status	
Income	
Personal	
Children	
Comment	
Effective Sales Method (1)	
Effective Sales Method (2)	
SOCIAL INTEREST CODE	
Theatre = 1	
Opera = 2	
Sporting = 3	
Travel = 4	
Books = 5	
Miscellaneous = 6	
Future Product Interest	
PAST MARKETING CODE	
Direct Mail = 1	

TABLE 3.5C, *continued*

RAW DATA ELEMENTS	CALCULATED DATA ELEMENTS
Personal Letter = 2 Brochures = 3 Technical Literature = 4 Journal Ad = 5 Trade Show = 6 Sales Rep = 7 Key Decision-Maker Total Consumer Estimate Market Class Market Segment	
L/H CODE L = Positive H = Negative	
VOLUME POTENTIAL 3 = 0-2 Units 2 = 3-4 Units 1 = More than 4 Units	
PROFILE GUIDE 1 = Highly Conservative 2 = Moderate 3 = Conservative 4 = Liberal 5 = Highly Liberal	
SERVICE NEED/SERVICE CODE 1 = First Service 2 = Second Service 3 = Third Service 4 = Greater than 3	
EXPECTED SERVICE CODE A = 1-2 years service expectation B = 3-4 years service expectation C = Greater than 4 years service expectation	

TABLE 3.5C, *Continued*

RAW DATA ELEMENTS	CALCULATED DATA ELEMENTS
RESEARCH CODE 1 = Primary 2 = Secondary	
PRODUCT CODE A = Maxi-Hypo B = Mini-Hypo C = All-Purpose	
STRATEGY Based on profile, research, product, market segment, and class code combinations	
SELECTION ATTRIBUTE TOTAL Sum of all numeric rankings	
SELECTION ATTRIBUTE MEAN Sum of each attribute ÷ the number of accounts	
SELECTION ATTRIBUTES CR PR SZ WR AC PP PS	
Distribution	
TOTAL PROFILE Sum of profile codes by segment	
TOTAL PRODUCT Sum of product codes by segment	
SELECTION ATTRIBUTES RANK Each attribute rank according to lowest mean by segment	

TABLE 3.5D
Data Elements for Market Data-Bank Report Applications

RAW DATA ELEMENTS

Total Market
Market Sales
Growth Rate/Segment
Market Growth (units and dollars)
Market Segment

MARKET CLASS CODE
L = Negative—$.20 earnings per share (EPS)
LM = $.21—$1.00 EPS
UM = Greater than $1.00 EPS

CONSUMER INCOME RANGE
$15,000-$25,000—Total N
$25,000-$35,000—N
Greater than $35,000 by segment

AGE DISTRIBUTION
25-30
31-40
41-60
Greater than 60 by segment

SOURCE CODE
1 = Annual Reports
2 = Trade Journals
3 = Product Literature or Price Lists
4 = Sales Force/Distributors
5 = Customer Feedback
6 = Product Purchase
7 = Shows/Exhibits
8 = Former Employees
9 = Special Industry Reports
10 = SEC Filings
11 = Seminars
12 = Other

CALCULATED DATA ELEMENTS

ACTUAL USERS
Total active accounts by segment

EQUIVALENT USERS
Total estimate of competitive accounts by segment

TOTAL USERS
Actual and equivalent users by segment

PENETRATION PERCENTAGE
Volume actual users ÷ total users

DEMOGRAPHIC RANK BY SEGMENT
Highest to lowest scaling

CONSUMER TARGET
Total consumer targets attempted by technique type

LEADS GENERATED
Total targets reached by technique type

PERCENT RESPONSE
(Leads generated ÷ consumer targets) × 100

TOTAL COSTS
Total expense associated with each technique type

TOTAL SALES
Total sales per consumer by technique type

RATING CODE
Reflects positive/negative sales trend correlation

TABLE 3.5D, ***continued***

RAW DATA ELEMENTS	CALCULATED DATA ELEMENTS
COMPETITION	*SALES-TREND CODE*
Name	A sales-trend code of either a plus (+) or minus (−) according to comparison of prior period to current period sales revenue
Address	
City	
State	
Zip Code	
Phone	*SEGMENT RANKING*
Product Line(s)	Rank market parameters by segment according to the "most," the "highest," and the most heavily weighted classification
Product Type	
Product Specifications	
Principal Officers	
Geographical Coverage	
Gross Sales (units)	*SEGMENT POTENTIAL*
Gross Sales (dollars)	Sum of weighted scores or segment rankings
Assets (total)	
Assets Range	
Revenue Range	
Earnings per Share (EPS)	
EPS History	
Total Employees	
Total Expenses	
Debt Structure	
Plant Capacity	
Current Production	
Area Representative(s)	
Area Distributor(s)	
Promotional Methodology	
Practices	
Platforms	
Quality History	
Performance History	
Field-Service Comment	
Share	
Research and Development	
Strengths	
Weaknesses	
Operating Advantage	

TABLE 3.5D, *continued*

RAW DATA ELEMENTS	CALCULATED DATA ELEMENTS
Operating Disadvantage	
Representative: Name/Segment	
Representative Address	
Distributor: Name/Segment	
Distributor Address	
Contact(s)	
SEGMENT	
Revenue Distribution	
Occupational Distribution	
Income Distribution	
Education Distribution	
Age Distribution	
DEMOGRAPHICS/SEGMENT	
Land Area	
Age (mean)	
Population (total)	
Population Breaks	
Population (square mile)	
Population Growth (%)	
White (%)	
Black (%)	
Other (%)	
Sex (%M, %F)	
Foreign	
Births	
Deaths	
Marital Status	
Divorces	
Children	
Civilian Labor	
Employment Total	
Employment (%)	
Public-School Enrollment	
Physicians	
Hospitals	
Number of hospital beds	
Income (per capita)	
Income (annual)	

TABLE 3.5D, *continued*

RAW DATA ELEMENTS	CALCULATED DATA ELEMENTS
Income (levels)	
Housing Code	
Crime Rate	
LEAD GENERATION/SEGMENT	
Account Name	
Geographical Area	
Date	
Follow-up Date	
SALES PROSPECT	
Name	
Address	
City	
State	
Zip Code	
Phone (b)	
Phone (h)	
Message	
Contact	
Result	
LEAD/PROSPECT CODE	
A = Personal Interview	
B = Direct Mail	
C = Conference	
D = Media	
E = Newspaper Clipping	
F = Journal/Magazine Return	
FOLLOW-UP CODE	
1 = Sales Force	
2 = Field Manager	
3 = Distributor	
4 = Product Manager	
5 = Service Manager	
6 = Technical Staff	
7 = Marketing Officer	
8 = Corporate	
Promotional Description	

TABLE 3.5D, *continued*

RAW DATA ELEMENTS	CALCULATED DATA ELEMENTS
Promotional Date	
Average Annual Purchases	
Total Market Sales by Segment (including competitors)	
Market Share Leader/Segment	
Average Order Size	
Total Advertising Expense/Segment	
Total Distribution and Logistics/Segment	
U.S. Statistical Abstracts (optional; used for industrial data)	

expanded data base.[4] These illustrations also show how a data base can be expanded.

The process of data comparison is in some respects more important than the actual elements. Every organizational data base will be unique; consequently, the data-base expansion offered in Table 3.5 A–D is merely an illustration of how the comparison process might evolve for one organization. However, the applications and benefits of an expanded data base should not be measured simply by the number of new and exciting reports generated. You, as manager, must differentiate and analyze the many new marketing reports and data to see if they provide a sufficient return on investment. As we stated at the beginning, an informed manager will be able to justify his decisions.

Action Plan

1. Identify specific marketing management objectives that an MKIS would satisfy.
2. Identify the specific tasks needed to achieve each objective.

4. Marketing-report applications will be discussed in detail in Chapters 6 through 9.

3. Establish firm operating-control procedures that will influence the direction and timing of each task.
4. Organize and formally document the resources that will be necessary to achieve your objectives.
5. Document the above to influence systematically the "need perception" of key decision-makers within your organization (see Table 3.2).
6. Determine MKIS data-element requirements through the development of your specific Marketing Philosophy (Table 3.3) and through a comparison of your existing data elements (Table 3.4) with your proposed elements (Tables 3.5 A–D).

SECTION II

DEVELOPMENT

System Design and Development

Designing Reports: Putting Your Data into Proper Perspective

CHAPTER 4

System Design and Development

Statement of Purpose for Your MKIS

Once you have determined that your present Marketing Information System is inadequate, you must decide what you want your new information system to accomplish. In a statement of purpose you should address the overall objective of the MKIS as well as establish its direct goal. This statement should also reflect time and budget considerations. An example: "The objective of XYZ's marketing department is to develop and maintain an ongoing Marketing Information System capable of providing marketing informational support by no later than (date) and to exceed no more than (dollars)."

As manager, you must identify your informational requirements and formally present them to upper management. Before you do this, however, it is important to remember that the time it takes you to realize you need additional information support is minuscule compared with upper management's time constraints. Because the development of an interactive MKIS is time-consuming and expensive, you must try to justify every element of the MKIS and its cost. If you begin with a formal unified statement of purpose that carefully describes the planning and objectives of the MKIS, you will be in a stronger position to justify your needs for support when you approach management.

The MKIS Design

The MKIS should effectively and objectively inform, service, and guide your marketing efforts. As manager, you have studied the data elements that comprise your current marketing reports, and you have followed the process outlined in Chapter 3. As a result, you have determined that you need a new Marketing Information System. The MKIS that you require will make it necessary to expand your current reporting data base (see Tables 3.5 A–D). The question now becomes: "How do you design the MKIS to do what you want it to do?"

TABLE 4.1
MKIS Input-Output Relationships

INPUT	OUTPUT
INTERNAL	*MARKETING ELEMENTS*
Sales-order entry	Corporate analysis
Customer service	ROI analysis
Manufacturing	Budget adherence
Engineering	Sales trends
Research and development	Industry trends
Personnel	Consumer profiles
Data processing	Consumer analysis
Government relations	Consumer targets
Marketing/sales	Consumer comparisons
	Consumer demand
EXTERNAL	Consumer trends
Annual reports	
Trade journals	*PRODUCT-LINE ELEMENTS*
Trade associations	Product-mix projections
Market research	Product-development program
Private research reports	Product life cycles
Database retrieval systems	Product distribution and logistics
Information brokers	
Information books	*MARKET ELEMENTS*
Government (Federal, State and local) reports, references, and databases	Market profile
	Market share
	Market trends
	Market growth
	Market index
	SALES ELEMENTS
	Sales by product
	Sales by location or cost center
	Sales by product line
	Sales by sales rep
	Sales by consumer segmentation
	Sales-rep profile
	Sales-management formats
	Sales budgets
	Sales forecast
	Sales planning

TABLE 4.1, *continued*

INPUT	OUTPUT
	PROMOTIONAL ELEMENTS
	Advertising analysis
	Promotion targets
	FINANCIAL ELEMENTS
	Credit policies
	Consignment activity
	Discount policies
	Promotional allowances
	Budgets
	ROI analysis
	GENERAL MARKETING ELEMENTS
	Hiring/turnover analysis
	Transfer policy
	Promotion policy
	Absenteeism effects

Source: Journal of Marketing, October 1969.

The logical first step in designing your MKIS is to link the flow of data that the MKIS will include. Table 4.1 illustrates the input-output relationships of the MKIS process. The inputs reflect both internal and external sources. Much of the data will originate internally from sources such as sales-order entry, manufacturing and data processing. Data will also be supplied through external sources such as trade journals, annual reports of competitors, and market research. Your outputs will vary depending on your organization and industry, but the output data in Table 4.1 shows how to begin the process.

Once you have formulated the input-output requirements, you must determine the format of your design establishing a framework as shown in Figure 4.1. In this example, the manager defines the Marketing Department as two departments, Marketing and Sales, each with specific applications.

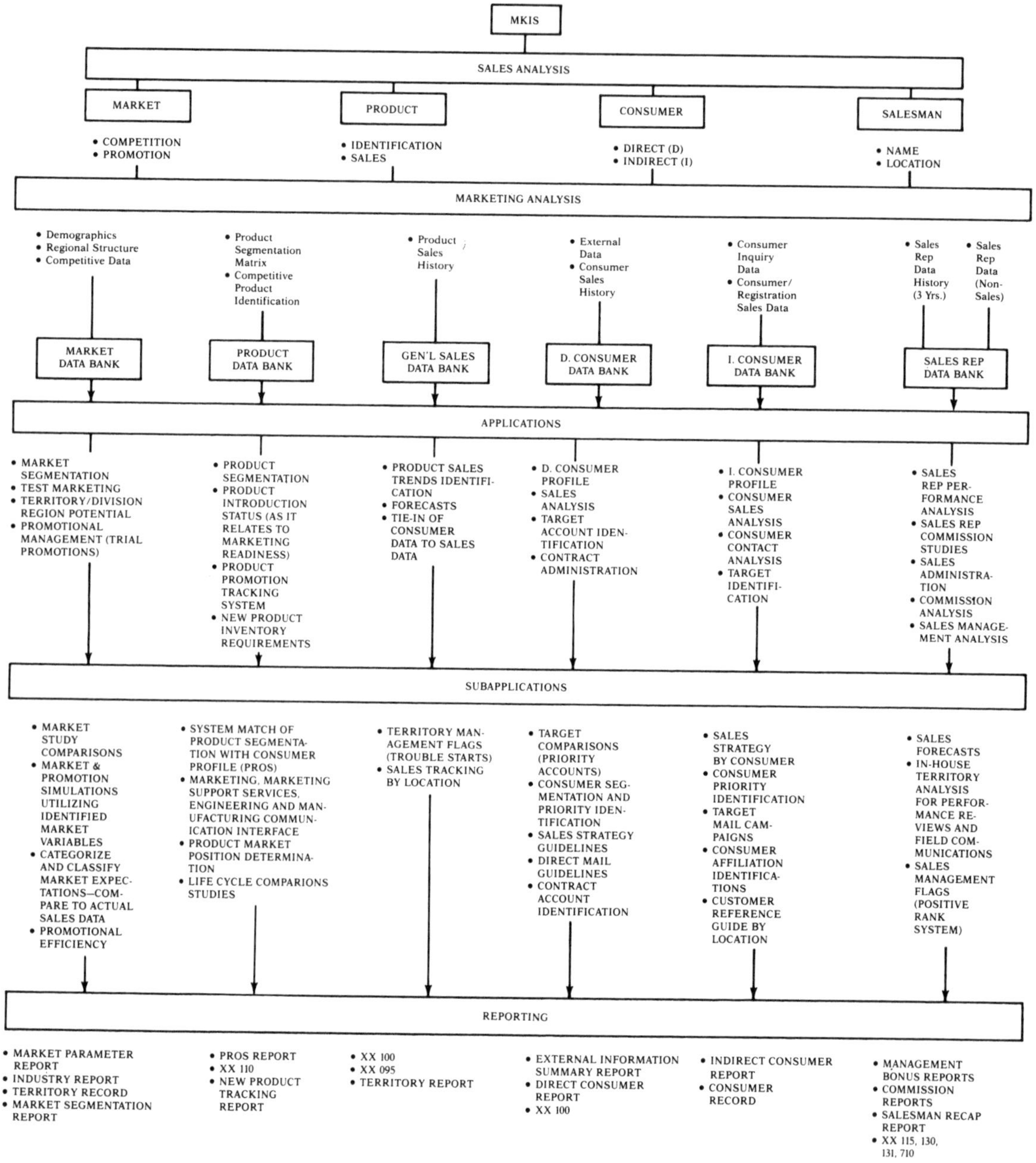

Figure 4.1 Marketing Information System framework illustration

The Application Headings (Market, Product, Consumer, Sales Force) are the actual core of the system and will appear throughout the entire MKIS. The Sales Analysis and Marketing Analysis applications, along with the many other support elements, will be contained in one or more data banks.[1] If you want, think of each data bank as a separate module in your overall system.

The term *data bank* is used in Figure 4.1 because this particular MKIS selectively links mini-information systems. In many ways, each data bank is self-contained within the overall data base of the organization, and most of the data are linked and interchangeable. One data bank, for example, may in fact utilize a time-sharing service for data input.

The applications are highlighted in this framework to show the core of the system. The MKIS framework also lists the reporting or processing function of the MKIS. The MKIS is now in a "workable" framework and portrays the following functional relationships:

1. Marketing departments
2. Output headings
3. Selected outputs
4. MKIS/Marketing Philosophy data banks
5. Applications
6. Subapplications
7. Reporting

Concentrating the design of the new system in a one-page framework is a challenging task. However, once you have done this, you can approach your Data Processing Department armed with specific inputs, outputs, data banks, and the design framework.

This preparation will be invaluable when it comes time to implement the MKIS because at that stage the framework becomes a reference tool for

1. The data banks were developed in part from the Marketing Philosophy/MKIS relationship as outlined in Chapter 3. You may want to use several additional data banks. We use only four data banks here for ease of interpretation.

other department managers. The unique design of the framework allows for a quick interpretation of the marketing components, marketing analyses and applications, data-storage locations, and system reports.

Working with Your Data Processing Department

After the Data Processing managers have recovered from the initial shock of your arrival with your arsenal of diagrams and frameworks, you still have a formidable task to perform. True, you are prepared and able to explain to the many programmers, systems analysts, and supervisors exactly what you require (and that preparation cannot be emphasized enough), but you will have to work with your Data Processing Department to examine, discuss, outline, plan, and design *every phase* of your MKIS development.

The first phase of your DP interface is more difficult than it first appears. You will have to design file formats or create data files with DP. Data must usually be stored on tape or on a disk so that the computer can read it quickly. Computer data stored on a disk or tape is divided into files. The information contained in these files are your data or marketing data elements. These data will be stored, created, assembled, formatted, manipulated, and ultimately communicated through reports and on-line terminals to you, the manager.[2]

Data files can be created in several ways. If your organization currently has a computer-based information system of any kind, there should exist a file system that you can analyze to determine why you are not getting the volume of information you require. As a starting point for determining the effectiveness of your current system, several output elements from that system were identified in Chapter 3 (see Table 3.4). Those elements were then compared with the expanded data base illustrated in Tables 3.5 A–D.

2. In today's systems environment, most files are placed in Mass Storage. Storage on disks offers relative compactness and high data-transfer capability, whereas storage on tapes is only used sequentially to access information. Both types of data access allow the DP user to combine data from any internal sources.

Taken together, these output elements will aid in the creation of the data files you will need for your new MKIS. Compare and contrast the data-file elements that are currently being employed by your DP Department. The task should become obvious: You must decide what additional data should be contained in the new data files to support the output that you have determined is necessary.

An equally effective means of determining how your data files should be structured is to design new report formats instead of your MKIS framework as presented in Figures 4.1 and 4.2. In other words, analyze the design of your current reports and detail the information they contain. In your MKIS preparation, you outlined several formats that displayed the kinds of information required for the future (see Tables 3.5 A–D). Again, the task is clear. Design your new reports with the information you think will be required now and in the future. These reports may in varying degrees be studied and reformatted by your DP Department. If you show DP the amount and diversity of the information you require, your chances of creating and using a mutually acceptable MKIS will increase significantly. Chapters 6 through 9 will illustrate and define the dynamics of reporting as it relates to marketing information.

Creating Marketing Files

When creating or expanding marketing-file structures, keep in mind exactly what you want each file to accomplish. In the Marketing Information Questionnaire in Chapter 2 (Tables 2.1 A–J), several questions were addressed to help you determine your data requirements. Specific data elements were thus identified through the development of the marketing philosophy and input-output relationships. Developing these desirable elements and bringing them on-line into your data system will ultimately provide an array of marketing-analysis routines consisting of:

1. The computation of recurring entries, i.e., sales invoice data and sales registration codes

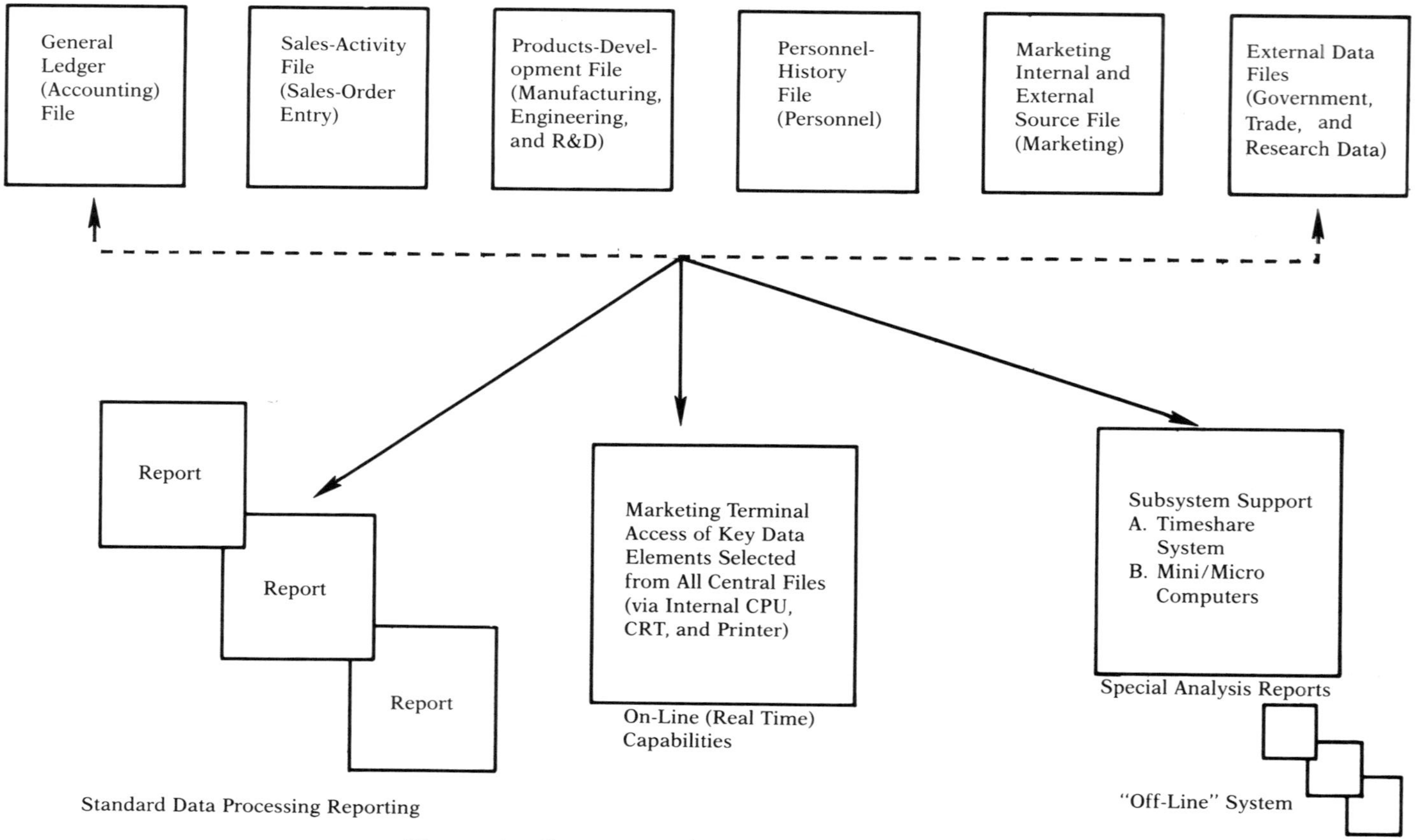

Figure 4.2 System overview: Marketing Information System

2. The generation of totals, mean values, variances, and standard deviations
3. The ability to compare and relate specific data over specific time periods
4. The ability to analyze and predict trends, impacts, declines, and growth

The task of designing marketing-file layouts is an extremely important phase in the development of the MKIS. Knowledge of a computer language and file structure is not important. What is important is that you, the marketing manager, understand and are able to communicate what marketing data elements you require. You may be asked to define, interpret, expand, and defend many of your requirements, so you should be prepared. Remember, the DP analysts will be classifying, organizing, and accumulating your required output, and they will need help from you. You will have to identify:

1. Output elements
2. Where the elements will be needed in specific applications
3. The recurrence of certain elements
4. Which elements will be updated
5. Field lengths (size of elements)
6. Code values where necessary
7. Security safeguards (file-access privileges)
8. Overlapping functions
9. Calculation requirements (Table 3.5)

Determining Edit Procedures, Codes, and System Maintenance

EDIT PROCEDURES

To ensure the integrity of the system, data-input edit programs should be designed by various DP staff members with your assistance. Basically, an edit is a check of the data entry. When the programmer designs the file program, he includes an instruction that all incoming data is to be examined for conformity to the data fields and parameters that you and the DP Department have agreed upon. This procedure is also important because it ensures a cross-checking or audit capability.

A simple example of an edit procedure is when you set up a code to record territory sales up to a maximum of five digits. If you attempt to input data of six or more digits, the data will be rejected. Another common edit feature is the rejection of alphabetical entries when the field is set up for only numerical data input. These simple edit functions are important because such items as account numbers, customer numbers, and invoice numbers all require edit, validation, and correction to maintain the accuracy of the MKIS data.

CODES

One technique employed by many organizations is the coding of range values. By assigning a code to these values, you can specify which range the data falls into. Thus, when the code appears, the user knows that a particular range is specified. This program procedure is used to save file space and allow the user to comprehend visually larger amounts of information with less interpretation. In an on-line application, these codes representing range values can be very efficient. For demographic data, such as population breaks, household income, or age values, a code can be assigned to represent value ranges. For example, a code of 1 could indicate the population range of 0–10, a 2 the range of 11–20, and so forth. Instead of printing the actual range parameters, you simply print the code(s) representing the value(s). When examining the hundreds of demographic range values, an entire demographic analysis can be represented on one CRT (cathode-ray-tube) screen.

The ability to scan such vast amounts of data is tempered, however, by an inability of many managers to learn what each code value represents. The design of the screen or report should visually present the code in such a way as to be aesthetically pleasing and not confusing.[3] Using codes to

3. See "Principles of Report Design" in the next chapter.

represent range values should be an option that you can use in those instances where ranges are preferred over an actual value.

MAINTENANCE

Perhaps the most overlooked function of any systems-development project is the maintenance provision. Each manager will put forth a great deal of effort in the development and the implementation of the MKIS, and the end result should be maintained with the same exactness and integrity. There are several ways to provide MKIS maintenance support. First, feedback from all environmental sources, both internal and external, must be provided to prevent the MKIS data from becoming insignificant over time. Second, internal edit features could be provided, such as built-in variance flags to alert the decision-maker when a sales figure shows a variance of, for example, three hundred percent. An error message at the bottom of the printout providing exception messages is also helpful. The manager should periodically scrutinize the MKIS data for errors.

Of course, system maintenance can also be enhanced by additional training of the personnel who will be responsible for data input and output. To ensure that the staff responsible keeps up-to-date with MKIS changes, in-house training programs and outside education are helpful. This is particularly significant if turnover is a factor, in that the users of the MKIS must remain in control of the system. Remember, these staff members will be responsible for such maintenance guidelines as determining error-notification techniques, input-rejection conditions, and system-recovery procedures. System integrity is essential in order to maximize the use of the MKIS.

File Example

Every file that is updated or developed will contain basic information about a field of data:

1. Name of field
2. Field Length

TABLE 4.2
Marketing Prospect File

PASSWORD	V.A.M.
PROGRAMMER	A.B.C.
PROC PARAMETER	NO JCL

HISTORY CARDS FOR THIS MODULE

10/28/80	ADDED FIELD NUMBERS TO RECORD
10/29/80	CHANGE FIELD NUMBER FROM POSITION 72 TO 73
11/04/80	INSERTED 03 RECORD-KEY, CHANGED CONSUMER-ID-NBR TO 05 LEVEL, MOVED AHP—STATE AFTER AHP—CONS-NAME

(1)			(2)	(3)	(4)	(5)
000010 01	AHP		—MARKETING-PROSPECT.		1	11/04/80
000020	03	AHP	—RECORD-KEY.		17	11/04/80
000030		05	AHP-AAA-CONSUMER-ID-NBR	PIC X (7).	2	11/04/80
000040	03	AHP	—CONS-NAME	PIC X (30).	6	11/04/80
000050	03	AHP	—CONS-STATE	PIC X (2).	10	11/04/80

TABLE 4.2, *continued*

(1)	(2)	(3)	(4)	(5)
000060	03 AHP —CONS-ADDR1	PIC X (30).	7	11/04/80
000070	03 AHP —CONS-ADDR2	PIC X (30).	8	11/04/80
000080	03 AHP —CONS-CITY	PIC X (23).	9	11/04/80
000090	03 AHP —CONS-ZIP	PIC X (9).	11	11/04/80
000100	03 AHP —XYZ-ACCT-KEY,		107	11/04/80
000110	05 AHP —COMPANY-CODE	PIC XX.	108	11/04/80
000120	05 AHP —BILL-TO-CUST	PIC X (5).	109	11/04/80
000130	05 AHP —SHIP-TO-CUST	PIC X (4).	110	11/04/80
000140	03 AHP —BUYER-NAME	PIC X (30).	13	11/04/80
000150	03 AHP —BUYER-PHONE		14	11/04/80
000160	05 AHP —AREA-CODE	PIC XXX.	15	11/04/80
000170	05 AHP —PHONE-EXCH	PIC XXX.	16	11/04/80
000180	05 AHP —PHONE-NBR	PIC X (4).	17	11/04/80
000190	05 AHP —PHONE-EXT	PIC X (2).	18	11/04/80
000200	03 AHP —MEMBER-TYPE-CDE	PIC X.	19	11/04/80
000210	03 AHP —OPERATION-CDE	PIC X.	20	11/04/80
000220	03 AHP —RESPONSE-CDE	PIC X.	21	11/04/80
000230	03 AHP —CONTRCL-CDE	PIC XX.	22	11/04/80
000240	03 AHP —SERVICE-CDE	PIC XX.	23	11/04/80

3. Field type
4. Field position (within the record)

Usually a data-based management system (DBMS) will contain a data dictionary component that maintains documented information on data elements such as name, type, length, alternate titles, cross-reference information, and application use. This level of documentation will provide users with a general sense of the scope of a data-base concept and the file structure itself. With or without a data dictionary component, the Data Processing Department will be able to explain file layouts and how they interact within the operating system.

The actual structure of the file is not an important consideration for many managers. However, a basic understanding of a file layout should lead to a better understanding of the system. Table 4.2 is an abbreviated example of the marketing prospect file. This is the same data that is shown in Figure 4.1 as the Consumer Data Bank. The file format as displayed in Table 4.2 is representative of the many file formats that you will encounter. Five main components of this file have corresponding numerical indicators. Column 1 is simply the sequential order of each field in the record (total file). The logic behind a sequential numbering system is to provide a cross-check capability for locating each field in the file.

Column 4 is another means of determining where each field is located. The numbers in this column represent the actual location within the record itself. For instance, the consumer name may be found in position six of the marketing-prospect file. Column 2 is simply the field description or marketing element previously defined. Column 3 is the length of each field within the record. For example, each consumer address may contain up to thirty positions in the record. Column 5 is the date each field item was created, or updated, within the file.

Organizational Interface

An intricate part of any MKIS is the ability of the system to interact with other departmental files and data banks. A marketing system does not stand alone. To gather information effectively from other internal sources, you must work with Data Processing. Too often, valuable information is never utilized because the current system was not designed to retrieve it. How, then, does the manager interface interdepartmental data?

Most managers, after designing their data files, will identify information that is still needed. This information is generally interdepartmental data, so it should not take long to find the missing data. Your DP Department should provide a flow chart of all existing interdepartmental files that "feed" into or are "fed" from your marketing files. Several examples of Interdepartmental Interface are presented in Figures 4.3–4.8.

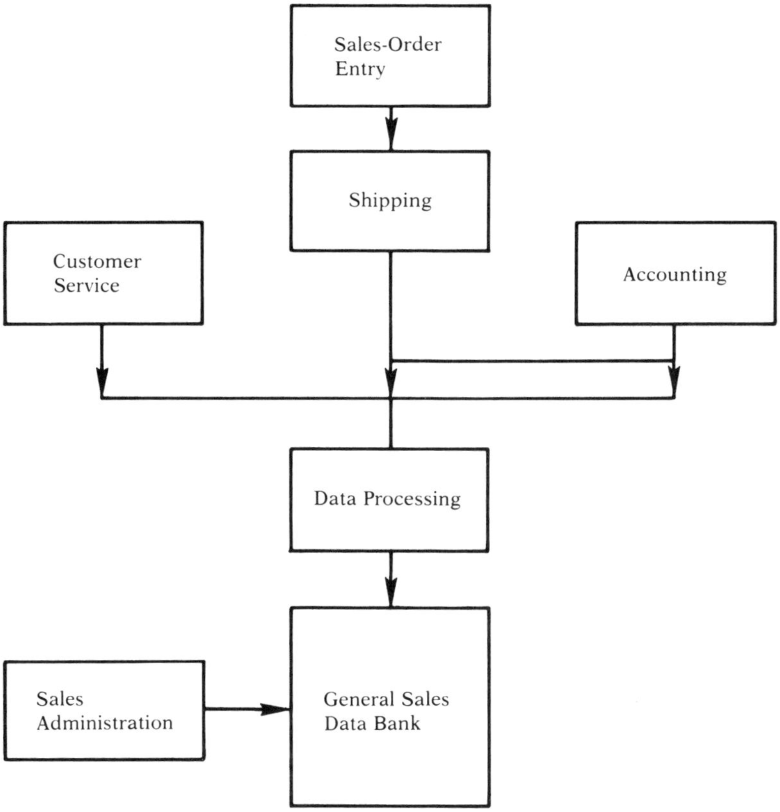

Figure 4.3 Departmental interface: general sales data bank

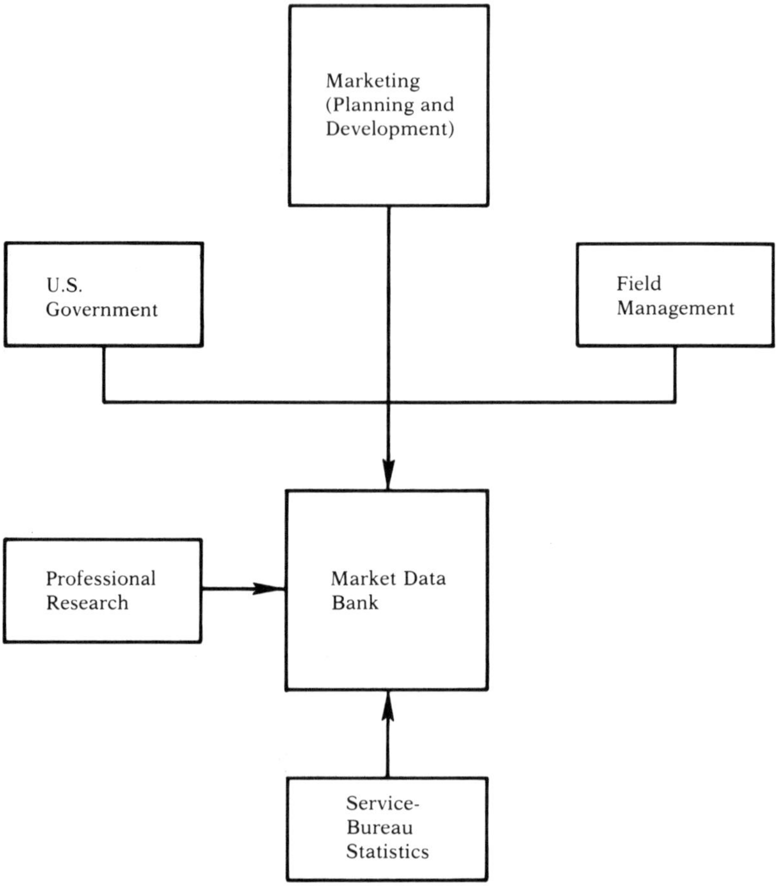

Figure 4.4 Departmental interfaces: market data bank

These interface flows show how the MKIS Data Banks (originally presented in the Framework in Figure 4.1) are accessed by many internal as well as external sources.

After you have determined the exact scope of your MKIS interface, you should hold several meetings with each department or source to determine exactly what information you seek and how you should secure it. Also, you

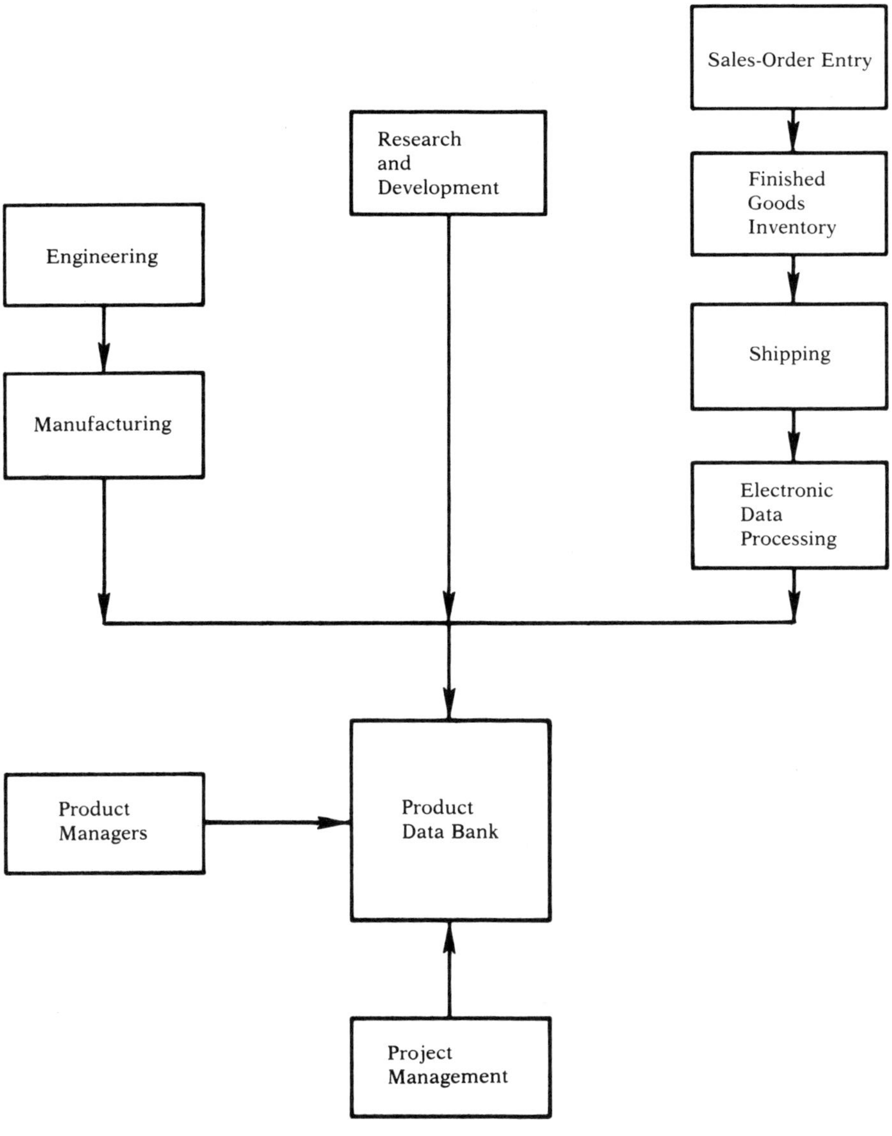

Figure 4.5 Departmental interface: product data bank

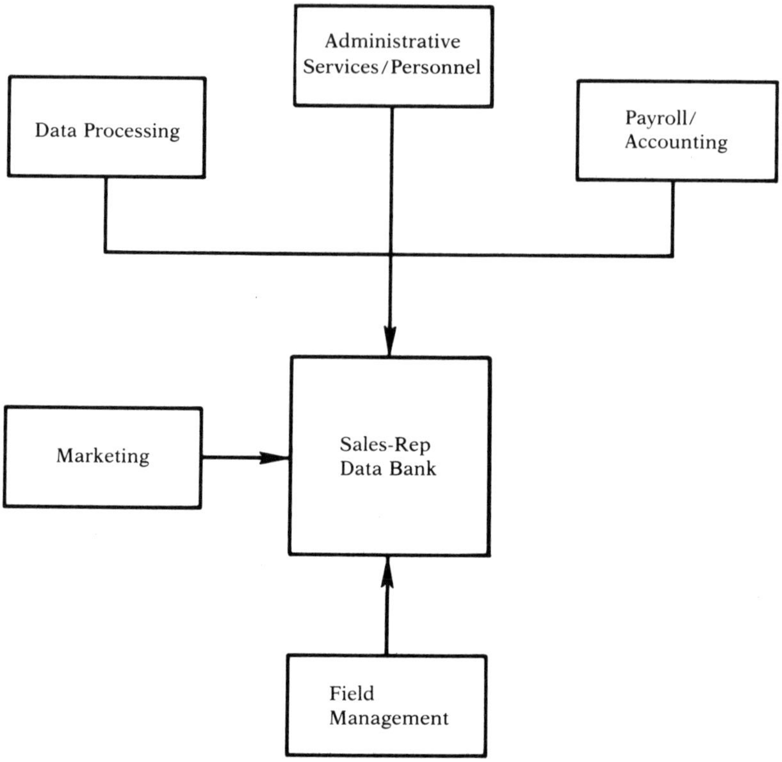

Figure 4.6 Departmental interface: sales rep data bank

will have to discuss how the information is to be maintained. Most managers are surprised to find just how much "extra" data that is vital in building their MKIS is uncovered during these meetings. Documenting exactly what information is available from interdepartmental sources is time-consuming and difficult in many organizations. However, the rewards of locating the information are tremendous. For example, many organizations require product registration and warranty data to be submitted by the buyer to the company upon purchase. In most cases, significant consumer-profile data can be retrieved by simply having the customer file(s) "feed" into the MKIS-processing operation.

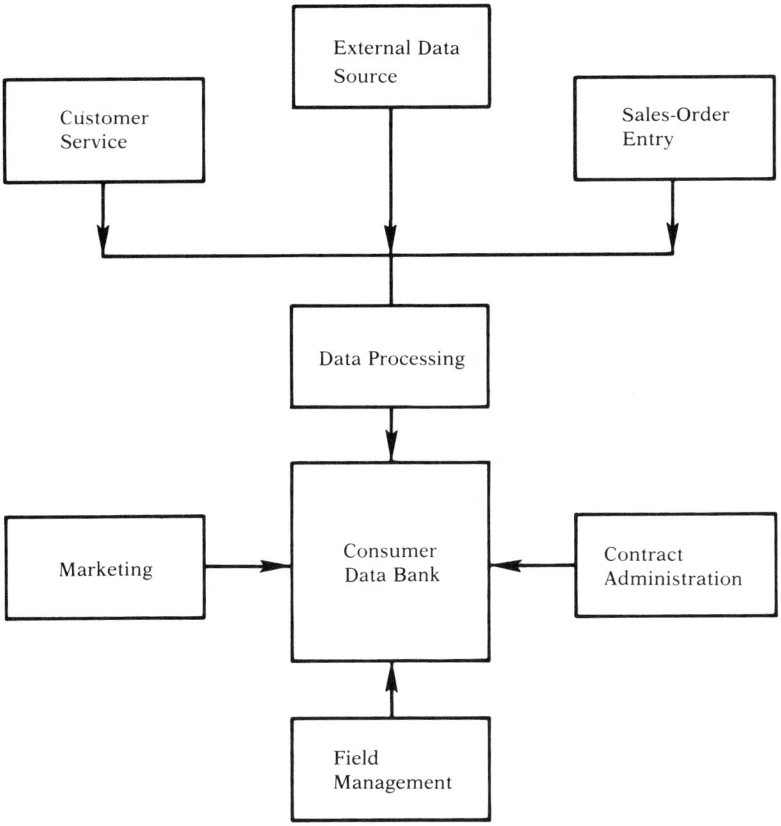

Figure 4.7 Departmental interface: direct-consumer data bank

Although every organization is unique, basic fundamentals exist upon which all departments operate. The departmental subsystem-interface examples presented in Figures 4.9–4.14 detail the three major components of interdepartmental-interface elements. The left-hand block represents general subsystem functions that may have informational importance to the MKIS. For example, in Figure 4.9, the general-ledger portion of general accounting is important to marketing because this subsystem function generates sales-rep expense data. This level of interface control can be

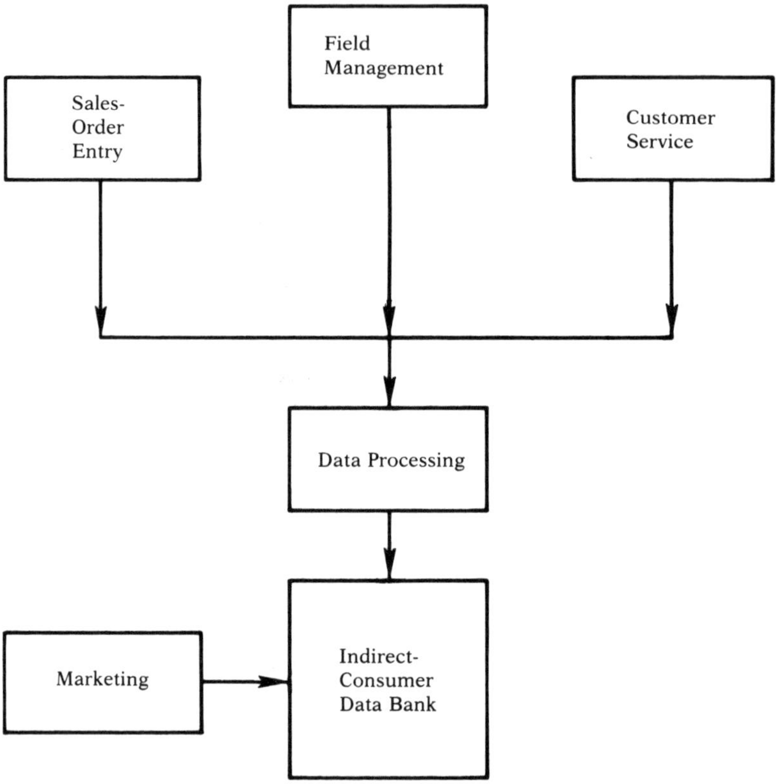

Figure 4.8 Departmental interface: indirect-consumer data bank

derived by working with other department managers to determine which areas of their operation generate data important to your MKIS. The middle block in Figure 4.9 illustrates common data that are likely to be shared by marketing through the use of the computer's central processing unit. The right-hand block represents typical Management Information System processing outputs (reports) that have relative informational importance to the MKIS.

The extent of the interdepartmental output utility is an interpretation

(Text continues on page 96)

GENERAL SUBSYSTEM FUNCTIONS

GENERAL LEDGER
- Transaction Posting
- Edit and Analysis
- Master Update
- Budget Distribution

ACCOUNTS PAYABLE
- Vendor Edit Control
- Invoice Register
- Tax Computation
- Check Production

PAYROLL
- Gross-Pay Calculations
- Gross-Pay Distribution
- Employee Record Control
- Payroll Data

ACCOUNTS RECEIVABLE
- Credit Determination
- Cash Receipts Data
- Collection Data
- Vendor Invoice Data
- Discount Policies
- Customer Billings

INVENTORY CONTROL
- Work in Process
- Raw Material Control
- Stock Control
- Cost-of-Goods Data
- Carrying-Cost Determination

COST ACCOUNTING
- Manufacturing Cost Data
- Direct Material Cost
- Direct Labor Cost
- Overhead Cost
- Standard Cost

COMMON DATA BASE

EXPENSE ANALYSIS
SALES EXPENSE DATA
SALES DATA
REVENUE ANALYSIS
CASH DISBURSEMENT DATA
ACCOUNTS DUE DATA
VENDOR INVOICES
W-2 DATA
GROSS EARNINGS
OFFICE PAYROLL
EARNINGS HISTORY
ACCOUNT BILLINGS
CONSUMER DATA
SALES REGISTER
ACCOUNT AGING
CONSIGNMENTS
INVENTORY DATA
WORK-IN-PROCESS DATA
FINISHED-GOODS INVENTORY
STERILE CONTROL STATUS
GOODS ON ORDER
SALES RECORDS
DIRECT COSTS
DIRECT LABOR
FACTORY OVERHEAD
STANDARD COST

MIS PROCESSING

GENERAL LEDGER
- Balance Sheet
- Income Statement
- Profit and Loss
- Cost Analysis
- Budget Variance/Analysis

ACCOUNTS PAYABLE
- Check Register
- Invoice Register
- Vendor Register

PAYROLL
- Employee Earnings
- W-2 Forms
- Payroll Record

ACCOUNTS RECEIVABLE
- Sales Register
- Account Activity
- Credit/Consignment Activity
- Billing Activity

INVENTORY CONTROL
- Inventory Status
- Product Status
- Work in Process

COST ACCOUNTING
- Production Cost
- Variance
- Standard Cost/Product
- Cost of Sales

Figure 4.9 Accounting subsystem interface

GENERAL SUBSYSTEM FUNCTIONS

MATERIALS MANAGEMENT
- Materials Requisition
- Quality Inspection

PRODUCTION
- Production Planning
- Daily Production
- Daily Orders
- Manufacturing Standards (Standard Costs)
- Manufacturing Costs (Direct, Indirect Overheads)
- Forecast
- Capacity Decisions

FINISHED-GOODS INVENTORY
- Customer Billings
- Plant Quality Control
- Product Control
- In-Process Inventory
- Final Inventory
- Consignments

PHYSICAL DISTRIBUTION
- Finished-Goods Data
- Current Orders
- Back-Order Status
- Shipping Data
- Reorder Point
- Order Control

COMMON DATA BASE

MANUFACTURING STANDARDS ANALYSIS
MACHINE SHOP ASSEMBLY DATA
MANUFACTURING STANDARDS
PRODUCTION DATA
PRODUCTION SCHEDULE
PRODUCTION COSTS
SALES/PRODUCTION FORECAST
UTILIZATION CAPACITY
MONTHLY BILLINGS
QUALITY-CONTROL DATA
FINISHED-PRODUCT DATA/INVENTORY
ORDER STATUS ANALYSIS
SHIPPING DATA
QUALITY-CONTROL DATA

MIS PROCESSING

MATERIALS MANAGEMENT
- Product Development Overhead (Indirect and Direct Cost Reports)

PRODUCTION
- Product Production Reports
- Daily Production Report
- Product Performance Report
- Standard Costs, Manufacturing, Direct and Indirect Product-Costs Report
- Production versus Forecast Report
- Production versus Sales Report

INVENTORY
- Daily Billings Report
- Work-in-Process Status Report
- Product Mix/Product Status Report

PHYSICAL DISTRIBUTION
- Finished-Goods Status Report
- Reorder Point Report
- Daily Shipment Report

Figure 4.10 Manufacturing subsystem interface

GENERAL SUBSYSTEM FUNCTIONS	COMMON DATA BASE	MIS PROCESSING
STAFFING AND RECRUITING • Sources of Labor • Selection PLACEMENT • Evaluation • Advancement COMPENSATION • Salary Administration • Performance Reviews • Incentive Plans EMPLOYEE RELATIONS • Grievance Administration • Discipline and Discharge • Corporate Services MANPOWER DEVELOPMENT • Management Improvement Programs • Instructional Support Programs	EDUCATIONAL HISTORY EMPLOYMENT HISTORY SALARY HISTORY REFERENCES PROMOTION RESULTS PAYROLL DATA PERSONNEL FORECASTS WAGE ADJUSTMENT FACTOR CONTRACT NEGOTIATION DATA PERFORMANCE RECORDS DISCHARGE ADMINISTRATION EMPLOYEE BENEFIT ADMINISTRATION SALES TRAINING MANAGERIAL TRAINING	EMPLOYEE INFORMATION REPORTS/DOCUMENTATION • Employee Salary Report • Employee Performance Review Reports • Payroll Distribution Reports • Employee Roster • Job Evaluation Report • Turnover Report • Employee Benefits Report

Figure 4.11 Administrative services/personnel subsystem interface

GENERAL SUBSYSTEM FUNCTIONS	COMMON DATA BASE	MIS PROCESSING
DATA COLLECTION:	CONSUMER:	CONSUMER DATA
	Name	• Active Consumer List
CONSUMER DATA	Address	• Inactive Consumer List
Name and Address	City	• Prospect List
Consumer Number	State	
Consumer Segment/Type	Zip	PRODUCT DATA
Purchase History	Phone	• Sales Catalog Summary
	Type/Number	• Field Inventory Report
PRODUCT DATA	Order History	• Field Items Ordered (not shipped)
Catalog Number		
Model Number	PRODUCT:	
Product Code/Territory	Number	SALES DATA
Price	Model	• Daily Sales Reports
Promotional Eligibility	Price	• Product-Billings Report
Description	Location	• Sales-Order Activity List
Inventory Type	Inventory Change	
Standard Cost Data	Labor Cost	DISTRIBUTION DATA
Break Price	Variable Cost	• Daily Shipment Activity
	Fixed Cost	• Monthly Shipment Activity
SALES DATA	Overhead Cost	
Units Billed	Quantity Discounts	
Bill to Company		
Number Orders YTD	SALES:	
Dates of Orders	Units Billed	
Contract Number	Order History	
Back-Order Allowance	Daily	
Sales Incentive Rate	Weekly	
	Monthly	
DISTRIBUTION DATA	Quarterly	
Quantity Shipped	Yearly	
Ship-to-Customer No.	Incentive Rates	
Location-Code	Back-Order Status	
STD Delivery Time		
	DISTRIBUTION:	
	Ship-to-Customer	
	Location Code	

Figure 4.12 Sales-Order Entry (S.O.E.) subsystem interface

GENERAL SUBSYSTEM FUNCTIONS	COMMON DATA BASE	MIS PROCESSING
RESEARCH DEVELOPMENT Marketing Feasibility Feedback Research Development Costs Research Design Detail Research Publication Research Data Valuation and Appraisal Product Differentiation Data	CURRENT RESEARCH PROJECTS PRODUCT SPECIFICATION DATA PRODUCT DIFFERENTIATION DATA PRODUCT DESIGN DATA START-UP EXPENSE DATA FEASIBILITY DATA APPLIED-RESEARCH DATA	RESEARCH DEVELOPMENT ● Research Status Report ● Product Specifications Report ● Competitive Comparison Tables (Guide) ● Design Review Status Report ● Marketing/New Product Report

Figure 4.13 Research and Development subsystem interface

GENERAL SUBSYSTEM FUNCTIONS	COMMON DATA BASE	MIS PROCESSING
PRODUCT DEVELOPMENT Research Status Product Design Product Evaluation Development Costs Valuation and Appraisal ENGINEERING SPECIFICATIONS Product Specifications Potential Product Weaknesses Product Differentiation Specifications Special Engineering Data	PRODUCT CHANGE SPECIFICATIONS REDESIGN SPECIFICATIONS PRODUCT FEASIBILITY DATA PRODUCT COST AND EXPENSE DATA PRODUCT SPECIFICATION DATA ENGINEERING ORDERS DATA PLANT ENGINEERING DATA	PRODUCT DEVELOPMENT Product Change Status Reports Engineering Design Review Status Reports Product Development Expense Summary SPECIFICATIONS Product Specifications Report-Engineer Specification Final Specifications Report

Figure 4.14 Engineering subsystem interface

for each manager. However, too many reports are not efficient in terms of data, space, and time consideration. You should concentrate your output whenever possible for ease of use and interpretation. A logical conclusion is that if you have reached the level of interdepartmental knowledge sufficient to require the streamlining of data output, your time has most likely been well spent.

Action Plan

1. Define the MKIS system's purpose. This should be built around your overall MKIS objectives.
2. Design the MKIS data structure to effectively inform, service and guide those who will use the system output.
3. Define the data requirements that will support your input-output relationships. (Table 4.1).
4. Design the MKIS Framework (Figure 4.1) to dramatize the MKIS as an information network. (Remember that the Framework consists of departments, outputs, data banks, applications and reports).
5. Re-evaluate your system structure and data linkages (Figure 4.2).
6. Define the MKIS data file elements. Use your accumulated design documentation as a reference guide.
7. Evaluate all edit procedures, codes and system maintenance provisions.
8. Evaluate Steps 1-7 with your DP analysts.
9. Examine all interdepartmental-interface requirements (Figures 4.3-4.8).
10. Initiate departmental interface workshops to determine common data use (Figures 4.9-4.14).
11. Develop a flow chart of your MKIS documentation to date.
12. Begin to document all MKIS detail and preliminary processing capabilities (reports).

CHAPTER 5

Designing Reports: Putting Your Data into Proper Perspective

Translating Your Marketing Philosophy into Specific Information Needs

Once you have determined your information needs, you can begin to design reports to satisfy those needs. In this chapter, and in the applications chapters (Chapters 6 through 9), we will refer to the "report" as the document of output for your data. Technically, data can be supplied in several different forms: hard-copy reports, cathode-ray-tube (CRT) screens, microfilm or microfiche, keypunch cards, or magnetic tape. The way in which the actual report is delivered in your organization most likely will be determined by the technical capabilities of your Marketing and Data Processing departments. However, regardless of the way in which data and information will be transferred to the user, the intent will remain the same. For the sake of consistency, we will refer to all applications as being comprised of information that is contained within a report, keeping in mind that the actual output may or may not be transferred to a hard-copy computer printout report.

To determine what reports you and your organization need, complete the following steps:

1. Relate your answers on the Marketing Questionnaire (Table 2.1) to your Marketing Philosophy (Table 3.3)
2. Devise your own version of the MKIS Framework (Figure 4.1)
3. Complete preliminary designs of reports that will provide the information being sought in your MKIS Framework
4. Determine which data elements must be present in order to satisfy the application sections of your MKIS Framework

These steps should help you order and structure your marketing information requirements.

If you follow the book sequentially, you will already have completed Steps 1 and 2. If you have not, you should review Chapters 1 through 4. Although many managers tend to jump right in to the report-design stage of a system, primarily because it is the most "fun," you can place your entire effort in jeopardy if your report applications do not tie to your Framework objectives. Contrary to popular custom, reports should not exist because they look nice or contain "neat" data. Reports should exist only because they contain information or data that will help marketing management make an intelligent decision about a problem or strategy.

Principles of Report Design

In Chapter 2, we analyzed data and information through the Marketing Information Questionnaire. In Chapter 3, we clarified data and information needs by establishing a Marketing Philosophy. However, knowing which questions you and your organization need answers to is only a small part of the MKIS implementation and development process. To be useful to the marketing-management decision-maker, information must be displayed in a way that will make it (1) timely, (2) effective, and (3) understandable.

First, the information you present must be timely. The time intervals at which information needs become available are a vital component of your system. If you or your staff make daily field product allocations based on previous sales data, for example, it will do little good to have sales results summarized solely on a monthly basis. On the other hand, if a system user needs sales data on existing product lines in order to prepare a long-range forecast, it is unlikely that sales data, detailed at a daily level, will do him much good. The time periods covered by the requests must match the levels at which the data are stored and retrieved. In other words, the application must fit the information needed.

Second, when information is reported to a user, it must effectively answer his questions. For example, if you are trying to measure your company's strengths versus the competition, having comparative-product technical literature will answer only part of the question. Most likely, you will also want to have access to sales history and customer and sales-representative feedback. In other words, the application must fit the information need. Information is effective only when it gives you input that can help answer questions and solve problems.

Third, the information reported must be understandable. A report will be of little value to the user if he cannot interpret it. All terminology, data-element descriptions, and calculations have to be explained to each user in order for the information to have its fullest impact. Misinterpretation of information is found particularly in calculated or derived fields on a report. A "trend," for example, could be calculated in dozens of different ways. Yet the way in which it is calculated may have different meanings to different users.

At this stage, you, the MKIS designer, have two primary tasks:

1. Of the hundreds of possible sales- and marketing-related questions, determine which are most appropriate to the organization and which can be answered by maintaining an ongoing information system
2. After completing the first task, determine how the information should be presented

Once you have systematically reviewed your Marketing Questionnaire, Marketing Philosophy, MKIS Framework, and existing system reports, you will be able to specify the ten, fifty, or three hundred functions that you want your MKIS to perform. But you still have additional work to do before you can begin your preliminary report designs. For example, you know that for sales-management purposes, the MKIS should be able to identify the best sales people. But "best" according to what criteria? Best in unit sales? Best in dollar sales? Best in profit contribution? Likewise, you might know that the Product Marketing Department in your company continually needs to identify, for promotion purposes, past purchases with customer profile. But for all products? For all customers? For what time periods?

As you begin to lay out your preliminary reports, you will discover many such questions that had not occurred to you before. Each report will prompt additional questions that relate to the specific data contained within it. Also, there are several general questions that relate to all reports, and these too should be considered:

1. Is the report currently being produced?
2. Is it prepared manually or by a computer?

3. Who uses the report? Who should use the report?
4. How often is it distributed?
5. What is the title of the report?
6. What applications does it provide within the MKIS Framework?
7. What type of a report is it? Into which subset (Sales Management, Product, Consumer, or Market) of your Framework does it fall?
8. What specific elements (sales units, customers) are included?
9. How should the data elements be presented?
10. What time period(s) should it cover?
11. Should the current data elements be compared against previous time periods, quotas, or standards?
12. What type of calculations should be included?

Once you know specifically what the report will contain, you can list your design ideas. For this purpose, you may want to use preprinted report layout sheets, which your DP Department should be able to provide. These forms will conform precisely to the characteristics of your DP shop's printer and will contain small blocks, with rows and columns, for all characters of the report. However, you can also design your report on a standard 8½ by 11-inch sheet of paper. Usually the physical appearance of the report will be modified several times, so at this stage you don't have to be exact.

There are three principles of good report design that you should try to follow:

1. The report should be kept simple by using as few data elements and calculations as possible.
2. Whenever possible, the report should have been prepared and tested several times manually before a final hard-copy conversion is authorized.
3. The report should be designed with a specific type of user in mind. A vice-president will want to see major trends and little detail, whereas an analyst may want the detail in order to interpret the trends.

Once the report design has been committed to paper, it should be documented and approved by the appropriate management group.

Report Name: *Product Performance Summary (by customer)* Number: *PSS-120*

Frequency: *Daily, Weekly, Monthly* Copies: 4

Purpose: *To provide a summary of unit and dollar purchases, by product, of each of our customers.*

File: *Sales Management Data Bank*

Report Data Elements:

1. *Customer Name*
2. *Customer Number*
3. *Territory Number*
4. *Units Shipped*
5. *Sales Amount*

Calculations: *None*

Totals: *By product, for units shipped, and $ sales amount*

Designed by: ______________________ (Report Designer)

Date: ____________

Approved by: ______________________ Vice President, Sales

______________________ Vice President, Data Processing

______________________ Systems Analyst

______________________ Others (as appropriate)

Figure 5.1 Report design

Whether you do this on an individual report basis or for all of the MKIS reports as a whole depends upon your situation. If you already have a working system that requires additions, then passing one report "through the approval loop" is appropriate. However, if you are designing an entire system, you will probably want to have all reports approved at one time. Nevertheless, you must create a design for each report. A sample of what you should include in this design is provided in Figure 5.1, which illustrates Report 6.3 in Chapter 6.

Relating Data Elements to Your Report Needs

The fundamental point in report design is that you cannot report data if you do not have it in your system. Therefore, once all reports are designed and approved, make a list of all data elements (and related reporting elements, i.e., the calculations derived from primary data elements) that do or will exist in your system. These elements will form the core of your system and become your MKIS data base. For convenience in reference and compilation, you can list them according to the appropriate data bank of your MKIS Framework.

Tables 3.5 A–D list all raw and derived data elements that are used in the reporting applications found in Chapters 6 through 9. The data-element listings are important for two reasons. First, they ensure that you are not duplicating your collection and storage efforts. Second, they will act as a dictionary for future uses when you review your system for application additions, deletions, and modifications.

Custom Report Writing

In concept, the calculation capabilities of a large mainframe computer are similar to those of a small calculator. Both can calculate large quantities of data in small periods of time. However, the large computer calculates, stores, and operates thousands of times faster. The only difficulty in dealing with the large computers is the communication process between the user and the central processing unit. How can the busy manager deal with "bytes," "records," and "fields" and custom design special data elements into meaningful reports? And how can he do this periodically without going to the Data Processing Department or a time-sharing service?

Fortunately, several information retrieval systems or, as they are sometimes referred to, custom report writers, are available. Any task can be accomplished that involves accessing data presently being stored in a data bank. Custom report writers use various forms of ordinary English-language commands to replace complex programming languages. The result is a program, produced in minutes, that enables the manager to satisfy information requirements. The report generated is exactly as requested.

Custom report writers require several days of orientation and several more days of practice to enable the user to custom-design special applications. Typically, a custom report writer requires that the user be familiar with:

1. Data storage location
2. Data availability
3. Calculations involved
4. Sequence specifications
5. Report format specifications

Basically knowing which data are contained in each data bank and understanding the report-writer condition clauses are all that are necessary.

Almost without exception, standard report distribution is insufficient for total decision-making support. Custom report writers allow you to design special information requests on a periodic-need basis. If any one of your special reports must be distributed regularly the actual programming by your systems group is reduced, because you in fact have already produced many of the specifications required for hard-copy production.

Action Plan*

1. Based upon your MKIS Framework (see Figure 4.1 in Chapter 4), make a list of the report applications that meet your overall information needs.

*Although you can complete these Action Plan items now, we suggest that you wait until after you review the applications in Chapters 6 through 9.

2. For each application, complete a first-draft copy of a support document explaining what the report contains and what it is intended to do.
3. Complete a preliminary design for each report application.
4. Determine which data elements, both new and derived, must exist in order to complete all of the applications.

SECTION III

APPLICATION

Sales-Management Report Applications

Product Data-Bank Report Applications

Consumer Data-Bank Report Applications

Market Data-Bank Report Applications

CHAPTER 6

Sales-Management Report Applications

Assumptions

Before we can discuss actual sales reports that you could derive from your MKIS, several ground rules must be established. Your actual applications may vary from those we present here; yet because the reports described are based on those most commonly found sales organizations, you should easily be able to modify them to fit your particular needs.

Let's establish a hypothetical sales organization (described in Figure 6.1) that has a national sales manager, four regional managers, twelve district managers, and sixty direct-sales representatives. The Hypo-Thetical Company sells all of its products directly to its customers through one sales force. Hypo's customer is the end user of the company's products. Because ultimately we will want to know the specific product sales of each sales representative, his territory, district, region, and the nation as a whole, we have assigned a five-digit numbering scheme for Hypo's sales organization:

Position(s)

1 Geographical area of the world. At Hypo, a 5 indicates national (United States).

2 Geographical area within national. Four geographical regions will fall into this position. At Hypo, 1 indicates the Eastern Region, 2 the Southern Region, 3 the Midwestern Region, and 4 the Western Region.

3 Further geographical breakdown within Position 2. At Hypo, this is the district level.

4–5 A specific territory or sales representative.

Under this scheme, each unit (nation, region, district, and sales representative/territory) is identified specifically. For example, all sales representatives in the Eastern Region will have a 51 prefix representing their territory numbers. Likewise, all sales representatives within District 1 of the Eastern Region will have a 511 prefix in their territory numbers.

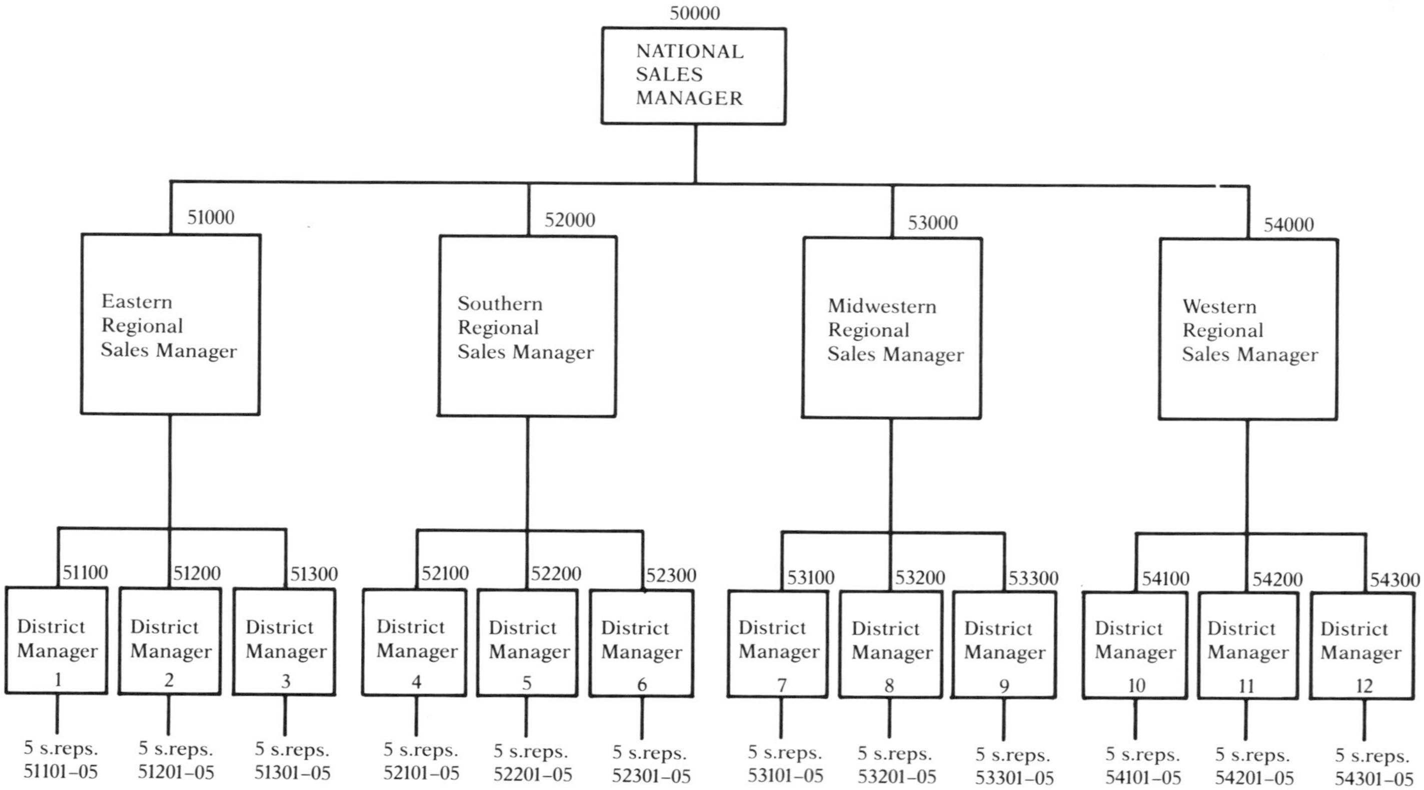

Figure 6.1 Sales organization of the Hypo-Thetical Company

Then, each sales representative in the same district will have a unique two-position identifier.

With this type of numbering structure, without using alphabetical characters, it is possible to divide the world into ten areas (0-9). At the regional level, you can divide the major geographical area (national-United States in this case) into nine separate regional areas (1-9). Then, each region can have up to nine districts (1-9), and each district can have a maximum of ninety-nine territories.

From a product standpoint, let's assume that Hypo manufactures and sells three products: the Maxi-Hypo, the Mini-Hypo, and the All-Purpose Hypo. The Maxi comes in three models: Deluxe (Model XL-101), Standard (Model MA-16), and Unusual (Model CP-302). The Mini has only one model, the Mini-Standard (Model STD-A1). The All-Purpose comes in six models (Models AP1 through AP6). The product types are summarized in Table 6.1.

The Framework for Sales-Management Reports

Even with a simple sales organization and a limited product line such as Hypo's, the need for a well-organized sales-report system is obvious. If you are unable to capture and report on the necessary data, you will be unable to make sound decisions on product and/or sales-force performance.[1]

In this regard, you should begin to consider the types of reports that will communicate exactly what you need to know. Effective sales-report applications of your MKIS should address the following:

1. Product/service performance by product/service type
2. Product/service performance by geographical area
3. Profit/loss performance by geographical area

1. The Sales-Management Reporting System is positioned on the far right side of the MKIS Framework (Figure 4.1) in Chapter 4.

TABLE 6.1
Product Mix for the Hypo-Thetical Company

NAME	CONFIGURATION/ DESCRIPTION	MODEL NUMBER
Maxi-Hypo	• Deluxe	XL-101
	• Standard	MA-16
	• Unusual	CP-302
Mini-Hypo	• Standard	STD-A1
All-Purpose Hypo		AP-1
		AP-2
		AP-3
		AP-4
		AP-5
		AP-6

4. Specialized reports for sales-rep information and commission payments
5. Sales-management performance flags
6. Ranking systems on key results
7. Ability to tie items 1-6 together and match/merge key data elements

The Organization of Sales-Management Report Applications

Each of these report applications falls into one, two, or three possible report levels: detailed, summary, or analytical. The Sales-Report Application Matrix (Table 6.2) outlines the sales reports that Hypo feels are important. Note that Hypo uses a report numbering system that easily relates the report to its function. For example, the Product/Service Performance reports have a PS prefix, followed by a "D" for Detailed, "S" for Summary, and "A" for Analytical reporting. Likewise, the report numbers tell how detailed or analytical the report actually is. The higher the number within the appropriate report level, the more summarized or

TABLE 6.2
Sales-Report Application Matrix for the Hypo-Thetical Company

REPORT APPLICATION LEVELS	DETAILED REPORT APPLICATION	SUMMARY REPORT APPLICATION	ANALYTICAL REPORT APPLICATION	
1. Product/Service Performance by Product/Service Type	PSD-100	PSS-110 PSS-120	PSA-130 PSA-140	
2. Product/Service Performance by Geographical Area	PSD-200	PSS-210(T) 211(D) 212(R) 213(N) PSS-220	PSA-230(T) 231(D) 232(R) 233(N)	PSA-240(T) 241(D) 242(R) 243(N) PSA-250
3. Profit/Loss Performance by Geographical Area		PLS-300(T) 301(D) 302(R) 303(N)	PLA-310(T) 311(D) 312(R) 313(N)	PLA-320(T) 321(D) 322(R) 323(N)
4. Specialized Reports for Sales-Representative Information and Commission Payments	SRD-400(T) 401(D) 402(R) 403(N)	SRS-410		
5. Sales-Management Flags		SFS-500 SFS-510		
6. Ranking Reports		SRS-600	SRA-610	
7. Summary Analysis Integration			SAA-700 SAA-710	

analytical the report is. And finally, where appropriate, Hypo has chosen to number sequentially the reports that are essentially the same but provide different versions for territory, district, region, and national sales reports. For example, Reports PSS-210 through PSS-213 have the same formats containing the same information, but at different geographical levels: PSS-210 is for territories, PSS-211 is for districts, and so on.

Before we review each of the sales-report applications, take a look at any one of the reports. In the upper right-hand corner of each report is a

Frequency option. This option indicates the reporting time periods that Hypo has available for that report. The frequency option used for each example appears in parentheses after the report number in the upper left-hand corner.

From a practical standpoint, it is not mandatory that you establish a report-numbering scheme like Hypo's. In fact, since you are likely to have parts of a sales-report system already in place, you might find it impossible. However, you do have to determine what your own sales-report application matrix should contain. You can certainly do without a uniform numbering system, but you cannot ignore the voids in your application matrix.

For reviewing each level of the report applications, we will consider four points, where appropriate: what is contained in the report (elements); where the elements originate;[2] how you (and who) should use the report; and possible variations of the report.

Product/Service Performance by Product/Service Type (100 Series)

The most basic reports classified under Sales-Management Report Applications are those that deal primarily with the detail of individual invoice transactions. These are the reports that will be most closely linked to your sales-order process. In fact, they may give just a listing of your actual sales-order invoices. The purpose of the Product/Service Performance by Product/Service Type reports is to provide an audit trail for you to use in cases where you need to refer to a specific invoice transaction.

PSD-100 (REPORT 6.1)

The Product Performance Detail Report is the lowest level of all sales reports. It shows every item that was shipped during a given day, week, or month, in invoice-number sequence. In some organizations, this report is referred to as the Invoice Register.

2. See Chapters 3 and 4 for the method of originating report elements and applications.

REPORT 6.1
Hypo-Thetical Company
Product Performance Detail
Period Ended 6/30/85

PSD-100 (Monthly)

Frequency: Daily
Weekly
Monthly

ORDER DATED	SHIP DATE	PRODUCT NAME	MODEL NO.	QUANTITY ORDERED	QUANTITY SHIPPED	SALE AMOUNT ($)	INVOICE NUMBER	P.O. NUMBER	CUSTOMER NUMBER
6-02-85	6-04-85	Maxi	XL-101	78	78	7,800.00	68394	30619	80001
6-02-85	6-04-85	Maxi	XL-101	135	130	6,500.00	68395	72814	94624
6-02-85	6-04-85	Mini	STD-A1	15	15	375.00	68396	64111	31122
6-03-85	6-07-85	A/P	AP-5	6	6	120.00	68397	12361	78214
⇕	⇕	⇕	⇕	⇕	⇕	⇕	⇕	⇕	⇕
6-30-85	6-30-85	A/P	AP-4	307	307	6,140.00	70462	0042	11669
Total Month	—	—	—	181,575	166,472	$4,661,812.00	—	—	—

Note: The arrows in this chart, and those that follow, stand for additional entries.

Note that in this sample monthly report three columns (Quantity Ordered, Quantity Shipped, and Sale Amount) have totals. The totals in the Sale Amount column obviously represent total gross sales for the month of June. However, the totals for Quantity Ordered and Quantity Shipped have a less direct meaning. Because we have mixed apples and oranges (or Minis and Maxis in this case), it does not mean much to say that Hypo shipped 166,472 units in June. If all of the units were Maxis, then Hypo had a tremendous month! But if they were mixed, Hypo had a dismal month. The *only* reason—but a very important one—that these totals are printed is for a cross-reference to other monthly reports. If, for example, when we add up all the units shipped, by territory, we do not get the same total as on the PSD-100 (Monthly), then we know that there has been an error in calculating at least one of these sets of reports. The inclusion and frequent use of these "control totals" in your system is very important.

This report will be derived most likely from your Sales-Order Entry system.[3] The report layout is secondary to its actual contents. You must ensure that every element of importance is included: what product was sold, when you sold it, and who bought it. If you can include these items (elements), you have the basis for an Invoice Register.

PSS-110 (REPORT 6.2)

The Product Performance Summary (By Product) Report is issued daily, weekly, or monthly to summarize the contents of Report 6.1, the Product Performance Detail (PSD-100), by product/model number for all products.

Whereas the detailed report will be most useful when troubleshooting a specific sales order, this summary report will be useful as a sales analysis tool. In the report, you can see how many of each model Hypo shipped during the month of June.

Much of the detail has been removed from the summary report so that you can focus on the direct results. Note that the control totals of this report are tied to the totals in Report 6.1 (PSD-100).

3. Refer to Figure 4.12, Sales-Order Entry Subsystem Interface, in Chapter 4 to determine exact data requirements.

REPORT 6.2
Hypo-Thetical Company
Product Performance Summary (By Product)
Period Ended 6/30/85

PSS-110 (Monthly)

Frequency: Daily
Weekly
Monthly

PRODUCT NAME	MODEL NO.	QUANTITY ORDERED	QUANTITY SHIPPED	SALE AMOUNT ($)
Maxi-Hypo	XL-101	8,753	8,600	860,000.00
	MA-16	1,500	1,500	135,000.00
	CP-302	1,000	1,000	80,000.00
Total Maxi-Hypo		11,253	11,100	1,075,000.00***
Mini-Hypo	STD-A1	84,950	81,000	2,025,000.00
Total Mini-Hypo		84,950	81,000	2,025,000.00***
All-Purpose Hypo	AP-1	58,372	58,372	1,167,440.00
	AP-2	3,000	0	0
	AP-3	18,000	10,000	200,000.00
	AP-4	0	0	0
	AP-5	6,000	6,000	120,000.00
	AP-6	0	0	0
Total All-Purpose Hypo		85,372	74,372	1,561,812.00***
Total All Products		181,575	166,472	4,661,812.00***

PSS-120 (REPORT 6.3)

The Product Performance Summary (By Customer) Report is a daily, weekly, or monthly report that explodes the information found in Report 6.2 (PSS-110) in order to include, by model number, summary sales data by each customer. This report looks at the sales volume (units shipped) of just one product, the XL-101 Maxi-Hypo, for all customers.

The report is useful when you want to analyze the impact of a sales promotion of a certain product. Are you reaching your target market? Are you achieving forecast? Note that the control totals in this report are tied to the XL-101 line item in Report 6.2 (PSS-110).

PSA-130 (REPORT 6.4)

A natural outgrowth of the previous summary examples is a more analytical report, the Historical Performance Summary (By Product) Report. This report allows you to track the trends of each product. Is your product following your projected life cycle? Are you ignoring products that have a high margin or potential?

On either a monthly or quarterly basis, by first examining a specific trend indicator, you can quickly spot those products that you want to analyze more carefully. Here, we will look at the average performance in the most recent two quarters and then compare this to the average of the previous four. You may want to use an indicator, as we have done here with the *** notation, to show where an increased or decreased performance level is above plus/minus a 100-percent change.

A variation to this report is to use dollar sales instead of units. In fact, by comparing the two reports, you can see the dollar and unit increases and study the impact of price changes.

PSA-140 (REPORT 6.5)

The Historical Performance Summary (By Customer) Report, when produced on a monthly or quarterly basis, provides a look at your customers' purchasing behavior and trends. The format is essentially the

REPORT 6.3
Hypo-Thetical Company
Product Performance Summary (By Customer)
Period Ended 6/30/85

Product Name: MAXI-HYPO
Model Number: XL–101

PSS–120 (Monthly)

Frequency: Daily
Weekly
Monthly

CUSTOMER NAME	CUSTOMER NUMBER	TERRITORY NUMBER	UNITS SHIPPED	SALE AMOUNT ($)
Acme Controls	69,362	51,104	375	37,500.00
Baker Labs	12,943	54,102	4,000	400,000.00
⇕	⇕	⇕	⇕	⇕
Wallace Pipe	16,169	53,102	75	7,500.00
Product Totals			8,600	860,000.00

REPORT 6.4
Hypo-Thetical Company
Historical Performance Summary (By Product)
Period Ended 6/30/85*

PSA-130 (Quarterly)

Frequency: Monthly
Quarterly

		UNIT SALES										
		FY 1983				FY 1984				FY 1985		PERCENTAGE CHANGE CURRENT 2-QUARTER AVERAGE VS PREVIOUS
PRODUCT NAME	MODEL NO.	Q1	Q2	Q3	Q4	Q1	Q2	Q3	Q4	Q1	Q2	4-QUARTER AVERAGE
Maxi-Hypo	XL-101	75	90	380	4,100	8,000	9,000	11,000	12,000	1,500	1,700	60.0
⇕	⇕	⇕	⇕	⇕	⇕	⇕	⇕	⇕	⇕	⇕	⇕	⇕
All-Purpose Hypo	AP-6	0	0	0	0	10	20	800	900	3,000	3,500	652.4***
Total All Products												

*Fiscal year is January–December.

REPORT 6.5
Hypo-Thetical Company
Historical Performance Summary (By Customer)
Period Ended 6/30/85*

Customer Name **Customer No.**
Acme Controls **69362**

PSA-140 (Quarterly) Frequency: Monthly
Quarterly

		UNIT SALES										PERCENTAGE CHANGE
		FY 1983				FY 1984				FY 1985		CURRENT 2-QUARTER AVERAGE VS PREVIOUS
PRODUCTS		Q1	Q2	Q3	Q4	Q1	Q2	Q3	Q4	Q1	Q2	4-QUARTER AVERAGE
Maxi-Hypo	XL-101	0	8	78	150	9	80	52	59	80	40	20.0
	⇕	⇕	⇕	⇕	⇕	⇕	⇕	⇕	⇕	⇕	⇕	
All-Purpose Hypo	AP-6	10	10	10	10	10	10	10	10	10	10	0.0

Total Customer 69362

*Fiscal Year is January-December.

same as Report 6.4 (PSA-130), but here you are looking at the history of each product within each customer.

You may want to confine your summary to only certain products or include an option in this report's print program that allows you to print just selected products. You can then alternate your products from month to month and avoid having a huge report that does not change substantially from one period to the next.

Product/Service Performance by Geographical Area (200 Series)

Like the 100 Series reports, the Product/Service Performance by Geographical Area reports offer the most detailed tools available in your MKIS, and in this case specifically at the territory, district, or regional levels. These reports are most widely used by the individual sales representative in following his sales orders. However, they are also excellent tools for in-house sales analysis, particularly when the user is interested in specific account- or territory-performance levels.

PSD-200 (REPORT 6.6)

The Product Performance Detail by Customer Within Territory Report is a daily and monthly sales recap for each sales representative. It reflects sales by customer, items ordered and shipped, sale amount, and the commission rate and amount to be paid on each order. The totals of all territories must be equal to the product-control totals found in the Series 100 product reports.

This report, issued on a daily basis, should be sent directly to the sales representative in the appropriate territory. On a monthly basis, the report should be distributed to sales management and the payroll department for commission calculations.

REPORT 6.6
Hypo-Thetical Company
Product Performance Detail
By Customer Within Territory
Period Ended 6/01/85

PSD-200 (Daily)
Territory 53201

Frequency: Daily
Monthly

CUSTOMER	ORDER NO.	INVOICE NO.	ORDER DATE	SHIP DATE	PRODUCT NAME	MODEL NO.	QUANTITY ORDERED	QUANTITY SHIPPED	SALE AMOUNT	INCENTIVE RATE	INCENTIVE AMOUNT
Albrecht Corp., P.O. Box 44463, Indianapolis, Indiana 47644											
94362	16169	44992	6/01	6/01	Maxi	XL-101	200	200	20,000.00	.10	2,000.00
	16169	44992	6/01	6/01	AP	AP-4	1	1	25.00	.05	1.25
Williams Computer, 1515 S. River Rd., South Bend, Indiana 47119											
13961	02114	48721	5/29	6/01	Maxi	XL-101	10	8	800.00	.05	40.00
	03961	48779	6/01	6/01	Maxi	XL-101	30	30	3,000.00	.075	225.00
Territory Totals							241	239	23,825.00		2,266.25

PSS-210 (REPORT 6.7)

The Product Performance Sales Summary Report provides an overview of sales for the month, quarter, or year for each territory, district, and region. For each product/model number, you have gross and net sales units and net sales dollars for the period and year-to-date. In addition, you may want to follow the example and include a Totals Section that looks at sales results only by the major product-line levels. If you do, you must make sure that the totals here correspond to the totals on the product reports.

PSS-220 (REPORT 6.8)

The Product Performance Summary by Customer Within Territory Report is a summary of the invoice data contained in Report 6.6 (PSD-200). It uses the format of Report 6.7, (PSD-210) but it has been broken down to the customer level.

PSA-231 (REPORT 6.9)

By using the same information provided in the earlier geographical area sales reports (Series 200), the Recap of Sales Performance Report looks at net unit and dollar sales by district and calculates a percentage change from a previous period. The report is essentially a field-sales management tool for monitoring individual performance and providing feedback to corporate management on the status of an area's progress toward goal achievement.

PSA-242 (REPORT 6.10)

The Sales to Forecast Comparison Report can be used by field management and corporate/marketing management to assess progress toward specific goals. In fact, this report, or one similar to it, is often used as one measure for determining a field manager's bonus. The report can be as general or specific as you care to make it, depending upon the confidence you have in your forecast. If your forecasting process is relatively

REPORT 6.7
Hypo-Thetical Company
Product Performance Monthly Sales Summary
Period Ended 6/30/85

PSS-210 (Monthly)
Region 51000 Eastern
District 51100
Territory 51104

Frequency: Monthly
Quarterly
Yearly

		MONTH TO DATE				YEAR TO DATE			
		UNITS				UNITS			
PRODUCT NAME	MODEL NO.	SOLD	RET	NET	NET $	SOLD	RET	NET	NET $
Maxi-Hypo Deluxe	XL-101	50	0	50	5,000	50	0	50	5,000
Maxi-Hypo Standard	MA-16	16	5	11	1,100	48	18	30	3,000
Maxi-Hypo Unusual	CP-702					100	40	60	6,000
Mini-Hypo Standard	STD-A1					50	0	50	2,500
All-Purpose	AP-1	100	50	50	1,250	100	50	50	1,250
All-Purpose	AP-2	75	75	0	0	75	75	0	0
All-Purpose	AP-3					80	0	80	2,000
All-Purpose	AP-4								
All-Purpose	AP-5								
All-Purpose	AP-6	75	0	75	1,875	160		160	4,000
Totals Section									
Maxi		66	5	61	6,100	198	58	140	14,000
Mini						50	0	50	2,500
All-Purpose		250	125	125	3,125	415	125	290	7,250
Total Territory		316	130	186	9,225	663	283	480	23,750

REPORT 6.8
Hypo-Thetical Company
Product Performance Summary
By Customer Within Territory
Period Ended 6/30/85

PSS-220 (Quarterly)
Region 51000 Eastern
District 51100
Territory 51104

Frequency: Monthly
Quarterly
Yearly

			QUARTERLY				YEAR TO DATE			
CUSTOMER	PRODUCT NAME	MODEL NO.	SOLD	RET	NET	NET $	SOLD	RET	NET	NET $
14663	Maxi	XL-101	300		300	30,000.00	300		300	30,000.00
Bartnow Con-		MA-16	900		900	90,000.00	900		900	90,000.00
struction Co.		CP-302	1,650	100	1,550	155,000.00	1,650	100	1,550	155,000.00
3319 N.E. 4th	Maxi Total		2,850	100	2,750	275,000.00	2,850	100	2,750	275,000.00
Court	Mini	STD-A1	180	30	150	3,750.00	180	30	150	3,750.00
ATT: Ac-	Mini Total		180	30	150	3,750.00	180	30	150	3,750.00
counts Pay-	AP	AP-1	3,000		3,000	60,000.00	3,000		3,000	60,000.00
able, Boston,		AP-2	15	5	10	200.00	15	5	10	200.00
MA 22150		AP-6	850		850	17,000.00	850		850	17,000.00
	AP Total		3,865	5	3,860	77,200.00	3,865	5	3,860	77,200.00
14663	Customer Total		6,895	135	6,760	355,950.00	6,895	135	6,760	355,950.00

REPORT 6.9
Hypo-Thetical Company
Product Performance Analysis
Recap of Sales Performance (By District)
Period Ended 6/30/85

PSA-231 (Monthly)
Region 54000 Western
District 54200

Frequency: Monthly
Quarterly
Yearly

		MONTH				YEAR TO DATE			
PRODUCT	MODEL NO.	NET UNITS	PERCENTAGE CHANGE FROM LAST MONTH	NET $	PERCENTAGE CHANGE FROM LAST MONTH	NET UNITS	PERCENTAGE CHANGE YTD LAST YEAR	NET $	PERCENTAGE CHANGE YTD LAST YEAR
Maxi	XL-101	1,600	15.4	160,000.00	16.9	1,600	13.5	160,000.00	14.8
	MA-16	1,000	−2.1	100,000.00	−3.2	9,000	6.2	900,000.00	6.2
	CP-302	850	3.0	85,000.00	3.0	8,762	7.9	876,200.00	8.5
Total Maxi		3,450	12.1	345,000.00	15.1	19,362	7.9	1,936,200.00	8.3
Mini	STD-A1	400	−16.9	10,000.00	−13.5	1,600	−3.1	40,000.00	0
Total Mini		400	−16.9	10,000.00	−13.5	1,600	−3.1	40,000.00	0
All-Purpose	AP-1	5,500	82.0	137,500.00	82.0	18,350	1.6	367,000.00	15.9
	AP-2	690	5.4	13,800.00	5.4	690	7.4	13,800.00	3.8
	AP-3	400	−10.9	8,000.00	−10.9	850	−8.6	17,000.00	−8.6
	AP-4	8,200	7.4	164,000.00	7.4	12,300	13.8	246,000.00	13.8
	AP-5	0	−100.0	0	−100.0	4,400	0	88,000.00	1.3
	AP-6	1,650	2.1	33,000.00	32.1	14,390	1.7	287,800.00	−16.4
Total AP		16,440	37.4	356,300.00	37.4	50,980	8.9	1,019,600.00	13.4
Total Products		20,290	21.5	711,300.00	23.1	71,942	6.8	2,995,800.00	7.1

REPORT 6.10
Hypo-Thetical Company
Product Performance Analysis
Sales to Forecast Comparison (By Region)
Period Ended 6/30/85

PSA-242 (Quarterly)
Region 53000 Midwestern

Frequency: Monthly
Quarterly
Yearly

	QUARTER			YEAR TO DATE		
PRODUCT	ACTUAL NET UNITS	FORECAST NET UNITS	PERCENTAGE ACHIEVEMENT	ACTUAL NET UNITS	FORECAST NET UNITS	PERCENTAGE ACHIEVEMENT
Maxi-Hypo	8,000	6,500	123.1	14,825	13,000	114.0
Mini-Hypo	750	980	76.5	980	1,265	77.5
All-Purpose Hypo	32,495	31,000	104.8	48,932	62,000	78.9
Total Products	41,245	38,480	107.2	64,737	76,265	84.9

unsophisticated and your confidence is low, then measuring actual achievements to a forecasted goal will not be very meaningful. However, regardless of the accuracy of your forecast, you should at least develop a rough measurement device, as Hypo has done here.

PSA-250 (REPORT 6.11)

The Unit-Sales Tracking Report is essentially the same as Report 6.5 (PSA-140), except that here the products are reviewed only by product lines and the customers are grouped by territories. The actual data values, however, are exactly the same.

At the bottom of this report, note that territory totals are provided. This type of final summary can become a meaningful tool for sales managers in assessing individual performance and in evaluating such opportunities as territory splits or customer-account realignments from one territory to another.

Profit-and-Loss Performance by Geographical Area (300 Series)

The purpose of the Profit and Loss reports is to offer a comprehensive view of a territory, district, or region in as little space as possible. These reports can contain a wealth of information about a given territory and are most widely used by senior field and in-house management.

PLS-303 (REPORT 6.12)

The Profit-and-Loss Summary utilizes a modified financial P&L statement to analyze profitability by each territory, district, and region, and the nation as a whole.

This type of report application for marketing and sales is a relative newcomer in corporate practice, but it is gaining in popularity because of its focus on bottom-line contributions. It offers one reason why companies

REPORT 6.11
Hypo-Thetical Company
Product Performance Analysis
Unit-Sales Tracking—Quarterly
Period Ended 6/30/85

PSA-250
Region 52000 Southern
District 52300
Territory 52301

Frequency: Quarterly

		FY 1983				FY 1984				FY 1985	
CUSTOMER	**PRODUCT**	**Q1**	**Q2**	**Q3**	**Q4**	**Q1**	**Q2**	**Q3**	**Q4**	**Q1**	**Q2**
AAA Products Miami, Fl.	Maxi	80	315	95	380	95	100	360	70	400	500
	Mini	100	100	100	0	0	0	100	100	100	0
	A/P	1,000	0	0	0	0	0	0	0	0	0
	TOTAL	1,180	415	195	380	95	100	460	170	500	500
Alphametro Inc. Ft. Lauderdale, Fl. ⇕	Maxi	0	0	0	0	0	0	0	0	0	0
	Mini	800	1,500	750	450	900	1,000	2,000	50	850	150
	A/P	0	0	15	0	0	0	80	0	15	450
	TOTAL	800	1,500	765	450	900	1,000	2,080	50	865	600
	⇕	⇕	⇕	⇕	⇕	⇕	⇕	⇕	⇕	⇕	⇕
Territory 52301	Maxi	150	315	120	400	190	200	390	70	400	500
	Mini	2,000	2,100	2,000	500	1,000	1,000	2,300	250	1,100	200
	A/P	1,500	740	630	400	30	500	145	90	0	550
	TOTAL	3,650	3,155	2,750	1,300	1,220	1,700	2,835	410	1,500	1,250

REPORT 6.12
Hypo-Thetical Company
Profit-and-Loss Summary—All Products
Period Ended 6/30/85 (Dollars)

PLS-303 (Quarterly)
National 50000

Frequency: Monthly
Quarterly

	Q2	YTD	PERCENTAGE CHANGE FROM Q1	PERCENTAGE CHANGE FROM Q2–FY 1984
Net Sales				
Maxi	18,000	31,085	37.6	49.1
Mini	2,400	4,300	26.3	53.4
AP	8,100	10,000	***	8.7
Total Net Sales	28,500	45,385	61.8	48.6
Manufacturing Costs	12,000	18,885	74.3	39.0
Gross Profits	16,500	26,500	65.0	51.0
Expenses, Controllable				
Travel and Entertainment	400	900	−25.0	5.8
Telephone	50	100	0	4.0
Samples	350	850	−30.0	10.8
Supplies/Rentals	10	25	−33.3	1.5
Literature, Shows, Exhibits	190	325	48.1	6.3
Total Controllable Expenses	1,000	2,200	−16.7	5.4
Expenses, Noncontrollable				
Auto Lease/Maintenance	85	185	−15.0	1.0
Customer Service	215	1,445	***	2.3
Salaries	1,500	2,950	3.4	7.5
Incentives	1,300	7,400	18.2	36.0
Building Rental	400	800	0	4.1
Insurance and Fees	10	20	0	10.8
Total Noncontrollable Expenses	3,500	7,800	−18.6	16.5
Total Expenses	4,500	10,000	−18.2	16.0
Profit Contribution	12,000	16,500	***	29.6

must look at more than just sales volume for measuring performance. The sales representative who sells more and spends more may not produce a greater profit contribution than the sales rep who sells less but also spends less.

Aside from its help in determining bottom-line results, a Territory (or District or Region) P&L provides a great deal of information in a small space, usually just one page. By reviewing this report, you can glean sales information by product line, manufacturing costs, and a variety of expense data. In addition, you can examine the trends of each line item. You can also quickly determine which areas are operating most efficiently (expense to sales)[4] and which are selling the most profitable products (manufacturing costs to sales).

PLA-311 (REPORT 6.13)

By including a report such as the Profit-and-Loss Analysis per Line Item, efficiency and profitability measures will be performed for you. In this example for a district, each line item (sales and expenses) is examined by how much, on a percentage basis, each territory contributes to it. The sales manager can easily pinpoint the contributors to his overall profitability.

PLA-322 (REPORT 6.14)

The Percentage of Net Sales Report is another useful tool. A Region example would show major P&L line items computed as a percentage of net sales for each district within the region.

Specialized Reports (400 Series)

Specialized sales-management reports can take many forms. Most often specialized reports fall into a catch-all section of the report system, and you

4. Referenced as "Efficiency Index" in Table 3.5 A in Chapter 3.

REPORT 6.13
Hypo-Thetical Company
Profit-and-Loss Analysis per Line Item
Period Ended 6/30/85 ($1,000s)

PLA-311 (Monthly)
Region 51000 Eastern
District 51200

Frequency: Monthly
Quarterly
Yearly

	ALL TERRITORIES JUNE	TERRITORY 51201	TERRITORY 51202	TERRITORY 51203	TERRITORY 51204	TERRITORY 51205
Net Sales						
Maxi	$ 750	15.5%	20.6%	12.4%	30.5%	21.0%
Mini	190	0	50.8	12.4	16.8	20.0
AP	160	31.1	20.6	12.4	20.0	15.9
Total Net Sales	1,100	15.0	23.5	12.4	28.5	20.6
Manufacturing Costs	400	20.0	19.8	18.5	28.5	13.2
Gross Profits	700	12.6	25.4	10.3	25.0	26.7
Expenses, Controllable						
Travel and Entertainment	45	15.0	32.6	6.9	25.5	20.0
Telephone	2	20.0	20.0	20.0	20.0	20.0
Samples	15	5.4	17.6	40.4	20.6	16.0
Supplies/Rentals	7	16.3	27.1	23.9	19.7	13.0
Literature, Shows, Exhibits	12	14.0	19.8	30.2	17.4	28.6
Total Controllable Expenses	81	19.6	25.4	26.2	20.8	18.0
Expenses, Noncontrollable						
Auto Lease/Maintenance	2	21.0	19.0	20.0	20.0	20.0
Customer Service	17	6.9	20.0	35.0	20.0	18.1
Salaries	28	22.4	18.6	19.5	19.5	21.0
Incentives	30	15.0	23.5	12.4	28.5	20.6
Building Rental	2	20.0	20.0	20.0	20.0	20.0
Insurance and Fees	1	20.0	20.0	20.0	20.0	20.0
Total Noncontrollable Expenses	80	19.1	18.6	22.3	20.0	20.0
Total Expenses	161	19.2	22.8	24.5	14.5	19.0
Profit Contribution	539	18.2	22.8	13.0	24.5	21.5

REPORT 6.14
Hypo-Thetical Company
Profit-and-Loss Analysis
Percentage of Net Sales
Period Ended 6/30/85

PLA-322 (Monthly)
Region 53000 Midwestern

Frequency: Monthly
Quarterly
Yearly

	53100	53200	53300
Net Sales			
Maxi	45.15	40.81	17.4
Mini	29.85	32.0	26.0
AP	25.0	27.19	56.6
Total Net Sales $	100.00	100.00	100.00
Manufacturing Costs	38.49	42.10	40.50
Gross Profits	61.51	57.90	59.50
Total Controllable Expenses	5.85	4.45	6.37
Total Noncontrollable Expenses	12.15	7.05	9.02
Total Expenses	18.0	11.50	15.39
Profit Contribution	43.51	46.40	44.11

can use them to analyze data elements stored in your MKIS that are important but are not included in other reports.

SRD-400 (REPORT 6.15)

The Commission Report brings together all elements of a commission program and presents them in one place. In this example, Hypo has three elements in its commission program: standard commissions, premium adjustments, and a bonus for obtaining new accounts. Because only the standard commissions were included elsewhere (in PSD-200, Report 6.6), Hypo includes this report for internal analysis and verification of payroll records.

SRS-410 (REPORT 6.16)

The Sales-Representative Information Report is a computerized version of an index-card system whereby certain data are kept, apart from those found in the Personnel Department, on each marketing and sales employee. Access to this report (or on-line file) is performed generally by top marketing-sales management and therefore can be used for as much confidential employee performance and miscellaneous information as practical or useful. This report (or file) can be used for anything from a departmental mailing list to a source for filling job openings.

Sales-Management Flag Reports (500 Series)

The purpose of sales-management flag reports is to provide the sales and marketing manager with a tool for identifying unusual circumstances quickly. The flag reports, if designed properly, should be the first reports the manager looks at each month. Once a problem is identified, he can then use other reports for specific back-up support.

REPORT 6.15
Hypo-Thetical Company
Commission Report
Period Ended 6/30/85

SRD-400
All Territories

Frequency: Monthly

REGION	DISTRICT	TERRITORY	NAME	STANDARD COMMISSION $	PREMIUM ADJUSTMENTS $	NEW-ACCOUNT BONUS $	TOTAL COMMISSIONS PAYABLE $
51000	51100	51101	Sawyer	789.40	149.80	215.00	1,154.20
		51102	Lackley	1,104.22	0	600.00	1,704.22
		⇕	⇕	⇕	⇕	⇕	⇕
		54305	OPEN				
Totals				115,000.00	7,894.15	18,360.00	141,254.15

REPORT 6.16
Hypo-Thetical Company
Sales-Representative Information Report
Period Ended 6/30/85

SRS–410

Frequency: Quarterly

REGION-DISTRICT-TERRITORY NAME-ADDRESS-PHONE	HIRE DATE	CURRENT STATUS DATE	CURRENT SALARY (ANNUAL) ($)	EFFICIENCY INDEX	COMMENTS
53000-53200-53205 Allison, Robert 601 N. Martin St. Muncie, Indiana 47306 (317) 284-9026	9/15/76	9/15/76	24,390	54.9	
54000-54000-54000 Almond, Robert 16669 S. Bayshore San Francisco, CA 91196 (804) 617-9942	12/05/70	12/16/76	59,870	316.8	(1) Named Region Manager of Year in FY 1984 (2) Was top sales rep three years running, 1971–73.

REPORT 6.17
Hypo-Thetical Company
Active Customers With Down Trends
For Last Six Quarters
Period Ended 6/30/85

Product: Mini-Hypo

SFS-500
Region 54000
District 54300
Territory 54305

Frequency: Quarterly

CUSTOMER NUMBER	CUSTOMER NAME	CITY	STATE	PERCENTAGE DOWN TREND	LAST FOUR-QUARTER UNITS
16773	All-City	Reno	Nevada	36.5	3,000
94316	STL Corp.	Las Vegas	Nevada	31.4	5,825
⇕	⇕	⇕	⇕	⇕	⇕
58329	TV Rental, Inc.	Reno	Nevada	0.8	1,500
Territory Totals	16*			19.7	3,600**

*Count of down-trend accounts.
**Average.

SFS-500 (REPORT 6.17)

The Active Customers with Down Trends Report should immediately highlight problem areas by account and by product. In this report, the district sales manager can examine one of his territories, 54305, and immediately know that for the Mini-Hypo, sixteen accounts have been trending down over the past six months.

Two statistics are important in this kind of report, and Hypo has included both. The first, Percentage Down Trend, looks at sales in the two most recent quarters (average) and compares them to sales in the previous four quarters (average). The report is ranked by highest to lowest Percentage Down Trend. The first statistic may at times become misleading without the help of a second one, such as Last Four-Quarter Units. By examining the second statistic, you can determine if the first is meaningful. In fact, you may want to limit a Down Trend report to only those customers who maintain a certain level of volume. It is of little use for a field sales manager to concern himself with a customer who has a down trend of 75 percent, but who only bought six units of a low-priced item last year.

If you want to key your flag to all products, you can vary this report to include dollars in place of units.

SFS-510 (REPORT 6.18)

Like Report 6.17, the Lost-Account Report is a good highlighting tool for the sales-management group. By setting up a particular time period (Hypo uses six months) that qualifies an account as "lost," the manager can quickly key in on trouble areas. Again, note that a qualifier statistic is included for each "lost" account so that the manager can concentrate on only those accounts of volume importance.

Ranking Reports (600 Series)

Ranking reports for sales management serve two purposes: (1) They provide information that can be used to assess progress when compared to

REPORT 6.18
Hypo-Thetical Company
Lost-Account Report: Dollars
No Activity for Two Quarters
Period Ended 6/30/85

SFS-510
Region 52000
District 52100
Territory 52104

Frequency: Quarterly

CUSTOMER NUMBER	CUSTOMER NAME	CITY	STATE	QUARTER AVERAGE PRIOR TO LOST
91114	R.S. Hardware	Hialeah	Florida	$8,450
74324	R.K. Computer Supply	Miami	Florida	6,990
⇕	⇕	⇕	⇕	⇕
83396	Allen Transfer	Miami	Florida	845
Territory Totals	14			$4,128

other units in the sales organization; and (2) they can help upper levels of marketing management feel the pulse of sales results. Ranking reports can be keyed to geographical sales areas, products, or customers, or to all three.

SRS-600 (REPORT 6.19)

The Trend Rankings: Units Report can be used to rank each territory, district, and region by its unit-trend increase in sales, here of Maxi-Hypo units. Dollar sales volume is not considered here, but it would be a natural corollary to this report.

SRS-610 (REPORT 6.20)

Another ranking example is the Profit-and-Loss Control Report. In this report, key revenue and expense items are ranked for each territory within the district. In subsequent report levels, the same kinds of rankings are done for districts within regions and then for regions within the nation.

In Report 6.20, each territory is ranked from 1-60[5] for each key item, with 1 being the highest (best) for the sales items and 1 being the lowest (best) for the expense items. Also, note that some index calculations are provided as well: Sales $ ÷ Sample $; Sales $ ÷ Total Expense $; and Profit Contribution $ ÷ Sales $. The indices, as well as their respective ranks, are included.

This report, as well as Report 6.19 (SRS-600), allows the user to gauge his performance levels against those of his colleagues. It also serves as an obvious performance-measurement tool for sales management.

Summary Analysis Integration Reports (700 Series)

The final group of reports that are classified under Sales-Management Report Applications are those that do not fit neatly under any other

5. 1-60 represents the number of sales territories at Hypo.

REPORT 6.19
Hypo-Thetical Company
Trend Rankings: Units
Period Ended 6/30/85

Product: Maxi-Hypo

SRS-600 (Quarterly)
All Territories, Districts,
and Regions

Frequency: Quarterly
Yearly

RANK	TERRITORY NO.	SALES REP NAME	UNIT TREND
Territory Level			
1	52101	W. Pepster	74.3%
⇕			
60			
District Level	District No.	District Manager Name	Unit Trend
1	53200	S. Long	36.4%
⇕			
12			
Region Level	Region No.	Region Manager Name	Unit Trend
1	53000	T. Beary	13.9%
⇕			
4			

REPORT 6.20
Hypo-Thetical Company
Profit-and-Loss Control Report (Dollars)
Period Ended 6/30/85

SRA-610 (Quarterly)
Region: 51000
District: 512000
Territories: All

Frequency: Quarterly
Yearly

RELATIVE TERRITORY STANDINGS	51201	51202	51203	51204	51205
Sales					
Maxi-Hypo (Rank)	16	4	59	17	39
Mini-Hypo (Rank)	24	1	60	21	19
All-Purpose Hypo (Rank)	8	39	46	9	51
TOTAL NET SALES (RANK)	15	8	49	12	40
Expenses/Profit					
Travel and Entertainment (Rank)	4	60	15	18	29
Samples (Rank)	1	19	23	14	37
Sales $/Sample $	374	196	872	439	119
—Rank	38	51	4	31	60
Sales $/Total Expense $	219	154	612	400	100
—Rank	37	48	3	24	59
Profit Contribution $/Sales $	.68	.54	.71	.69	.49
—Rank	12	38	4	11	49

heading. These reports provide information about each territory, district, and region, and they are drawn from several sources. What the flag reports are to sales management, the analysis/integration reports should be to top marketing/sales management. These should be *the* reports used first and foremost by the vice-president of sales and the national sales manager.

SAA-700 (REPORT 6.21)

The Territory Summary Analysis Report shows the number of customers in each territory, how many of those customers have purchased a product from each of the product lines over the course of the reporting period, the size of the average customer, and the general direction of sales in each territory.

This report also provides a tool for assessing territory potential by listing the number of customers that use only one or two of the company's products. Because sales analysis has shown that a buyer of one of Hypo's product lines uses either Hypo's or a competitor's other product lines, the greater the number of customers buying fewer product lines within a territory, the greater the potential of that territory, all else being equal.

Although it is not shown in this report, you should include in your report the same information for the district, region, and nation.

SAA-710 (REPORT 6.22)

The Territory/Account Summary Analysis Report is actually an extension of Report 6.21 (SAA-700), but it focuses specifically on the account activity of each territory, district, and region.

The Account Status section of the report shows the number of accounts in each territory that are considered active/mature, inactive/lost, new, or reactivated. The classifications are mutually exclusive, with the total of the four categories representing the total number of customers within the territory.

The definition of the classifications should be unique to your specific needs. Hypo uses the four terms: (1) Active/Mature: An account that has

REPORT 6.21
Hypo-Thetical Company
Territory Summary Analysis
Period Ended 6/30/85

SAA-700 (Quarterly) — Frequency: Quarterly, Yearly
All Territories, Districts, and Regions

REGION	DISTRICT	TERRITORY	TOTAL NO. ALL CUSTOMERS	TOTAL NO. MAXI CUSTOMERS	TOTAL NO. MINI CUSTOMERS	TOTAL NO. AP CUSTOMERS	AVERAGE DOLLAR CUSTOMER	TERRITORY TREND DOLLAR PERCENTAGE CHANGE	NO. CUSTOMERS BUYING ONLY 1 PRODUCT	NO. CUSTOMERS BUYING ONLY 2 PRODUCTS
51000	51100	51101	73	61	14	49	$1,300	+5.6%	17	50
		↕	↕	↕	↕	↕	↕	↕	↕	↕
54000	54300	54305	94	16	37	74	600	−4.8	70	16
Totals			6,842	1,945	3,372	2,316	11,750	+18.9	3,817	2,054

REPORT 6.22
Hypo-Thetical Company
Territory/Account Summary Analysis
Period Ended 6/30/85

SAA-710 (Quarterly)
All Territories, Districts, and Regions

Frequency: Quarterly
Yearly

			ACCOUNT STATUS				ACCOUNT TRENDS			
REGION	DISTRICT	TERRITORY	ACTIVE/ MATURE	INACTIVE/ LOST	NEW	REACTIVATED	UP	DOWN	NO CHANGE	NO ACTIVITY
51000	51100	51101	13	17	2	8	5	15	17	3
		⇕	⇕	⇕	⇕	⇕	⇕	⇕	⇕	⇕
54000	54300	54305	27	4	1	9	21	6	8	6
Totals			3,740	1,845	102	1,155	3,319	1,723	980	820

made a purchase in six of the last eight quarters and one of the last two; (2) Inactive/Lost: An account that has not purchased any products in three of the last eight quarters and in neither of the last two; (3) New: An account that has never purchased a product until this reporting period; (4) Reactivated: An account that has purchased a product this reporting period but had not done so for two previous periods.

The Account Trends section of the report looks at customers from a purchasing-trend standpoint and classifies each customer as trending up or down or showing no change or no activity. Again, these classifications are mutually exclusive, and the total represents the total number of accounts within the territory. For its directional-trend classifications, Hypo uses a percentage change in the last two periods (average) over the previous four periods (average).

Other Considerations

DISTRIBUTION

The Distribution Chart for Sales-Management Reports (Table 6.3) shows who or what group in the organization should receive each report. Having useful information is not enough unless it is disseminated to the appropriate decision-makers.

Because of the hierarchical nature of the typical sales organization, a general rule for the distribution of sales reports is to give only those reports that are at the same level or one level below the individual receiving the report. For example, the national sales manager should receive only national and regional sales reports. Lower levels of sales reports are of course always available to him, but they should not be included in his normal distribution.

One error many organizations make is to overwhelm management decision-makers with too much information and data. In fact, a common complaint among report users today is not that they have too little information, but that they have too much. The only exception to this

TABLE 6.3
Distribution Chart for Sales-Management Reports

REPORT LEVEL	REPORT NO.	DISTRIBUTION
1. Product/Service Performance by Product/Service Type (100 Series)	PSD-100	Billing Control; Sales Analysis
	PSS-110	Sales Analysis; Product Manager
	PSS-120	Sales Analysis; Product Manager
	PSS-130	Sales Analysis; Product Manager
	PSA-140	Sales Analysis
2. Product/Service Performance by Geographical Area (200 Series)	PSD-200	Sales Rep; Sales Analysis
	PSS-210	Sales Rep; District Manager; Sales Analysis
	-211	District Mgr; Region Mgr; Sales Analysis
	-212	Region Mgr; National Mgr; Sales Analysis
	-213	National Sales Mgr; VP Sales/Mkt
	PSS-220	Sales Rep; District Mgr; Sales Analysis
	PSA-230	Sales Rep; District Mgr; Sales Analysis
	-231	District Mgr; Region Mgr; Sales Analysis
	-232	Region Mgr; National Mgr; Sales Analysis
	-233	National Sales Mgr; VP Sales/Mkt
	PSA-240	Sales Rep; District Mgr; Sales Analysis
	-241	District Mgr; Region Mgr; Sales Analysis
	-242	Region Mgr; National Mgr; Sales Analysis
	-243	National Sales Mgr; VP Sales/Mkt
	PSA-250	Sales Rep; District Mgr; Sales Analysis
3. Profit-and-Loss Performance by Geographical Area (300 Series)	PLS-300	Sales Rep; District Mgr; Sales Analysis
	-301	District Mgr; Region Mgr; Sales Analysis
	-302	Region Mgr; National Mgr; Sales Analysis
	-303	National Sales Mgr; VP Sales/Mkt
	PLA-310	Sales Rep; District Mgr; Sales Analysis
	-311	District Mgr; Region Mgr; Sales Analysis
	-312	Region Mgr; National Mgr; Sales Analysis
	-313	National Sales Mgr; VP Sales/Mkt
	PLA-320	Sales Rep; District Mgr; Sales Analysis
	-321	District Mgr; Region Mgr; Sales Analysis
	-322	Region Mgr; National Mgr; Sales Analysis
	-323	National Sales Mgr; VP Sales/Mkt

TABLE 6.3, ***continued***

REPORT LEVEL	REPORT NO.	DISTRIBUTION
4. Specialized Reports for Sales-Representative Information and Commission Payments (400 Series)	SRD-400	Payroll; Sales Analysis
	-401	Payroll; Sales Analysis
	-402	Payroll; Sales Analysis
	-403	Payroll; Sales Analysis
	SRS-410	VP Sales/Marketing
5. Sales-Management Flags (500 Series)	SFS-500	District Mgr; Region Mgr
	SFS-510	District Mgr; Region Mgr
6. Ranking Reports (600 Series)	SRS-600	Region Mgr; VP Sales/Mkt; Sales Analysis
	-610	Sales Rep; District Mgr; Sales Analysis
	-611	District Mgr; Region Mgr; Sales Analysis
	-612	Region Mgr; National Mgr; Sales Analysis
	-613	National Sales Mgr; VP Sales/Mkt
7. Summary Analysis Integration (700 Series)	SAA-700	Sales Management; Sales Analysis
	SAA-710	Sales Management; Sales Analysis

general rule of report distribution is the sales/market analysis group. This group is essentially the "keeper of the data," and it needs all levels of data/information at hand in order to prepare analyses for all levels of management.

REPORT SELECTION AND STORAGE MEDIA

As you reviewed the report examples in this or in earlier chapters, two areas of concern probably surfaced. You may feel that many of the examples provided are inappropriate for your organization and that we have excluded many that are appropriate. But remember, our attempt is to present examples that are commonly found in many business organizations. No one organization will have exactly the same reports included here. Many will have more, and many will have less. A service organization may have drastically different reports, although the questions of who? where? and how much? that the reports help answer will most likely be similar.

Or perhaps you think we are the victims of too many three-martini lunches—*no* organization can function with so *much* information. If this thought has occurred to you, you have begun to understand and apply the principles of sales reports to your organization. We are not suggesting that you run to your Data Processing Department and present them with a list of twenty-two report specifications. Rather, you must examine the total scope of your requirements first and then design the reports that will provide you with maximum information and efficiency.

Regardless of the amount of sales information you require, you are going to have a lot of it. Modern data-processing capabilities and the ease of accessing data at nearly every level of detail and analysis is a fact of life in every organization today. Therefore, in order to use your data/information effectively, you must distribute it properly and store it cautiously. This means that, where you can convince your DP Department to accommodate you, you may want to store your data in on-line files and access it via a video screen (CRT) or terminal. Of course, some data will have to be in a hard-copy report (or microfiche) format for ease of use. But, in general, most information can be accessed from a terminal and thus free you from reams of paper. A word of caution though: Try to retrieve all of the data/information you require, but make it accessible in the most convenient form.

UNITS VS. DOLLARS

In some sample reports, you will notice that we use unit sales as a measure of performance, and in others we use dollar sales. For any given report, you may want to use units or dollars, or both. You should review your requirements and determine which is most appropriate in each case.

TIMING/FREQUENCY

On each sample report, the Frequency notation that appears in the upper right-hand corner is simply our recommendation. You must weigh it against your own requirements. In some cases, you will want to see information on a daily basis, whereas in other cases quarterly updates will be sufficient. The less frequent a report, the less analysis that will be required. If you can operate effectively with fewer updates, by all means do so. But remember, you do not want to jeopardize your decision-making by the lack of timely information and reports.

Action Plan

1. Obtain or devise the following, and put them together in a common file.
   a. A sales-management structure (organization chart) for your organization
   b. A product price list for all products
   c. A distribution list of all sales reports used in your organization
2. Develop a list of sales-management reports that you want to include in this module of your MKIS. Use whatever is appropriate from those that you are currently using. Add to it what you have learned from this chapter and whatever else you think is important.
3. With your new list, "interview" all users of the existing or proposed reports and include their comments and recommendations in your list.
4. Using the principles described in Chapter 5, design your preliminary sales-report specifications.
5. Review your preliminary report specifications with the appropriate users and obtain whatever form of approval is required.
6. Armed with your specifications, meet with your Data Processing Department to discuss implementation of this module. Make sure that you, the users, and DP understand each step of the module's implementation process. Document it, in writing, with a work schedule.

CHAPTER 7

Product Data-Bank Report Applications

The Purpose of the Product Report System

In any product (and/or service) report system, the manager should understand the five key components in the system: (1) product performance, (2) product competition, (3) product profitability, (4) new-product tracking, and (5) product forecasting.

1. Before you can obtain useful information from product report analyses, you must know how your products differ from one another, not so much from a technical standpoint, but rather according to the performance you expect from them in the marketplace. For example, if you have a product that sells consistently year after year and goes through very little physical change, simple sales analyses may be sufficient to evaluate the product's performance. If, however, you have introduced a new product that is aimed at a new market, you will probably want to monitor how fast it is gaining acceptance, to what extent it is replacing your competitor's products, who is buying it and why, and so on. In effect, you must put on your marketing-planning hat when developing product report applications. Whereas sales reports may be sufficient for the sales team, the marketing manager will require more specialized types of reports.

2. A related component of marketing planning and strategy lies in understanding competitive products and how they perform in the marketplace. Once you have developed a system to track your sales effectively, you will then have to focus on your products' impact on the overall market. You will want to track your success against that of your competitor, and you will also want to keep a handle on the actual components, functional and cosmetic, of your competitor's products.

3. A vital area of the product report system is product profitability. Although this area typically is considered to be a function of the Accounting Department, you may have to review your product's performance in a slightly different light. While Accounting will probably be able to tell you which product lines contribute what portion of the bottom line, it cannot tell you which products *should be* contributing, or by how much,

to your bottom line. Only the marketing manager knows where and how much the product mix should be contributing, and only the marketing group can evaluate product success based on competitive factors and market potential.

4. Your product report system should incorporate new products in all phases of their development cycles from conception to market introduction. In particular, if you are considering a complex mix of new products for new markets, your MKIS design will have to include product-status tracking and scheduling. Again, because this area will overlap with other functional areas in your organization, principally with Research & Development, other departments may become involved in new-product-development tracking. However, the ultimate fate of any product lies in the hands of the marketing unit, and thus marketing users of the MKIS will require special report applications.

5. The ability to forecast products accurately is closely linked to overall corporate profitability because most organizations plan all levels of operation based upon planned or forecasted sales.

Table 7.1 highlights these five principal components for most product report applications.

Product Life-Cycle Overview

The product life-cycle concept will be used throughout this chapter to analyze product report applications. Although many marketing practitioners may debate the usefulness of applying strategies based on life-cycle stages, every organization applies some strategy, either implicit or explicit, to each of its products. We are not suggesting particular strategies that you should or should not use at each life-cycle stage. However, where given strategies exist, the marketing manager needs product-performance information in order to evaluate any alternative marketing strategies.

Figure 7.1, the Typical Product Life-Cycle Curve, illustrates the various

TABLE 7.1
Requirements of the Typical Product Report System

YOUR PRODUCT REPORT SYSTEM SHOULD HELP YOU:

1. Determine if you are properly matching product and strategy over time.
2. Identify and monitor each product's key competitive strengths and weaknesses.
3. Analyze product profitability.
4. Provide guidelines for monitoring new product ideas, development, and introductions.
5. Provide an efficient link with your organization's forecasting model or process.

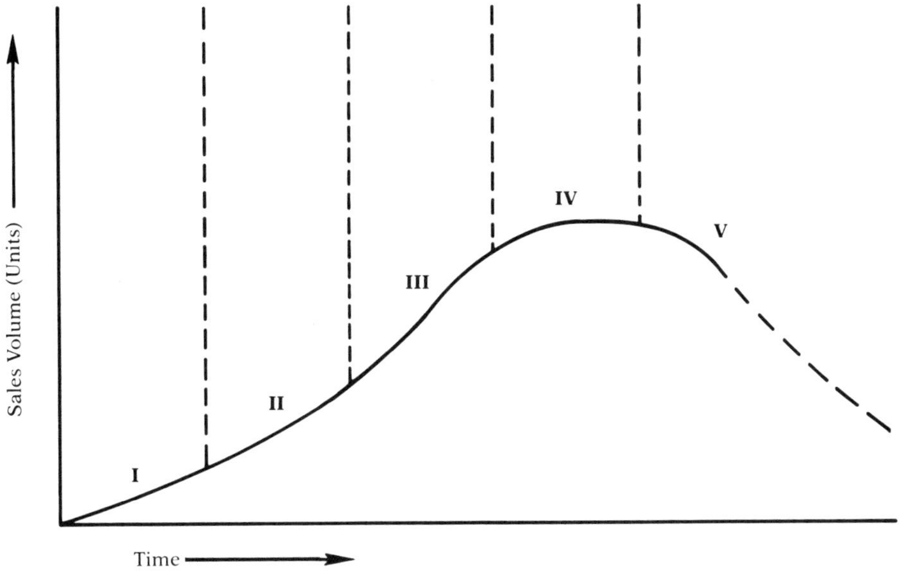

Stages
I. Product Conception and Development
II. Product Introduction—Early Market Acceptance
III. Sales-Volume Growth—Product Takeoff
IV. Maturity—Early Market Saturation
V. Sales Decline—Product/Market Phaseout

Figure 7.1 Typical product life-cycle curve

TABLE 7.2
Product Conception and Development

CHARACTERISTICS OF STAGE I PRODUCTS	MKIS IMPLICATIONS
1. Initial product idea or discovery	• Product-development data banks • Competition file
2. New-product idea evaluation	• New-product idea tracking system • Product-idea development status
3. Final approval of new product idea (by management)	• Competition file • Financial pro formas • Sales analyses of similar products
4. Transformation of the new-product idea into a prototype	• Expansion of the new product idea tracking system
5. Business and market plans for new-product introduction	• Profit-and-loss planning for new products (break-even analysis) • Market-planning system for new products

TABLE 7.3
Product Introduction—Early Market Acceptance

CHARACTERISTICS OF STAGE II PRODUCTS	MKIS IMPLICATIONS
1. Low sales volume (units)	• Company product performance of previous introductions and competitive units • Reevaluate selected market
2. Competition is limited	• Evaluate market potential index
3. Sales are made to the trend setters, innovators, and high-income groups	• Test to see if products are reaching the targeted audience (product-segmentation match to consumer profile)
4. Several product changes	• Evaluate sales results of various product versions • Monitor product-mix positioning
5. High marketing/sales costs and heavy promotion expenses	• Evaluation of planned vs. actual expenses • ROI analysis
6. Limited distribution	• Analysis of distribution channels and product inventory levels
7. Relatively high prices	• Competition file

TABLE 7.4
Sales-Volume Growth—Product "Takeoff"

CHARACTERISTICS OF STAGE III PRODUCTS	MKIS IMPLICATIONS
1. Rapid sales growth	• Determine high-growth products
2. Continued purchase by early customers	• Product purchases by targeted group(s) • Differentiate group profile/attribute
3. Large number of new customers	• Product purchases by new market segments (new profile data)
4. New competitors enter market	• Evaluation of competitive position (life-cycle position, product differentiation, consumer strengths)
5. Increased product features and/or improvements	• Competitive product evaluation • Life-cycle impact evaluation • Cash-management evaluation
6. Prices remain high or fall slightly	• Competitive price evaluation • Market-impact evaluation
7. Continued high promotion expenses	• Budget monitoring • ROI Evaluation
8. High profitability	• Product P&L statements

stages of growth during a product's life cycle.[1] Of course, these stages may vary in duration and intensity. Some products may never go beyond Stage I, whereas fad products, such as Hula-Hoops and pet rocks, may skip Stage II altogether and go to Stage III. In this case, the line on the life-cycle curve becomes almost vertical. But no matter where the product lies on the life-cycle curve, certain marketing strategies must be developed. In many cases, marketing management can make product-strategy decisions without explicitly considering product life cycles, yet there are many implications for the MKIS product reports. By examining each growth stage, you can determine whether you will need more product-performance information in order to make better strategy decisions. If you require more detailed information, you should allow for this when you design your MKIS.

1. For a more detailed description of the characteristics of each life-cycle stage, refer to the appropriate chapters in the Kotler and Staudt books listed in the Bibliography.

TABLE 7.5
Maturity—Early Market Saturation

CHARACTERISTICS OF STAGE IV PRODUCTS	MKIS IMPLICATIONS
1. Sales begin to taper off or show only sporadic growth	• Accurate sales analysis and inventory analysis become key • Special promotional considerations
2. Competition intensified A. Stiff price competition (mark-downs begin) B. Weaker competition drops out C. High-entry barriers for competitive entry	• Competitive price tracking • Continued maintenance of the competition file
3. Trade-ins and replacement sales begin to dominate the market	• Product sales analysis
4. Market becomes highly segmented	• Market-segment purchase analysis • Product-introduction cycle evaluation
5. Costs increase A. Promotion budget up B. R&D seeks new ways to apply product	• Continued budget monitoring

Tables 7.2 through 7.6 show the characteristics of products in each stage of the life cycle that have implications for your MKIS.

Products at the Premarket Stage (Stage I)

When products are in Stage I, the conception and development stages (see Table 7.2), five essential steps must be completed before the product can be released to the market. The product must be conceived or developed, evaluated, receive management approval, be physically made into mockups or prototypes, and be reviewed in the context of the organization's marketing plan.

What information should marketing management have access to in order to evaluate the new product during Stage I? Once you have the idea

TABLE 7.6
Sales Decline—Product Market "Phaseout"

CHARACTERISTICS OF STAGE V PRODUCTS	MKIS IMPLICATIONS
1. Volume decline becomes permanent	• Sales analysis
2. Competition decreases drastically	• Competition file
3. Survivors (competitors) become specialists	
4. Choices for consumer narrow	
5. Consumers limited to the core markets	
6. Promotion budget is reduced	• Budget monitoring
7. Product prices are reduced	• Price monitoring

for a new product, that product will have to compete with all other new products for attention. This requires a report system for tracking new-product development. A system could be devised similar to Report 7.1. For each product that has been accepted for market consideration, Report 7.1 shows a planned and actual column for both "start" and "finish" dates. The basic steps the product must follow to market release are listed in the left-hand column.

During Stage I of the product's life cycle, marketing management will have to consider the competition. What products are already on the market? How well are they doing? If your organization is continually asking such questions, then an important component of your MKIS should be a Competitive Data Base. What you include in this data base will depend entirely on your need for sophisticated and/or detailed information. Table 7.7 lists several key elements that you will want to consider for your Competitive Data Base. An effective on-line entry and update system or good manual storage system will serve most situations. If you are thinking about introducing a new product to the fast-food market and want to know something about every hamburger franchise in the United States, obviously you should have access to a computer. Even then, your needs may be too large to handle through your own system, so you may

REPORT 7.1
Hi-Tech, Inc.

New Product Development/Availability Status
NPD-601

Frequency: Monthly
Quarterly

STEPS/ACTIVITY	PRODUCT A			
	START DATE		*FINISH DATE*	
	PLANNED	*ACTUAL*	*PLANNED*	*ACTUAL*
A. IDEA GENERATION				
Product Conceptualization				
B. PRODUCT SCREENING				
C. FEASIBILITY RESEARCH				
1. Product Objective				
2. Present Business Situation				
3. Define Opportunities				
4. Define Problems				
5. Situation Analysis				
6. Market-Share Analysis				
7. Competitive-Product Studies				
8. Strategic Alternatives				
9. Profitability Applications				
10. Resource Allocations				
11. Expenditure Justification				
D. BUSINESS ANALYSIS				
1. Define Market Size				
2. Define Market Trend				
3. Define Anticipated Trend				
4. Competitive Analysis				
5. Demographic Analysis				
6. Identify Consumer Targets				
7. Differentiate Product				
8. Determine Selling Price				
9. Identify Break-Even				
10. Inventory Considerations				
E. PROTOTYPE TESTING AND RESEARCH & DEVELOPMENT				
Engineering Design				
F. TEST MARKETING				
Results Measurement				
G. FULL PRODUCT RELEASE				

TABLE 7.7
Competitive Data-Base Elements

Name and addresses
Product(s) line/mix
Product specifications
Principal officers/executives/contacts
Geographical coverage
Gross sales (1–3 years)
Gross earnings (EPS history)
Plant and warehouse capacity
Production capabilities
Total sales representatives, distributors, and employees
Share of market (trend)
Identified selling and promotion methods
Competitive practices (i.e., allowances, terms, discounts, etc.)
Advertising platforms (key words, phrases)
Quality, performance, and reliability history
Field-service capability
Research & development capability
Strengths and weaknesses of competitive products
Operating advantages/disadvantages
Guarantees/warranties

need access to commercial data bases. (We will discuss these data bases in greater detail in Chapter 11.) Table 7.8 lists some of the sources available for securing competitive information.

After your initial research, you should formally evaluate your new idea. Cochrane Chase and Kenneth Barasch[2] have devised a unique way to evaluate new-product ideas. The result is Report 7.2, the New-Product Evaluation Report. By looking at the six fundamental components guiding a new product's potential success (company operations, potential market, marketability, engineering/production, finance, and legal), Chase and Barasch weigh the merits of the product idea to arrive at an overall numerical evaluation. On a scale of 1 to 5, they rate each characteristic

2. Cochrane Chase and Kenneth L. Barasch. *Marketing Problem Solver.* (Radnor, Pa.: Chilton Book Company, 1978).

REPORT 7.2
New-Product Evaluation Report Prepared
NPD-604

Frequency: On Request

(1) CHARACTERISTIC	(2) RELATIVE IMPORTANCE WEIGHT	(3) RATING (1,2,3,4, or 5)	(4) VALUE COL (2) × COL (3)
A. COMPANY OPERATIONS			
1. Compatibility	0.6	___	___
2. Safe Product	0.6	___	___
3. No Interruption	0.4	___	___
4. Long-Range Growth	1.4	___	___
TOTAL (A)	3.0		═══
B. POTENTIAL MARKET			
1. Industry Growth	1.2	___	___
2. Market Diversity	0.6	___	___
3. Dependence on Economy	0.4	___	___
4. Seasonal	0.2	___	___
5. Geographical	0.3	___	___
6. Purchasing Patterns	0.3	___	___
TOTAL (B)	3.0		═══
C. MARKETABILITY			
1. Channel Cost/Effectiveness	0.4	___	___
2. Price/Quality	0.4	___	___
3. Promotable	0.4	___	___
4. Discounts/Deals	0.2	___	___
5. Marketing Management	0.3	___	___
6. Customer Loyalty	0.3	___	___
7. Product Differentiation	0.3	___	___
8. Market Life	0.2	___	___
9. Competition	0.4	___	___
10. Customer Acceptance	0.4	___	___
11. Sales to Present Customers	0.2	___	___
12. Knowledge of Customers	0.4	___	___
13. Packaging	0.1	___	___
TOTAL (C)	4.0		═══

REPORT 7.2, *continued*
New-Product Evaluation Report Prepared
NPD-604

Frequency: On Request

(1) CHARACTERISTIC	(2) RELATIVE IMPORTANCE WEIGHT	(3) RATING (1,2,3,4, or 5)	(4) VALUE COL (2) × COL (3)
D. ENGINEERING/PRODUCTION			
1. Access to Resource	0.4	___	___
2. Manufacturing Expertise	0.5	___	___
3. Marketable Cost	0.4	___	___
4. Storage Requirements	0.2	___	___
5. Entry Requirements	0.4	___	___
6. Serviceability	0.3	___	___
7. Durability	0.2	___	___
8. Research Budget	0.2	___	___
9. Byproducts	0.2	___	___
10. Operating Cost	0.2	___	___
TOTAL (D)	3.0		═══
E. FINANCE			
1. Profitability	1.6	___	___
2. Payback	0.6	___	___
3. Available Capital	1.0	___	___
4. Best Use of Capital	0.8	___	___
TOTAL (E)	4.0		═══
F. LEGAL			
1. Patent Protection	0.8	___	___
2. Meets Products, Label, and Advertising Restrictions	0.8	___	___
3. Trademark Protected	0.6	___	___
4. Royalties Settled	0.2	___	___
5. Labor Relations	0.2	___	___
6. Other Legislation	0.4	___	___
TOTAL (F)	3.0		═══
GRAND TOTAL	20.0		═══

Instructions: In Column (3), enter the numerical ratings of each corresponding characteristic as given on the rating charts. Multiply the numbers in Columns (2) and (3) and enter the products in Column (4). Enter the total of Column (4). The total of Column (4) is the weighted rating. A total weighted rating of 80 points corresponds to an "Above Average" rating.

TABLE 7.8
Sources for Gathering Competitive Information

1. Annual reports
2. Trade journals and magazines
3. Company product literature and price lists
4. Your sales force and distributors
5. Feedback from customers
6. Purchasing products
7. Shows and exhibits
8. Former employees of competitors
9. Purchase of special industry reports
10. Securities and Exchange Commission filings
11. Seminars

Key: Gather these data from as many sources as you can.

within each of the six component areas. Tables 7.9 through 7.14 describe the ranking system for each component. Here again, you may find that this application does not have to be computerized. However, if you systematically evaluate dozens of new-product ideas each year, you may find that if you develop a new-product-evaluation model, all you have to do is plug in the numbers each time you want to run an evaluation.

Stage I products will also require some form of corporate management approval before you can pursue the development project. Information gathered from the Competitive Data Base may be required. It may also be necessary to provide financial pro formas of predicted success. Of course, your MKIS cannot perform magic and create such a document, but it can provide guidelines for sales analyses and profitability of similar products.[3]

Finally, the Stage I product will be transformed into a prototype, and marketing/business plans will be proposed and eventually introduced. With an effective new-product tracking system, you will be able to monitor your idea to ensure that it is being brought along on schedule. For your business plan, you may want to use sales analyses from existing similar products derived from your sales-report applications.

3. See Chapter 6 on sales-management report applications.

(Text continues on page 178)

TABLE 7.9
New-Product Appraisal: (A) Company Operations

CHARACTERISTIC	EXCELLENT 5	ABOVE AVERAGE 4	AVERAGE 3	BELOW AVERAGE 2	POOR 1	POINTS
1. Compatibility with current product line(s).	Complements and reinforces an otherwise incomplete line.	Easily fits current line, but not necessary.	Fits current line, but may compete with it.	Does not fit well. Competes with and may decrease sales of current line.	Does not fit at all. Endangers or replaces an otherwise successful line.	
2. Ability to produce a safe product. (Also environmental concerns.)	Completely feasible. No functional or environmental hazards to overcome.	Mostly feasible. Only slight functional or environmental hazards to overcome.	Possible. Several functional or environmental hazards to overcome.	Difficult. Many functional or environmental hazards to overcome.	Impossible to overcome all functional or environmental hazards.	
3. Interruption of present activities.	No interruption.	Little interruption but correctable or acceptable.	Little interruption, only some of which is correctable or acceptable.	Great interruptions resulting in hard-to-improve economy.	Complete interruption resulting in chaos.	
4. Long-range growth and security of firm.	Definitely helpful.	Somewhat helpful.	Maybe helpful.	Not at all helpful.	Hindrance.	

From *The Marketing Problem Solver* by Cochrane Chase and Kenneth L. Barasch. Copyright 1978 by the authors. Reprinted with the permission of the publisher, Chilton Book Company, Radnor, Pennsylvania.

TABLE 7.10
New-Product Appraisal: (B) Potential Market (Feasibility)

CHARACTERISTIC	EXCELLENT 5	ABOVE AVERAGE 4	AVERAGE 3	BELOW AVERAGE 2	POOR 1	POINTS
1. Industry growth and structure.	In growth stage. Increasing sales and profits at an increasing rate. Increasing demand.	Reaching maturity stage. Increasing sales and profits at a decreasing rate.	Turning from maturity to saturation stage. Leveling out of sales and profits.	Sales and profits have begun to decline.	Sales and profits are decreasing at an increasing rate. Decreasing demand.	
2. Market diversity and stability.	Covers many industries. Highly stable.	Covers several industries, with a growing number of uses.	Covers a few industries with a static number of uses.	Covers a limited number of industries, with a decreasing number of uses. Unsteady.	Reaching obsolescent stage.	

TABLE 7.10, *continued*

CHARACTERISTIC	EXCELLENT 5	ABOVE AVERAGE 4	AVERAGE 3	BELOW AVERAGE 2	POOR 1	POINTS
3. Dependence on general economy (recession-proof)	No reliance on economy.	Large degree of resistance to economic change.	Some resistance and some sensitivity to economic change.	Moderately sensitive to economic changes.	Highly sensitive to economic changes.	
4. Seasonal variation of sales.	None.	Minor.	Predictable.	Varying intensity.	Severe fluctuations.	
5. Geographical dispersion of customers.	Easy-to-reach concentrations.	Slight dispersion, but mostly concentrated.	Some concentrations and some dispersions.	Mostly dispersed.	Very sparse concentration and highly dispersed.	
6. Purchasing patterns across various industries.	Similar purchasing patterns.	Only slight differences in purchasing patterns.	Differences, but easy to adjust.	Somewhat different purchasing patterns.	Completely different purchasing patterns.	

TABLE 7.11
New-Product Appraisal: (C) Marketability

CHARACTERISTICS	EXCELLENT 5	ABOVE AVERAGE 4	AVERAGE 3	BELOW AVERAGE 2	POOR 1	POINTS
1. Cost/effectiveness and availability of existing or new channels of distribution.	Readily distributable to major markets through present channels.	Can use present channels for majority of major markets, plus some new channels.	Must utilize new and present channels equally.	Requires many new channels to be developed.	Requires all new channels, none of which are compatible with existing channels.	
2. Can be attractively priced/quality with competitive products (initial and maintenance)	Better quality and lower cost than all competitors.	Either lower priced and equal quality or equal price and better quality than competition.	Equal price and same quality as competition.	Either higher priced or lower quality than competition.	Both higher priced and lower quality than competition.	
3. Suitability and potential of methods and costs of promotional tools.	Selling attributes are superior to competing products. Lends itself to existing promotion and advertising techniques.	Features compare favorably with competition; has demonstrable characteristics. Can utilize some current promotional techniques.	Equal to competing products' features. Slight similarities in promotion required.	Few promotable features. Must develop new promotional tools.	Does not compare favorably with competitive products. All new promotion techniques are required.	

TABLE 7.11, *continued*

CHARACTERISTICS	EXCELLENT 5	ABOVE AVERAGE 4	AVERAGE 3	BELOW AVERAGE 2	POOR 1	POINTS
4. Possible discount allowances and deals over and above competition.	Easily accomplished.	Can beat out smaller competition.	Most firms already offer substantial discounts.	Would make company appear to be discount house.	No increase in sales would result, since products are bought solely on quality.	
5. Executive talent and marketing management.	Complete and qualified staff currently available.	Large part of qualified staff available.	Some adequate staff available.	Need many new staff members.	Need totally new staff.	
6. Replacement market/brand loyalty.	Lends itself to repeat purchases.	May repeat if conditions merit.	Equal chance of repeat or switching.	Little chance of repeat purchases.	"One shot" only.	
7. Product differentiation (unique).	Fills a need not currently satisfied; is original, a leader.	Improvement over existing competition, an adaptation.	Some individual appeal, but basically a copy of another product with minor differentiation.	Barely distinguishable from competitors.	Same as competitor's product. No distinctive or unique advantages.	
8. Market life/obsolescence (longevity, durability).	Significantly longer life than competition.	Slightly longer life than competition.	Equal life to competition.	Slightly shorter life span than competition.	Significantly shorter life than competition.	

TABLE 7.11, *continued*

CHARACTERISTICS	EXCELLENT 5	ABOVE AVERAGE 4	AVERAGE 3	BELOW AVERAGE 2	POOR 1	POINTS
9. Degree of competition, established or potential.	No competitive or substitute products foreseen.	Only slight competition from alternatives.	Several competitors to different extents.	Many competitors.	Would be completely outclassed. Other firms are entrenched.	
10. Customer acceptance.	Readily accepted by customers.	Only slight resistance.	Moderate resistance.	Appreciable customer education needed.	Extensive customer education needed.	
11. Sales to present customers.	All present customers.	Most of present customers.	Some present customers.	Few present customers.	Entirely different customers.	
12. Knowledge of purchase, consumption, and use patterns of customers.	Complete knowledge.	Extensive knowledge.	Partial knowledge.	Little knowledge.	No knowledge.	

TABLE 7.11, ***continued***

CHARACTERISTICS	EXCELLENT 5	ABOVE AVERAGE 4	AVERAGE 3	BELOW AVERAGE 2	POOR 1	POINTS
13. Packaging available to provide (a) Product protection in shipping, storage, and handling; (b) customer convenience, and (c) manageable cost.	Meets all criteria.	Satisfies most criteria.	Satisfies half of criteria.	Satisfies few criteria.	Satisfies none of criteria.	

TABLE 7.12
New-Product Appraisal: (D) Engineering/Production

CHARACTERISTICS	EXCELLENT 5	ABOVE AVERAGE 4	AVERAGE 3	BELOW AVERAGE 2	POOR 1	POINTS
1. Economical access to resources: raw materials, facilities, personnel, capital, and production know-how.	Adequate amounts are readily available through dependable sources. Present idle plant is usable. Substitutes are available if needed.	Little new equipment and other resources sources are required. Plant may require slight additions.	Some new equipment, personnel, and other resources are needed.	Mostly new equipment, personnel, and resources are needed.	Limited supplies. All new plant, personnel, and resources needed.	
2. Technical know-how in manufacturing, technical support, process familiarity.	Currently available and qualified.	Most available.	Some available.	Need additional know-how.	Need all new know-how.	
3. Can be manufactured at a marketable cost.	All sources are obtainable and can be processed at lower than competitive costs.	Most resources are obtainable and can be processed at a lower than competitive cost.	Some resources are converted into finished product at lower than competitive cost.	Few resources are convertible at competitive costs.	No resources can be processed competitively.	

TABLE 7.12, *continued*

CHARACTERISTICS	EXCELLENT 5	ABOVE AVERAGE 4	AVERAGE 3	BELOW AVERAGE 2	POOR 1	POINTS
4. Adequate storage facilities.	Space to spare.	Some available after reorganizing inventories.	Can be obtained after inventory reorganization or space acquisition.	Little space available now or in the future.	No space available.	
5. Industry entry requirements.	Excellent fit available at low cost through internal development or acquisition. Few other companies can enter.	Good fit available at low cost through internal development or acquisition.	Partial fit available, but high cost.	Rarely available at any cost. Many companies can enter.	Poor fit. Can be made by any size firm.	
6. After-sale service requirements.	Present service organization adequate in personnel and facilities.	Minor reinforcement in personnel and/or facilities will present no serious problems.	Moderate adjustments needed, but can be accommodated.	Major adjustment of service organization needed.	Present service capability totally inadequate.	
7. Ability to produce a durable product (temperature, impact, abrasion, tearing, resist deterioration).	Completely feasible to withstand conditions of use and environment.	Mostly feasible to withstand conditions of use and environment.	Somewhat feasible to withstand conditions of use and environment.	Difficult to withstand conditions of use and environment.	Impossible to withstand conditions of use and environment.	

TABLE 7.12, *continued*

CHARACTERISTICS	EXCELLENT 5	ABOVE AVERAGE 4	AVERAGE 3	BELOW AVERAGE 2	POOR 1	POINTS
8. Dollars and time estimates for research are within budget constraints.	Completely within budget.	Mostly within budget.	Possible and probably within budget.	Difficult to accomplish within budget.	Impossible without major budget increase.	
9. Byproducts.	Can completely utilize byproducts that otherwise would have been extremely expensive to purchase.	Partial utilization of byproducts at a cost savings.	Some use of byproducts at no particular savings.	No use of byproducts.	Problem in storage and disposal of byproducts.	
10. Operating cost.	Significantly less than competing products.	Slightly less than competing products.	About same as competing products.	Slightly more than competing products.	Significantly more than competing products.	

TABLE 7.13
New-Product Appraisal: (E) Finance

CHARACTERISTIC	EXCELLENT 5	ABOVE AVERAGE 4	AVERAGE 3	BELOW AVERAGE 2	POOR 1	POINTS
1. Profitability: expected return-on-investment (before taxes).	Over 20 percent per year.	10–19 percent per year.	6–9 percent per year.	3–5 percent per year.	2 percent and under per year.	
2. Payback period.	Less than 2 years.	2–3 years.	4–5 years.	6–7 years.	8 years or more.	
3. Availability of dollars for capital expenditures and working capital.	Abundant.	Easily obtainable.	Obtainable at high interest rates.	Difficult to obtain at any interest rate.	Impossible to obtain.	
4. Putting capital to best use.	Cannot be invested in a more lucrative venture.	There may be other ventures equally as lucrative.	There are several equally lucrative ventures.	There are many other more lucrative ventures.	Can be invested in much more lucrative ventures.	

TABLE 7.14
New-Product Appraisal: (F) Legal

CHARACTERISTIC	EXCELLENT 5	ABOVE AVERAGE 4	AVERAGE 3	BELOW AVERAGE 2	POOR 1	POINTS
1. Patent protection.	Impregnable. Exclusive license or rights.	Some resistance to infringement, but not foolproof. Few firms have similar patents.	Probably not patentable, but defies replication. Patent issue is unsettled.	Not patentable; can copy some attributes; open field.	Easy to copy with no problems. Many licenses are outstanding.	
2. Meets legal restrictions applying to product, label, advertising, and shipment.	Meets all.	Meets most.	Meets some.	Meets few.	Meets none.	
3. Trademark/copyright protected.	Impregnable.	Some light copying of mark.	Several infringements may occasionally arise.	Many infringements on mark, or no trademark allowed.	Trademark not allowed; some firm already owns mark.	

TABLE 7.14, *continued*

CHARACTER-ISTIC	EXCELLENT 5	ABOVE AVERAGE 4	AVERAGE 3	BELOW AVERAGE 2	POOR 1	POINTS
4. Claims to royalties or other indemnities.	Completely settled.	Tentative agreement reached.	Still in negotiating stage.	Minor disagreements as to claims.	Major disagreements as to claims.	
5. Labor/union relations.	Complete contract settlements are in accord and favorable to company.	Contracts are resolved, but not completely favorable to company.	Still in negotiating stage.	Major negotiating problems.	Complete impasse.	
6. Existing or impending legislation that could affect product.	Completely favorable.	Somewhat favorable.	Hard to determine effect.	Some problems will result.	Completely detrimental.	

From *The Marketing Problem Solver* by Cochrane Chase and Kenneth L. Barasch. Copyright 1978 by the authors. Reprinted with the permission of the publisher, Chilton Book Company, Radnor, Pennsylvania.

Products after Market Entry (Stage II)

Once products have been released, they are in Stage II of their life cycles. (See Table 7.3 for highlights of the seven frequent characteristics of Stage II products and their implications for your MKIS.) In general, Stage II products are relatively high priced, have limited distribution and competition, and bear heavy promotion and other market/sales-entry expenses. They also tend to go through several product changes (many of which are cosmetic) and sell relatively few units. The product is usually purchased by trend-setting and high-income consumers.

What information does the marketing manager require in order to evaluate Stage II products? Although all of the seven major Stage II product characteristics have MKIS implications, we will focus on the three most important ones: sales volume, competition, and the initial consumers. The other four characteristics in Table 7.3 also require information in order to be reviewed, but specific applications for these are included in the discussion of the other life-cycle stages.

To illustrate additional applications of the product report system, we will use the example of Hi-Tech, Inc., a hypothetical company engaged in manufacturing and marketing data-processing equipment. Here we will focus only on Hi-Tech's printer division. Table 7.15 summarizes the Hi-Tech Printer Division product line.

TABLE 7.15
Hi-Tech, Inc., Printer Division's Product Line
(5 printer market segments, 19 products)

COMPUTER PRINTER PRODUCT SEGMENTS	MODEL NUMBERS
• Hi-Speed Printers for Large Main-Frame Computers	HSP 101–107
• Mini-Computer Printers	MNP 112–116
• Micro-Computer Printers	MCP 120–122
• Word-Processing Printers	WPP 125
• Specialty Printers (Graphics)	SPP 132–133

As in all stages of the life cycle after market entry (Stages II–V), the crucial variable for evaluation is unit sales. Through analysis of all sales reports available through your sales-management report applications (Chapter 6), you can evaluate your product's early market acceptance. You can also compare a new product's unit sales volume to planned results or to similar products in their entry stages. Then you can go one step further and evaluate a product or product segment's success versus the marketplace. Report 7.3 (PSA–201) compares Hi-Tech's unit sales volume in a given quarter to the sales volume of the entire market. The report also computes a percentage of the market share and a change in that share from the last period. When broken down to an individual product level, the relative changes in market share can help you to determine if your product is performing as expected.

Because products in Stage II are still relatively new, competition is generally limited. However, you will still want to monitor your competition file and keep it updated so that you will be aware of any important sales trends. If your sales of a Stage II product have dropped or leveled off, is it because of competition or because you misjudged your product's entry into the market? Whatever the case, you may want to monitor sales by the stage of the product life cycle (see Report 7.5 regarding Stage III products) in order to spot differences between planned and actual sales results.

Another important characteristic of Stage II products is that initial sales are most often made to the trend setters and higher income groups. In order to monitor which consumer is indeed the purchaser of your product, you will have to match your product segmentation to your consumer profile. We will discuss this application further in Chapter 8. For now, we will focus on a product-line application of the Consumer Segment-Product Segment Matrix. In a very concise format, Report 7.4 (PSA–301) provides an effective means of measuring how each of Hi-Tech's product segments stacks up across consumer segments. This application answers the questions: Are we selling our products to the intended consumers? Should we shift our strategy to promote a particular product line to other

REPORT 7.3
Hi-Tech, Inc., Printer Division
Product-Sales Analysis (Units)
By Product Segment
Period Ended Q1, FY 1982

PSA-201

Frequency: Quarterly

PRODUCT SEGMENT	Q1 HI-TECH	Q1 TOTAL MARKET ESTIMATE	Q1 PERCENTAGE MARKET SHARE	PERCENTAGE CHANGE MARKET SHARE
Hi-Speed	600	6,000	10	0.1
Mini	2,000	4,500	44.4	−1.4
Micro	150	2,000	7.5	2.5
Word-Processing	40	850	4.7	−5.6
Specialty	180	280	64.3	11.4
Total	2,970	13,630	21.8	2.1

REPORT 7.4
Hi-Tech, Inc., Printer Division
Product Segment—Consumer Segment Matrix
Period Ended Q1, FY 1982

PSA-301 Frequency: Quarterly

	CONSUMER SEGMENTS						
	INDUSTRIAL ORIGINAL EQUIPMENT MANUFAC-TURER (OEM)	INDUSTRIAL END USER	RETAIL	DISTRIBUTOR	MAIL ORDER INDIVIDUAL	UNIDENTIFIED	TOTALS*
Product Segments							
Hi-Speed	0	250	50	300	0	0	600
Mini	800	100	600	400	10	90	2,000
Micro	0	0	0	50	80	20	150
Word-Processing	0	0	0	25	10	5	40
Specialty	0	180	0	0	0	0	180
Totals*	800	530	650	775	100	115	2,970

*Must tie to PSA-201 Totals.

REPORT 7.5
Hi-Tech, Inc., Printer Division
Product-Sales Analysis (Units)
By Product Type by Growth Stage
Period Ended Q2, FY 1983

PSA–103
Stage III Products

Frequency: Monthly
Quarterly
Yearly

	FY 1982				FY 1983		PERCENTAGE SALES INCREASE/DECREASE 2-QUARTER AVERAGE— 4-QUARTER AVERAGE
PRODUCT	Q1	Q2	Q3	Q4	Q1	Q2	
HSP101	300	300	350	350	480	590	64.6
HSP102	1,500	1,700	1,800	1,800	1,900	1,500	0
⇕							
WPP125	100	100	200	200	175	175	16.7

segments? And to review the same information from another perspective, you may want to calculate percentages of sales contributing to each of the consumer segments in addition to reporting just the raw data.

Products Showing Sales Growth (Stage III)

When products begin to increase in sales volume, they enter Stage III of their life cycles. Of the many characteristics common to Stage III products, eight have MKIS implications. These eight characteristics and implications are highlighted in Table 7.4.

Rapid product sales growth is the easiest characteristic to identify. It is also the most critical for Stage III products. Because you may want to associate different marketing strategies with products in different stages of their life cycles, you will have to monitor product sales activity very closely. Are the increased sales of your product being purchased by the customer who will sustain long-term purchases? Are there many repeat purchases? Dozens of other questions could also be asked. But it is up to you to ask the right questions for your organization.

Report 7.5 (PSA-103) looks at sales trends for each Stage III product. This report obviously is valid for products in other life-cycle stages as well, but for Stage III products, it can act as a watchdog for those products that either are not performing up to your expectations or are not in line with your promotion strategies. Alternatively, you can use a similar version of this report to rank your product sales (by individual product for all products) by percentage sales increase. You can also compare your products that are increasing in sales volume to the appropriate strategies for Stage III products and do the same for products that have lower and higher sales-volume increases in order to determine if you are matching each product to its proper strategy.

Another common characteristic of products in Stage III relates to the purchaser. In most cases, the initial buyers of the Stage I product will continue to buy. Also, because of large increases in unit sales volume during Stage III, there will be large numbers of new first-time buyers. One of the applications used in Chapter 6, Report 6.5 (PSA-140), is an ideal tool for measuring these two expected phenomena. This report tracks individual product sales by purchaser over several quarters, and it will immediately highlight the continued buying habits of your initial customers as well as identify new customers.

Of the eight characteristics of Stage III products, the competitive factor is the major one with direct MKIS implications, for it is at this point in your product's life cycle that the majority of competitors enter the market. Thus you will have to adjust your competition files in order to show the key ingredients that differentiate your products from your competitor's.

Products That Are Maturing (Stage IV)

As unit sales begin to level off, the product is usually entering Stage IV, the maturity period, of its life cycle. Of the five Stage IV characteristics that have MKIS ramifications, three of the most critical are intensified competition, cost increases, and market segmentation (see Table 7.5).

Because all of the competitors who entered the market during Stage III are now seeing a falloff in overall market growth in Stage IV, each competitor increases his efforts to maintain market share. As he does so, prices often decrease. Therefore, a subset of your competition file at this point should include product-price tracking.

Of course, if prices fall, marketing management will begin to focus its attention on overall product or product-line profitability. By modifying the territory P&Ls presented in Chapter 6, you can arrive at Report 7.6 (PPL-501). The items in this report can be identical to the territory P&Ls, the only difference being that the column headings represent products or product lines. Two points of caution, however:

1. Because this type of report crosses over into Accounting's domain, you should check to see what types of analyses already are being

performed. In many cases, though, you will find that while Accounting does provide product-line P&Ls, it will do so only through the gross-profits level. Accounting usually is concerned with standard and variance manufacturing costs at the individual product level and marketing expenses at more macro levels.

2. The more detailed the level of P&L reports, the greater the chance that the data will become increasingly meaningless. Thus an overall marketing P&L will be more accurate than a product-line P&L. Likewise, the product-line P&L will be more accurate than an individual product P&L. As profit-and-loss analyses become more detailed, more and more arbitrary expense allocations begin to appear. Therefore, you should review your P&L applications in order to ensure that you are not "overreporting."

Regardless of their form, profit-and-loss analyses applied to the marketing sector can be extremely useful tools. In addition to Report 7.6, you may want to show each P&L report line item as a percentage change from a previous period, as a percentage of all products or product lines, or within a single column as a percentage of net sales.

The third critical characteristic of Stage IV products is that the market tends to become segmented. At this point, some organizations will begin to focus their marketing efforts toward a single or a few groups of buyers. The real significance of consumer and market data-bank report applications will be discussed in Chapters 8 and 9. However, a general type of summary report is appropriate here. Report 7.7 (CFR-401) compares Hi-Tech's market share on a geographical basis against that of its competitors. It also compares percentage-unit growth rate, by geographical segment, and product prices for the current quarter and the previous year.

Products That Are Being Phased Out (Stage V)

All of the characteristics for Stage V products (see Table 7.6), meaning products that show a continued unit-sales decline, have been dealt with

REPORT 7.6
Hi-Tech, Inc.,
Profit-and-Loss Summary by Product Line
Month Ended 6/30/83
(Dollars in Millions)

PPL-501

Frequency: Monthly
Quarterly
Yearly

	COMPUTERS	PRINTERS	SUPPLIES	TOTAL
Gross Sales (less returns and warranties)	18.6	12.4	15.9	46.9
Net Sales				
Manufacturing Costs				
Gross Profits				
Expenses, Controllable				
Travel and entertainment				
Telephone				
Samples				
Supplies/rentals				
Literature, shows, exhibits				
Advertising				
Total controllable				
Expenses, Noncontrollable				
Auto				
Customer service				
Salaries				
Incentives				
Building change/overhead				
Insurance fees				
Miscellaneous				
Total Noncontrollable				
Total Expenses				
Profit Contribution	9.4	5.3	10.8	25.5

REPORT 7.7
Hi-Tech, Inc., Printer Division
Microcomputer Printer Segment
Period Ended Q3, FY 1980

CFR-401

Frequency: Quarterly

	MARKET SHARE (PERCENT)					UNIT GROWTH RATE/YEAR (PERCENT)					PRICE RANGES ($1,000s)	
COMPETITOR	NATIONAL	EAST	SOUTH	CENTRAL	WEST	NATIONAL	EAST	SOUTH	CENTRAL	WEST	Q3	LAST FY
Century Printers	8	4	24	5	8	100	108	65	110	94	4-9	4-5
IDM Technology	15	20	12	27	20	69	37	86	49	71	4-11	4-5
Porath Printer Co.	30	45	7	25	25	42	19	81	36	48	5-7	5-6
Tigerprint Inc.	12	12	12	10	15	15	8	32	14	32	9-14	9-13
All Others	25	10	30	18	24	25	37	8	29	40	3-11	3-10
Hi-Tech	10	9	15	15	8	20	40	49	15	12	5-6	5-6
Total	100	100	100	100	100	55	42	79	62	49		

earlier in this chapter. Although the report examples were used to illustrate specific life-cycle concepts, they are pertinent to all products at any life-cycle stage. In fact, to use these or modified report applications, you do not have to do so within the confines of the product life-cycle concept. You could view them as four separate levels of product reporting: (1) product sales analysis, (2) competitive reporting, (3) profitability reporting, and (4) new-product analysis. Table 7.16 shows how this product-report matrix is organized at Hi-Tech, Inc.

A Note about Forecasting and Your MKIS

Forecasting models are an enhancement to your basic MKIS system. You cannot design your system without first understanding the forecasting needs of your organization. If you do any statistical forecasting, whether manually or through a computer system, you must know which data elements will be components within the forecast model, and you must be sure that you have all of the necessary data elements in your system before you can utilize your forecasting models. For example, if you are using a Weighted Moving Average Formula and the number of time periods in your formula is thirty-six monthly periods, you will have to have thirty-six

TABLE 7.16
Product Report Matrix for Hi-Tech, Inc.

REPORT-APPLICATION LEVELS	DETAILED REPORT APPLICATION	SUMMARY REPORT APPLICATION	ANALYTICAL REPORT APPLICATION
1. Product-sales analyses			PSA-103
			PSA-201
			PSA-301
2. Competitive report			CFR-401
3. Profitability report		PPL-501	
4. New-product analyses		NPD-601	NPA-604

months of data. And of course the same is true for all other variable components in the model.

Action Plan

1. Review the concepts of the product life cycle and develop a set of relationships between each of your products (or product lines) and your specific marketing-management strategies.
2. From Step 1, for each product-strategy relationship, make a list of those items, questions, or problems that must be resolved and determine what information you need to resolve them. (These are your MKIS product implications.)
3. Having defined your information needs in Step 2, develop a list of the product reports that you want to include as part of your MKIS.
4. Follow Steps 3 through 6 as outlined in the Action Plan for Chapter 6.

CHAPTER 8

Consumer Data-Bank Report Applications

The Consumer

Marketing in its purest sense is the ability to communicate the proper mix of product or service information to create a controlled consumer response. Philip Kotler suggests that each organization should be responsible in part to sense, service, and quantifiably satisfy consumer wants.[1] To satisfy specific consumer needs, every organization must be able to answer the following:

- *Who* is our consumer?
- *Where* does our consumer live?
- *Why* does our consumer buy from us?
- *How often* does our consumer purchase our product or service?
- *Where* does our consumer purchase our product or service?

These simple consumer parameters will result in several consumer applications. Table 8.1 shows what an effective MKIS consumer report system can accomplish. For example, by identifying the consumer, you will be able to develop a complete consumer segmentation and profile. Understanding why the consumer buys from you is less quantifiable and somewhat more subjective. However, by identifying how Carl Consumer reacts to certain marketing stimuli (promotional campaigns, product features, or sales incentives), a pattern will emerge. These purchase patterns should stimulate future product development, promotional considerations, or incentive offerings. How often and where Carl Consumer buys your product or service is a function of his past and present buying patterns. Basic demand calculations from the point of sale and the time of sale may be used to project future sales.

The more you and your organization understand about the consumer, the better able you will be to provide significant and meaningful report applications and develop effective control and planning reports. The

1. Philip Kotler, *Marketing Management Analysis, Planning and Control* (Englewood Cliffs, N.J.: Prentice-Hall, 1976), p. 15.

TABLE 8.1
MKIS Consumer Applications

- Identifies Carl Consumer, and why, when, where, and how much he buys (consumer segmentation and profile)
- Identifies consumer demand (past, present, and future)
- Identifies consumer locations that are the most profitable and offer the greatest contribution potential
- Identifies and predicts consumer reaction to product marketing applications and programs
- Assists in establishing effective forecasting techniques through the use of the computer and simulation
- Assists in identifying specific consumer targets for promotion and sales programs
- Assists in transferring future consumer needs and values to Research & Development
- Assists Customer Service in consumer complaints and consumer identifications
- Offers the best possible match through a program of product segmentation and consumer-profile match (matching customer with product).

consumer reports in this chapter have a letter and numbering scheme similar to the reports in Chapters 6 and 7. The consumer report matrix shown in Table 8.2 depicts the report system. Every report system matrix will be different, based on the specific set of data elements and applications selected for the purpose of the report.

Basic Consumer-Identification Reports (100 Series)

Direct mail is a highly efficient means of advertising if you know your target. However, inaccurate mailing addresses, product interests, selection attributes, and last contact dates will result in an unproductive direct-mail program. Basic consumer identification requires a great deal of market and sales research along with consistent report maintenance. But this research will result in effective consumer mailing lists. Effective consumer lists are a prerequisite for conducting primary market research, test-marketing, and product-acceptance or investigation testing. To develop a mailing list for consumer identification and maintenance, you should use several sources

TABLE 8.2
Consumer Reporting Matrix

REPORT APPLICATION LEVELS	DETAILED REPORT APPLICATION	SUMMARY REPORT APPLICATION	ANALYTICAL REPORT APPLICATION
1. Basic Consumer Identification	CID-100	CIS-102	CIA-101
2. Consumer Potential/Profile	CPD-200	CPS-202	CPA-203
3. Consumer Service Record			CSA-300
4. Consumer Sales Strategy	CSD-420		CSA-410
5. Consumer Profile and Segmentation		CSS-501	CSA-503

TABLE 8.3
Direct-Mail Guide (Mailing-List Sources)

Seminar brokers (AMA, Penton)
Publishing firms (books, journals, newspapers)
Brokers (who sell mailing lists)
Sales records
Shipping records
Telephone inquiries
Sales representatives' call reports
Advertising inquiries
Prior lead-producing publicity
Trade-show registrants
Current consumer recommendations
Product/warranty registrations
Yellow Pages
Business/industrial directories
Thomas Register of Manufacturers
Standard & Poor's Register/Moody's Industrial Manual
Association membership rosters
Stockholders
Dealers/distributors
Subscriber lists (purchased from magazines)
Trade association and union mailing lists

on a trial basis to test their effectiveness. Table 8.3 lists some of the mailing-list sources.

The consumers in the following report examples are structured for both industrial and general consumer classification. Many organizations maintain both a direct consumer list and an indirect one. In Report 8.1, Cheryl Lynn Dupui will be considered an indirect consumer. The primary or direct consumer is the Swift Control Data Corporation. All subsequent profiles and segmentation applications will revolve around either consumer classification. If your organization is strictly consumer, then Cheryl Lynn Dupui is your direct consumer. If your organization is purely industrial, then Swift Control Data Corporation will be considered your direct consumer. For purposes of illustration, we include both in the report examples.

CID-100 (REPORT 8.1)

The Consumer Master Identification Report is simply the master consumer list or customer file. All consumer or account-number designations should be maintained on a master list of this type. All future consumer identification should be verified for accuracy against the customer master. This report should be maintained through sales-order entry, customer-service registration, or sales-force maintenance routines.

CIA-101 (REPORT 8.2)

The Consumer Profile Guide is an upgrading of the Consumer Master Identification Report in that profile data is now reflected. In this report, the actual geographical location is now merged with either consumer demographic and psychographic data or industrial profile data. In our example, we provide both. Examples of consumer profile data could include age, sex, marital status, income bracket, occupational status, education, number of children, and so forth. Examples of industrial profile data could include organization size (a code is useful, as discussed in Chapter 4), assets, total revenue, number of employees, earnings per share (EPS), product mix, debt structure, and so on. The relevant profile parameters will be somewhat unique depending on your consumer classification and product or service requirements. This report is maintained through sales-order entry, customer-service records, sales-force input, and market research techniques.

CIS-102 (REPORT 8.3)

The Consumer Profile Summary is a composite of all consumer profile records, and it produces an overall evaluation of the consumer base. This summary can be produced at the territory or cost-center level, the district, region, or, as shown, the national level. The parameters will be unique for each organization. Our example utilizes both an indirect and a direct consumer base for illustration only.

The objective of the report is to help market research and product managers determine whether the total consumer profile for either a

REPORT 8.1
Consumer Master Identification
Hypo-Thetical Company
Period Ended 6/11/85
CID-100 (Quarterly)
Territory
District
Region

Frequency: Monthly
Quarterly

	MAILING LABEL			
ACCOUNT NUMBER	**NAME**	**ADDRESS**	**PHONE**	**PRIMARY CONTACT LOCATION**
69362	Cheryl Lynn Dupui Requisitions Manager	35 East Jackson Clearwater, FL 33589	555-2121	Swift Control Data Corporation U.S. 19 Clearwater, FL 33569
⇕	⇕	⇕	⇕	⇕

REPORT 8.2
Hypo-Thetical Company
Consumer Profile Guide
Period Ended 6/1/85
CIA-101 (Monthly)
Territory

Frequency: Monthly
Quarterly

ACCOUNT NUMBER	NAME	ADDRESS	PROFILE/STATUS
69362	Cheryl Lynn Dupui	35 East Jackson, Clearwater, FL 33589	Consumer Age: 36 Sex: Female Marital Status: M Income: Middle Occupation Status: Professional Title: Acquisitions Manager Education: MBA 1975 Industrial Size: Small Assets: $75M Revenue: $35M Employees: 175 EPS: $.75 Products: Communications Equipment

REPORT 8.3
Hypo-Thetical Company
Consumer Profile Summary
Period Ended 6/11/85

CIS-102
National

Frequency: Quarterly

INDIRECT CONSUMER

AGE

MEAN	MEDIAN	RANGE
39	36	26-66

INCOME

MEAN	MEDIAN	RANGE
$27,100	$25,000	$21,000-$96,000

EDUCATION

HIGH SCHOOL	COLLEGE	GRAD
9%	78%	13%

OCCUPATIONAL DISTRIBUTION

ACQ MGR	MKT MGR	MIS MGR	OFFICER	DP MGR
13%	10%	20%	14%	43%

CHILDREN

1	2	3	4
40%	30%	10%	10%

INCOME DISTRIBUTION

$21,000-30,000	$30,000-40,000	$40,000+
73%	20%	7%

AGE DISTRIBUTION

25-30	31-40	41-60	60+
11%	49%	37%	3%

SEX

MALE	FEMALE
71%	29%

MARITAL

YES	NO
71%	29%

DIRECT CONSUMER

SIZE/CODE DISTRIBUTION

L	M	S
17%	50%	33%

ASSETS RANGE

$1-50M	$51-100M	$101-200M	$201-400M	$401-600M	$600M+
17%	16%	20%	20%	10%	17%

EPS HISTORY

1979	1980	1981	1982	1983	1984
$1.21	$1.15	$1.79	$ .69	$ .55	$ .51

REVENUE DISTRIBUTION

$1-25M	$26-50M	$51-100M	$101-200M	$201-300M	$300M+
6%	16%	30%	20%	15%	13%

territory or national level is consistent with the target of your promotional efforts. If it is not, you may want to reexamine your promotional programs, product pricing, and packaging.

Consumer-Potential Profiles (200 Series)

The Consumer-Potential Profile reports show consumer volume potential and provide an encapsulated product-purchase history, a calculation of period sales trends by product type, and total dollar rank by product. However, these are more than sales reports. By analyzing these simple reports, you will uncover several marketing-related applications.

CPD-200 (REPORT 8.4)

The Consumer Sales Expansion Report highlights each consumer's product-purchase trend and his degree of satisfaction with each product line. By understanding each consumer's past purchase pattern by product and time, you will be able to predict future purchase patterns and new product-line acceptance. Distinct consumer segments within geographical boundaries can also be extracted from this report. Marketing managers sometimes find it difficult to assess segmented consumer groups by product and location. By inserting a code indicator (Love-Hate Code), the manager can determine who buys which product, where the buyer resides, and his degree of product satisfaction. For example, Mr. Porath at Mastertech now reflects a negative satisfaction code with Product AP-2. We must find the reason why the AP-1 was satisfactory and why the AP-2 was not.

This report will be derived from your Consumer Data Bank and a sales-order entry interface. The Consumer Data Bank (Table 3.5C) is designed to accumulate consumer information. As such, the fields' names, addresses, and L/H code are identified through an access of this file while the sales order interface can provide product history. The report can be used by product managers, market planners, product planners, and promo-

REPORT 8.4
Hypo-Thetical Company
Consumer Sales Expansion
Period Ended 6/1/85
CPD-200
Region 51000
District 51100
Territory 51104

Frequency: Monthly

ACCOUNT NUMBER	NAME	ADDRESS	CITY/STATE/ZIP	PHONE	PRODUCT HISTORY	TREND INDICA-TOR	L/H CODE
06111	Douglas Porath Operations Mgr. Mastertech, Inc.	112 Marlin	Miami, FL 33157	555-0158	1/12/69—AP-1 3/17/71—AP-1 12/1/77—AP-1 10/9/78—AP-2 10/4/80—AP-2	.44	L-10/9/78 H-8/04/81

tion managers. The promotion manager may want to segment distinct consumer groups by product preference and geographical location and reproduce this information using computer graphic displays.

CPS-202 (REPORT 8.5)

The Consumer Volume Potential Report provides a summary of each account's purchase patterns, market-penetration status, and volume potential. The volume potential is built into the consumer file by range values and corresponding code values. A range of 0–2 units is classified as a code 3, or low volume potential. However, as the product history grows, any increase in product-purchase increments could move the consumer into a new range value, as illustrated. For inactive status or lost accounts, the volume potential is based on the last date of purchase and volume total.

Consumer segmentation based on activity status, volume potential, and product segment is the primary function of this report. For example, Mastertech begins as "just an account number" and becomes an account with a specific product segment history and a corresponding future-volume indicator. The market penetration or status code is also an effective tool for aiding the sales force in identifying lost accounts and the value of those accounts. This report will be accessed through the Consumer Data Bank and sales-order-entry data files.

CPA-203 (REPORT 8.6)

The Consumer Rank by Territory Report is a sales-order-entry-generated summary of each territory account and the value of the account. Field representatives or managers can use this report to establish certain priorities among all accounts based on each account's total dollar rank. If your organization maintains a contracts administration function within Marketing, this report should be used as a basis of price quotations and contracts negotiation. The report can also be used to evaluate the effect of certain contracts, price adjustments, quantity discounts, and promotions on units shipped and revenue change.

REPORT 8.5
Hypo-Thetical Company
Consumer Volume Potential
Period Ended 6/1/85
CPS-202 (Monthly)
Region 51000
District 51100
Territory 51104

Frequency: Monthly
Quarterly

ACCOUNT NUMBER	NAME	PRODUCT IDENTIFICATION	SALES VOLUME	MARKET PENETRATION	VOLUME POTENTIAL
06111	Mastertech	10/9/81—AP-2		Active Status	3
		10/4/83—AP-2	AP-2/2		
		10/5/84—AP-3	AP-3/3		
		10/6/84—AP-4	AP-4/6		2
06113	Datatech	10/16/81—MA-16		Inactive Status	1
		01/05/82—AP-2	AP-2/10		

REPORT 8.6
Hypo-Thetical Company
Consumer Rank by Territory
Period Ended 6/30/85
CPA-203
Region 51000
District 51100
Territory 51104

Frequency: Quarterly

		PRODUCT UNIT SALES—QUARTER						
ACCOUNT NUMBER	CUSTOMER	TOTAL UNITS (A)	TOTAL UNITS (B)	TOTAL UNITS (C)	TOTAL UNITS	TOTAL DOLLARS	RANK CURRENT	RANK LAST
06111	Mastertech	6	5	0	11	550,000	1	2
69362	Swift Control	5	4	0	9	396,001	2	1
00112	Hi-Technotech	4	3	1	8	352,000	3	5
71557	Datatech	3	4	1	8	339,115	4	10
71555	Ally Chemical	2	4	1	7	304,440	5	20

Consumer Service Records (300 Series)

High medical technology or pharmaceutical organizations continue to enjoy the advantage of having the consumer or physician complete product registrations as required by law. Other organizations must rely on their customer-service or warranty departments, basic market research, or sales input to establish reliable customer-service records.

In any event, reliable customer service information has intrinsic benefits that are difficult to measure but may help to produce bottom-line results. Typically, a better consumer understanding emerges, which may indicate prospects for future sales generation.

CSA-300 (REPORT 8.7)

The Customer Service Record Report is an excellent tool for sales management and product managers in planning sales strategies and product forecasts. The primary benefit of this report is the service-need section, which highlights each consumer's service record and expected service and sales codes.

In the report example, Ultra-tech should be expected either to replace the AP-1 with the AP-5 on June 11, 1984, or require AP-1 service on or by June 11, 1984. The code 1 AP-1 is a special indicator for a first-time service on 6/11/80. The expected service code (4B) designates that service is expected within four years. The installation record indicates product AP-5 as the recommended replacement on approximately 6/11/84.

This report is useful to sales managers because it shows who and where the consumer is and what his needs are. The promotion manager can use the report totals to identify the need for a direct-mail follow-up by knowing when particular consumer segments require new products. If your organization does not maintain a sales force, a direct communication from your customer-service department or distributor may be equally effective. The consumer profile code should represent a profile value or designation associated with specific types of consumer background. For example, in Report 8.7 the profile code 2 represents a moderately high industrial-

REPORT 8.7
Hypo-Thetical Company
Consumer Service Record
Period Ended 6/1/85
CSA-300 (Monthly)
Region 51000
District 51100
Territory 51104

Frequency: Monthly
Quarterly

				SERVICE NEED		
ACCOUNT NUMBER	NAME	ADDRESS	CONSUMER PROFILE CODE	SERVICE CODE	EXPECTED SERVICE CODE	INSTALLATION RECORD
00112	Peter Manakus Systems Manager Ultra-Tech	3 Elm Street Gainesville, FL 33689	2	1 AP-1 (6/11/80)	4B	AP-5 (6/11/84)

type consumer profile with respect to such attributes as company size (employee number, assets, or revenue), purchasing habits, or types of products bought and sold. This report is accessed through the Consumer Data Bank, customer-service file, and the Product Data Bank.

Consumer Sales Strategy Reports (400 Series)

The previous report examples identify who, where, why, and when. But how does the manager take full advantage of this consumer profile? The answer involves a commitment to strategy and how a given set of profile parameters correlate to a specific strategy or alternative. Market-segmentation, consumer profiles, selection attributes, and market-class designations all may be used in strategy formulation. Lumping your consumers into one customer file and using one marketing strategy is too narrow in scope. You must utilize as much consumer information as possible to determine distinct marketing strategies for specific groups of consumers. By combining your different marketing strategies (after taking into consideration the composites of consumer profile data), a range of unique strategies for different market segments should emerge.

CSA-410 (REPORT 8.8)

The Consumer Sales Strategy Matrix Report is somewhat complex to program and maintain, but the rewards are extraordinary. This report is a composite by consumer of profile code, research code, product code, market-segment code, and market class. These code designations will be unique to your organization. The profile code used in this example simply designates high-profile consumers (1) to new or low-profile groups (5). The market-research code signifies how the data were obtained and formulated. For example, primary research input would be code 1, and secondary input would be code 2.

The product code is the Maxi-Hypo (A), Mini-Hypo (B), and All-Purpose Hypo (C). The market segment refers to occupation classification

REPORT 8.8
Hypo-Thetical Company
Consumer Sales Strategy Matrix
Period Ended 6/11/85
CSA-410
Region 51000
District 51100
Territory 51104

Frequency: Quarterly

ACCOUNT NUMBER	NAME	PROFILE CODE	MARKET RESEARCH CODE	PRODUCT CODE	MARKET SEGMENT	MARKET CLASS	STRATEGY NUMBER
71555	Ally Chemical	5	1	A	B	L	16
71557	Datatech	4	1	A,B	B	LM	27
71559	Bureau Service	1	1	B,C	C	UM	15
71661	Gains University	3	1	A,B,C	C	UM	1
	⇕	⇕	⇕	⇕	⇕	⇕	⇕

or job title segments. The market class is generated from the market data bank and ranks companies or individuals according to their financial status. Earnings per share, net assets, and gross revenue or income are the preferred indicators. For example, the "L" market class indicates a low EPS (or gross revenue), while a "UM" (upper middle) would indicate a very sound financial position. The code "LM" (lower middle) reflects a moderate or stable position.

Each consumer is given a profile code value to summarize his overall profile at a glance. By assigning a unique strategy to one or several profiles, you can open the marketing door to accommodate a seemingly endless array of strategies. The computer can generate thousands of different combinations, but you must define a manageable combination of profiles.

By summarizing the total for each strategy number, you can then use the marketing strategies that are most appropriate for both specific and large consumer segments. This is an extremely efficient means of reaching your total consumer base or segments with the most effective marketing plan.

CSD-420 (REPORT 8.9)

The Consumer Attributes Master Report details each consumer's "hot buttons" or important selection criteria. These attributes reflect the importance each consumer may give to such selection parameters as:

Company reputation	(CR)
Product reliability	(PR)
Product size	(SZ)
Product warranty	(WR)
Product appearance/color	(AC)
Product price	(PP)
Product service	(PS)

The benefit of the report is found in the Total and Mean (average) section at the bottom. Since each attribute is scaled (1 to 7) according to its relative importance in the selection process, a final ranking per geograph-

REPORT 8.9
Hypo-Thetical Company
Consumer Attributes Master
Period Ended 6/11/85
CSD-420
Region 51000
District 51100
Territory 51104

Frequency: Quarterly

ACCOUNT NUMBER	NAME	SELECTION ATTRIBUTES						
		CR	PR	SZ	WR	AC	PP	PS
71555	Ally Chemical	3	5	4	7	1	2	6
71557	Datatech	1	6	4	5	2	3	7
71559	Bureau Service	4	3	2	5	6	1	7
71661	Gains University	3	5	4	6	2	1	7
Total	4	11	19	14	23	11	7	27
Mean		2.75	4.75	3.50	5.75	2.75	1.75	6.75

ical area is possible. The lower the mean, the more important the selection attribute. For example, Ally Chemical's sale is based on appearance/color and price, respectively. While the total reveals price and then appearance, to the promotion manager and field representative, these differences are important. The promotion manager has price discount policies in mind, while the sales representative sells appearance and color coordination. By totaling these attribute lists for different market segments, territories, or products, you can determine which promotional incentive to use for which area. Selection attributes are collected by field, in-house, or conference research and by customer registration input.

Consumer-Profile and Segmentation Reports (500 Series)

Why did American auto manufacturers fail to maintain gross profits in the late 1970s and early 1980s? Because they, and other organizations, failed to respect what consumer research dictated or what a lack of consumer research did not dictate. Carefully evaluating what your consumers want and why they want it are two specialized areas of the marketing concept. The marketing concept is the attempt to calculate systematically total consumer behavior and response patterns. The automobile manufacturers obviously calculated incorrectly or failed to accept what research was telling them. It is likely that no organization will ever know too much about its consumer base. Typically, the opposite is true. Organizations always require greater amounts of consumer-identification information. Simple data-gathering techniques such as field research,[2] on-line data-base research, outside customer research, and in-house research will in most cases provide sufficient data for consumer profile or segmentation.

2. See, for example, the Consumer Maintenance/Referral Data in Table 8.4.

CSS-501 REPORT 8.10)

The Consumer Segmentation and Profile Summary Report summarizes key consumer-segmentation and profile codes by distinct geographical areas while highlighting the total consumer-base profile. In the example, territory 104 has 100 accounts. The majority of these accounts demand product STD-A1 and fall into market segment C. The "selection attributes total" section is a summation of the scaled rankings (1 to 7) divided by the total number of accounts. The result is an attribute ranking within territory. For example, "PP" (product price) is the most important selection attribute among the total consumer base in territory 104.

This report is an exceptional tool for estimating new-product acceptance, promotion acceptance and effectiveness, sales effectiveness, and overall marketing strategy. Some firms use a similar report to analyze territory expansion and realignment. Product managers, department directors, vice-presidents, presidents, and field managers all would require this report on a quarterly or semiannual basis. Each would benefit from the concise geographical profile this report offers.

CSA-503 (REPORT 8.11)

The Segment Profile Analysis Report is similar to Report 8.3 (CIS-102) except that here we include territory in the profile analysis. This report is meaningful because of the side-by-side geographical comparisons of territories, districts, or regions. A final analysis or composite, summarizing all territory analyses by district, region, or total domestic, also can be prepared. To an advertising director, for example, the consumer distinctions between one territory and another may necessitate different campaign strategies. To the sales manager, offering special incentives with the STD-A1 in one territory may be self-defeating, but it possibly would be effective in another. Marketing planners will find this report especially useful for estimating new-product acceptance, territory promotional testing, product-position studies, and territory-management analysis.

REPORT 8.10
Hypo-Thetical Company
Consumer Segmentation and Profile Summary
Period Ended 6/11/85

CSS-501 — Frequency: Quarterly

Region 51000
District 51100
Territory 51104

Number of Accounts: 100

Total Profile: 1: 13 2: 21 3: 18 4: 41 5: 7

Total market/Product code:	Product STD-A1: 37	Product MA-16: 11	Product CP-302: 28
	Product AP-1: 9	Product AP-3: 10	Product AP-5: 6
Total market segment:	Segment A: 14	Segment B: 27	Segment C: 34
	Segment D: 9	Segment E: 16	
Number market class:	LM: 36	UM 13	L: 51

Total selection attributes:	C/295	PR/475	SZ/377	WR/590	AC/275	PP/198	PS/660
Average:	2.95	4.75	3.77	5.90	2.75	1.98	6.60
Rank:	3	5	4	6	2	1	7

REPORT 8.11
Hypo-Thetical Company
Segment Profile Analysis
Period Ended 6/11/85
CSA-503
District 51100
Region 51000

Frequency: Semiannually

TERRITORY	TOTAL BASE/ TOTAL PERCENTAGE	TITLE DISTRIBUTION PERCENTAGES	PRODUCT-LINE PERCENTAGES	PROFILE DISTRIBUTION PERCENTAGES	PRODUCT SEGMENT PERCENTAGES	SELECTION DETERMINATES DISTRIBUTION
104	100/.006	DP Mgr = 40	STD-AI = 66	4 = 61	C = 47	PP = 1
		Mkt Mgr = 10	CP 302 = 34	2 = 21	B = 27	AC = 2
		Acq Mgr = 15		3 = 18	E = 26	CR = 3
105	220/.009	Acq Mgr = 36	MA-16 = 73.5	4 = 37.5	A = 62.5	AC = 1
		DP Mgr = 34	AP-1 = 26.5	3 = 33	D = 21.5	CR = 2
		Mis Mgr = 18		2 = 30	C = 16.0	SZ = 3
106	175/.008	Mis Mgr = 57	AP-5 = 40	1 = 66	E = 100	CR = 1
		DP Mgr = 43	AP-6 = 60	2 = 34		PR = 2
						SZ = 3
⇕	⇕	⇕	⇕	⇕	⇕	⇕

TABLE 8.4
Consumer Maintenance Referral Data

Name:
Address:
City:
State:
Zip Code:

1. Personal Likes:
   Dislikes:
2. Married (yes or no):
3. Children (yes or no) (number):
4. Social Interests:
   Theater:
   Opera:
   Sporting Events:
   Travel:
   Books:
   Misc.:
5. Most Effective Sales Methods/Approach:
6. Least Effective Sales Methods/Approach:
7. Past Marketing-Effort Effectiveness (yes or no):
   Direct Mail:
   Personal Letter:
   Brochures:
   Technical Literature:
   Journal Advertising:
   Trade Show Advertising:
   Sales-Rep Support:
8. Future Product Interests:
9. Profile Update Information (use update forms):
10. Selection Attributes Rank:
11. Who makes the key decisions regarding product selection?
12. Profile Code:
13. Market Segment:

Summary

Depending on the size of your data base, entering and maintaining consumer data is an extremely disciplined effort. Identifying who, where, why, when, and how often takes several months and different combinations of input origination. Many organizations rely on information brokers to identify and profile their consumers. Some organizations rely on field managers and sales representatives for the data. And still others buy special research reports and add their own conclusions. Regardless of how you identify and enter your data, you must maintain the data's integrity. Using a Consumer Maintenance Referral sheet (Table 8.4) is a must if you are to maintain the accuracy of your original input. Remember the old computer saying "garbage in, garbage out." You should expend as much energy and use as many resources to maintain your data as you did to secure it.

Action Plan

1. Describe your current consumer and detail the informational requirements to service and satisfy your total consumer base.
2. Develop a consumer-marketing-strategy relationship and describe the informational requirements necessary for identification, profile, segmentation, and strategy.
3. From Step 1 and 2, develop a Consumer Data Bank using Table 3.5C in Chapter 3 as a guide. Using this base, develop a list of the consumer reports you want to include as part of your MKIS.
4. Follow Steps 3 through 6 as outlined in the Action Plan for Chapter 6.

CHAPTER 9

Market Data-Bank Report Applications

Market Structure

When you ask marketing executives why their organizations are successful in terms of sales, a common response is "we're able to keep abreast and even stay one step ahead." But what does "staying ahead" actually mean? Most marketing executives would agree that quantitative measurements of both the consumer and the market are an absolute necessity. But measuring the past, present, and future market conditions are also essential in taking full advantage of planning requirements, strategy formulation, and opportunities. Only by measuring selected market parameters over periods of time is one able to "stay ahead."

Often the marketing manager relies on research opinions, various consumer or market tests, special statistical analyses, sales-representative data, and surveys to analyze the state of the market. The market-data requirements of today are so encompassing that the marketing manager should not merely rely on research techniques. He should rely on information brokers, data-base services, government data banks, and various other data publishers as well.[1] Although market parameters as they pertain to each organization are unique, the market structure (economic, demographic, political, technological, informational, and cultural) is usually similar. Today's marketing manager faces a host of market variables within this structure that typically he has little or no control over.

The objective is for the marketing manager to identify the market structure and market parameters that should be controlled through measurement and then through reaction. Understanding how a change in population and income affects your sales for a particular geographical area is one application. In addition, knowing exactly when and how to react to a given set of parameter changes is another.

Table 9.1 identifies a general group of market applications using the Market Data Bank.[2] The applications presented are general enough to

(Text continues on page 222)

1. See Appendix B, The Business Research and Information Guide.
2. The Market Data Bank data elements are presented in Table 3.5D in Chapter 3.

TABLE 9.1
Market Data-Bank Applications: The MKIS Results of Effective Market Applications

- To segment and profile specific market characteristics
- To identify and react to changes in the market
- To identify trends (short- and long-term) in the market
- To calculate market potential by geographical location
- To measure specific market variables for profitability impact
- To calculate market penetration by product
- To calculate competitive activity by market and geographical location
- To aid in market-research programs
- To identify specific market needs, perceptions, and values for promotional considerations

REPORT 9.1A
Market Management Guide (MMG)

(For any geographical area, territory, cost center, market, or consumer or product segment)

INDIRECT CONSUMER

1. Name
   Address
2. Title
3. Profile category
4. Occupation/Specialization
5. Account numbers
6. Account history (purchase profile by product—last two years)
7. Product category
8. Identified market segment
9. Preference category
10. Selection-attributes ranking
11. Social distinction

REPORT 9.1B
Market Management Guide (MMG)

(For any geographical area, territory, cost center, market, or consumer or product segment)

DIRECT CONSUMER

1. Name
   Address
   Phone
2. Account number
3. Purchase history (total summary)
4. Contact name
   Phone
5. Employee size
6. General facilities and services
7. Financial status:
   Total expenses
   Total revenues
   Long-term debt status
   EPS
8. Growth projections (unit sales, dollar sales, market and industry)
9. Key decision-makers

REPORT 9.1C
Market Management Guide (MMG)

(For any geographical area, territory, cost center, market, or consumer or product segment)

MARKET PROFILE

1. Market growth projections (units)
2. Population
   Total
   Per square mile
   1-24 (actual and percentage of total)
   25-30
   31-40
   41-60
   60
   Percent white
   Percent black
   Percent female
   Percent male
   Percent urban
   Percent with high school education
   Percent with college education
3. Per-capita income
   Rank in U.S.
   Total
   Average annual
4. Median values, family income
   Rank in U.S.
   Total
5. Percent income
   $15,000
   $15,001-24,999
   $25,000-30,000
   $30,000
6. Total prospects (total market less current account base)
7. Company sales, total by product (trend)
8. Regional sales trends, competition (by product)
9. Company product-specification tables
   vs.
   Competitive product-specification tables
10. Competitive market-share estimate (list)

REPORT 9.1C, *continued*
MARKET PROFILE

11. Efficiency index
(total sales ÷ total expenses)
12. Current price-sensitive accounts
13. Current contract accounts
14. Total accounts
15. Total active accounts
16. Total inactive accounts
17. Key accounts

apply to most organizations. How you use the Market Data Bank is of course determined by the requirements of your particular applications. The Market Report Matrix is outlined in Table 9.2. Market identification and segmentation, competitive profiles, promotion effectiveness, and so forth are the types of controls that are often absent from even the most sophisticated MKIS.

TABLE 9.2
Market Report Matrix

REPORT APPLICATION LEVELS	DETAILED REPORT APPLICATION	SUMMARY REPORT APPLICATION	ANALYTICAL REPORT APPLICATION
1. Market identification, profile, and segmentation		Market Management Guide (MMG) MMS-100	MIA-101
2. Competitive analysis		MCS-200	
3. Market parameters/statistics		MRS-300 MRS-300.1 MRS-301	
4. Market service data (promotional effectiveness)	MSD-400 MSD-401	MRS-402	
5. Market analysis		MRS-500	MAA-505

While examining the market report system, you should visualize the extent to which these examples can or cannot be applied to your organization. As in Chapters 6, 7, and 8, the report-system matrix in Table 9.2 is only a representation of how a report system revolves around previously identified applications.

Market Identification, Profile, and Segmentation Reports (100 Series)

The need to identify, classify, and segment important market parameters into a manageable report is a fundamental application. The values of such an identification report could include:

1. Basic territory management
2. Account prospect guide
3. Field management sales analysis
4. A tool for better communication between in-house marketing personnel and the sales force.

The Series 100 reports, which complement one another with respect to marketing management, present general market, profile, and segmentation information. The ultimate objective of each report is to generate sales potential through a greater understanding of market conditions, opportunities, and planning.

THE MANAGEMENT MARKET GUIDE

The Management Market Guide (MMG) (Reports 9.1 A–C) documents an organization's key market parameters. The parameters can include market demographics, psychographics, consumer-profile data, or organizational statistics. In our MMG outline, the individual (indirect consumer), the organization (direct consumer), and the market constitute the classification headings. The key parameters of each will be assigned different values by your organization's members according to their needs. For example, the sales representative, no matter how experienced, will require consumer-profile information (whether the consumer is an individual or an enterprise) as a prerequisite for sales calls. By combining consumer-profile information with relevant market information, the sales representative can plan his sales strategies and marketing activities. The information contained in the MMG is especially helpful for new or realigned sales representatives.

If the sales force uses the MMG as a prospect list, you should attach an update or comment section. Field managers find the MMG especially valuable as an aid in determining sales-force efficiency and realignments. Sales representative John Jones may generate low-revenue production, but his market profile may indicate a need to realign the territory because of a limited market potential. A territory market comparison is one method of determining market capacity by location. The MMG is particularly valuable for marketing directors, market planning managers, and other in-house marketing personnel for communicating with field managers and sales-force personnel.

The MMG is a composite of all MKIS data banks. While the Consumer Data Bank is obviously accessed, the Market, Product, and Sales Data Banks are also used in the MMG. The MMG example here of course will not meet all the informational requirements of every organization; it is merely a guide that you can use in developing your own. The MMG provides a composite profile of any given geographical area, territory, cost center, consumer, market, or product segment. The MMGs in Reports 9.1 A-C represent three functional reports: the Indirect Consumer (Report 9.1A), the Direct Consumer Profile (Report 9.1B), and the Market Profile (Report 9.1C).

MSS-100 (REPORT 9.2)

The Market Profile and Product Analysis Report distinguishes the potentials of both products and market segments. Market segments can represent a number of different designations. Instead of consumer type, we use market segment as representative of a particular geographical area.

The report should provide a measure of each product's potential

REPORT 9.2
Market Profile and Product Analysis
Period Ended 6/11/85
MSS-100 (Quarterly)

Frequency: Monthly
Quarterly

	PRODUCT A	PRODUCT B	PRODUCT C
Total Market			
Gross Sales:			
Units			
Dllars			
Market Sales:			
Actual Users			
Equivalent Users			
Total User Estimate			
Percent of Current Penetration			
Growth-Rate Projection			
Market Segment A			
Gross Sales:			
Units			
Dollars			
Market Sales:			
Actual			
Equivalent			
Total			
Penetration			
Growth			
Region Sales (Units):			
Northeast			
Northern			
Mid-Atlantic			

within the total market as well as within particular segments. Gross sales of course is actual dollars and units. Both primary and secondary research reports are used for the market-data input. Actual Users represents the total number of active accounts within the consumer file. Equivalent Users represents an estimate of the consumer market that buys equivalent competitors' products. Total User Estimate is the total consumer market. The difference between Actual Users and Equivalent Users represents short-term prospects or potential. Penetration Percentage is the percent of the Actual Users divided by the Total User Estimate.

The purpose of this report is to track your penetration position as well as to correlate your penetration and growth rate. Your penetration percent may be improving, but this will mean little if the market growth has started to decline or shift interest toward new technology. However, if the penetration percentage is increasing at the same time that growth is increasing, your potential for sustained segment or product sales is promising.

MIA-101 (REPORT 9.3)

The Market Segmentation Matrix Report is a product-line segment analysis of significant market-profile parameters by competitor. The report shows the relationship of key market indicators of your organization and your competitors. To examine the Market Segmentation Matrix, you should ask such questions as:

1. Do our competitors target the same consumer group?
2. Are we targeting equivalent product specifications to equivalent consumer groups?
3. Why is Competitor B doing so well in the South?

These questions and others must be examined routinely by marketing planning groups or committees.

The report should be used for product-position analysis, profitability analysis, product technology comparisons, consumer-profile comparisons, and market area comparisons. Significant variations from competitors' positions would indicate the need for further market research.

REPORT 9.3
Market Segmentation Matrix
Period Ended 6/11/85
MIA-101

Frequency: Quarterly

PRODUCT-LINE MARKET	YOUR ORGANIZATION	COMPETITOR A	COMPETITOR B	COMPETITOR C
Total Sales:				
Units				
Dollars				
Total Market Sales:				
Units				
Dollars				
Market Share				
Market Growth (Percent)				
Units				
Dollars				
Product Specifications				
Total Consumer Estimate				
Total Consumers by Income:				
15,000–25,000				
25,000–35,000				
35,000+				
Total Consumers by Age:				
25–30				
31–40				
41–60				
60+				
North (include market share)				
South (include market share)				
East (include market share)				
West (include market share)				
Attributes				

Competitive Analysis Reports (200 Series)

Most organizations today, no matter how sophisticated their information or research departments, conduct ongoing analyses of the competition. In fact, this is likely to be the most common marketing function today. Many organizations rely on the manual tracking and updating of competitive profiles. By systematically reviewing competitive information, the user will know where the information originated, the date of input, and the importance of the information. A uniform system of collection, input, and output offers a better alternative than looking up the information in several different locations.

MCS-200 (REPORT 9.4)

The Competitive Summary Report presents key competitor parameters as they relate to your organization. Report 9.4 is presented in outline form for convenience of interpretation. The actual report may be several pages in length, depending on product comparisons per competitor.

Obviously you will have to do a preliminary analysis of which parameters you want to include under competitor data. The report will contain competitor data and your organizational data for the same parameters. The source code on the right-hand side of the report indicates the actual source of the competitor data.[3] For example, product-line comparison data can be generated by using competitive product literature and price lists. Plant-capacity estimates can be generated from special industry reports.

Product managers, research managers, company officials, product planners, and even Wall Street analysts would find a competitive summary report useful. The input for this report is either batch (manual entry by keypunched cards) or on-line. The preferred method is via on-line entry with an update screen. This allows every competitor parameter to be updated, and it offers convenience to the manager because the data are stored in one place.

3. See Table 7.8, Sources for Gathering Competitive Information, for actual source-code values.

REPORT 9.4
Competitive Summary Report
MCS-200
Territory

Frequency: Quarterly
Yearly

COMPETITIVE DATA	COMPETITOR	YOUR DATA	SOURCE CODE*
Name			
Product(s) Line			
Product(s) Mix			
Product Specifications			
Geographical Coverage			
Gross Sales			
Plant Capacity (Estimation)			
Total: Area Representatives, Distributors, Etc.			
Share of Market and Trend			
Identified Promotion/Selling Methodology			
Practices (i.e., Allowances, Terms, Discounts)			
Advertising Platforms			
Quality, Performance, and Reliability History			
Field-Service Capability			

*See Table 7.8.

Market Parameters and Statistics Reports (300 Series)

Organizational decision-makers never seem to have enough information. And certainly two information requirements that often are neglected by many firms is market parameter and statistical identification. Understanding the market involves demographics and economics as well as competitive, technological, and political information. While demographic and economic data are readily available,[4] models for the use of such data are not. A wide range of opinion exists regarding the merits of using demographics and economics for decision-making and policy direction. There are two primary reasons for disenchantment with demographics. One reason is that the elaborate models used in many instances to verify their validity are seen as both suspect and as more trouble than they're worth. Second is the opinion that "demographics are not applicable to our organization."

Assuming demographics and other market parameters are applicable, and most managers believe they are, how do you use these data to evaluate markets and predict the future? By applying basic statistical measurements to market parameters, applications such as geographical potential, geographical influences, area efficiency ratings, and geographical realignment are possible.

MRS-300 AND MRS-300.1 (REPORTS 9.5 AND 9.6)

The Demographics Comparison and Demographic Rank Reports are simple in format but big on applications. Report 9.5 should offer territory descriptions of market parameters that you feel affect sales generation for a particular location. Parameters such as population, age, and sex are compared for each territory within a district to identify more accurately a territory's overall sales potential. The comparison of variance percentages for each parameter can use average values, percentages, or totals. For example, territory 011 may have an average age value of 43, whereas

4. See the first two sections of Appendix B, The Business Research and Information Guide.

REPORT 9.5
Demographic Comparison
Period Ended 6/11/85
MRS-300
Region
District

Frequency: Annually

	DEMOGRAPHICS									
			SEX		RACE				OCCUPATION	
TERRITORY	POPULATION TOTAL/ GROWTH	AGE (MEAN)	PERCENT MALE	PERCENT FEMALE	PERCENT WHITE	PERCENT BLACK	INCOME (MEAN/MEDIAN)	EDUCATION (MEAN/ MEDIAN)	PERCENT WHITE	PERCENT BLUE
011	70,000/.17	43	47	53	66	30	$15,100/17,000	12.1/12.5	51	49
012	400,000/.19	50	50	50	72	16	$17,300/19,510	10.8/11.5	66	34
013	150,000/.14	46	49	51	68	19	$16,100/18,000	10.7/11.4	60	40

REPORT 9.6
Demographic Rank
Period Ended 6/11/85
MRS-300.1
Region
District

Frequency: Annually

	DEMOGRAPHICS						
				OCCUPATION			
TERRITORY	POPULATION TOTAL/ GROWTH	INCOME (MEAN)	EDUCA- TION (MEAN)	PERCENT WHITE	PERCENT BLUE	BIRTH RATE (PERCENT)	OVERALL RANK
012	1/1	1	2	1	1	2	1
013	2/3	2	3	2	2	1	2
011	3/2	3	1	3	3	3	3

territory 012 may have a value of 50. The district (sum of a designated group of territories) average may be 43, and therefore territory 012 has a variance of 7 years. This may be significant if your market is directed at older consumers. If enough negative variances are found to exist in any one territory, you might want to consider a territory realignment.

A ranking system such as Report 9.6 should be created to provide an initial territory-potential estimation. In the following example, each territory is ranked against the other territories.

PARAMETER	TERRITORY 001	R	TERRITORY 012	R	TERRITORY 013	R
Age	43	3	50	1	46	2
Population	70,000	3	400,000	1	150,000	2

If the product is directed toward older consumers, obviously territory 012 would have the highest ranking or largest potential, all other parameters being equal. The objective of course is to rank every parameter by territory and sum the rankings to yield an overall territory rank of parameter values. Again, you want to look for any consistent discrepancies in territory values.

Marketing Services Reports: Measuring Promotion and Lead Effectiveness (400 Series)

The measurement of promotional and lead effectiveness is one of the most complicated marketing requirements. How does a promotion manager evaluate the effectiveness of his advertising campaign? One highly respected marketing-management book comments on the issue: "No matter how you analyze it, the proof is in the pudding. The overall evaluation of the ad campaign should measure the effect of the campaign on total sales."[5] Lead and prospect efficiency should also measure success by virtue of a sales correlation.

5. James A. Constantin, Rodney E. Evans, and Malcolm L. Morris, *Marketing Strategy and Management* (Dallas: Business Publications, Inc., 1976), p. 162.

The elements of advertising and lead analysis include (1) planning and development, (2) the identification of the message or lead, (3) preliminary evaluation, (4) organization or consumer activity response, and (5) sales correlation.

MSD-400 (REPORT 9.7)

The Lead Analysis Report is a tool that can be used by marketing planners and directors to identify and control lead prospects more effectively. The report has several lead-generation-technique codes, including sales-representative input and direct-mail promotion-piece returns. Each consumer or location should have a lead-technique code next to the date of input. The lead-technique code identifies the method of lead generation. The computer should arrange the prospect list according to the date of lead receipt. A few lead-technique codes are:

Personal interviews = Code A
Direct-mail piece = Code B
Trade show/conference inquiry = Code C
Television spot = Code D
Newspaper clipping = Code E
Journal advertisement clipping = Code F

When a lead is followed up, the date of the follow-up should be submitted for data entry and subsequent report production.

Report 9.7 shows the lead follow-up in greater detail. The area totals that will appear on the last page reflect the totals for consumer target, leads generated, cost per technique, and sales for each consumer/technique type. For example, let's assume that twenty consumer prospects were generated by technique A, personal interviews. Twenty-five of the total prospects were generated by technique B, direct-mail returns. By accessing the sales order or sales data bank, we are able to total the sales for both quarters for each consumer name or, if applicable, for each account number. These data are calculated by totaling all consumers by lead-technique code and generating a sales-correlation total per technique code. By calculating the

REPORT 9.7
Product A
Lead Analysis Report
(Period)

MSD-400

Frequency: Quarterly

CONSUMER NAME OR GEOGRAPHICAL LOCATION	DATE(S)	LEAD-GENERATION CODE	FOLLOW-UP DATE	FOLLOW-UP CODE	SALES/QUARTER		
					LAST	CURRENT	TREND
John B. Jones	1/24/85	A	3/07/85	1	14,000	15,000	+1.07
Harry Jones	1/25/85	B	5/07/85	2	14,000	13,000	− .93
William Jones	1/25/85	B	5/16/85	3	12,000	14,000	+1.16

Area Totals (Quarter)

Total Consumer Target:	Total Leads Generated:	Percent Response:	Total Cost:	Total Sales:
A	A	A	A	A
B	B	B	B	B
C	C	C	C	C
D	D	D	D	D
E	E	E	E	E
F	F	F	F	F

total cost for each lead-generation technique with percent sales gain, the promotion manager now has a quantifiable measurement of how effective each lead technique has been. However, remember that there are no absolute measurements of promotion effectiveness. You will have to temper your analyses with subjective considerations of how various promotion/lead methods interact to produce a sale.

Report 9-7 is produced by accessing the Sales Order/Sales Data Bank as well as the Consumer Data Bank and the Market Data Bank. Sales service managers, product managers, and marketing managers can use this report as a sales control and planning tool.

MSD-401 (REPORT 9.8)

The Sales Prospect Report is produced simultaneously with Report 9.7 (MSD-400). The purposes of the report are to produce a lead-prospect follow-up, to document the result, and to identify the responsible individual. The report should be produced on a three-part carbon. One copy should be held in-house, one for return by the salesman to the office, and one for the individual responsible for the follow-up.

The Sales Prospect Report should provide prospect information that can be used for the follow-up. The lead-technique code used in Report 9.7 (MSD-400) becomes the response code. The individual responsible for the follow-up should identify himself as one of the following codes:

1 = Sales force
2 = Field manager
3 = Distributor
4 = Product manager
5 = Service manager
6 = Technical staff
7 = Marketing officer
8 = Corporate

It is best to have the responsible individual complete the prospect report immediately following contact.

REPORT 9.8
Sales Prospect
Period Ended 6/11/85
MSD-401
Territory

Frequency: Daily

PROSPECT	RESPONSE CODE	CONTACT	RESULT CODE
Mr. Norman R. Baker 511 Prospect Street Miami, Florida 33157	B	-15 days -30 days -45 days	—Not able to reach —Change of Address
B: (305) 555-1212 H: (305) 555-1234			—Only General Interest —Complaint —Competition —Wanted Specifications —Purchase —Other
Consumer Profile: 2 Title: Director Marketing Products: Maxi Series Selection: Cost Size Message: Have prospect identify long-term selection attributes and objectives. Identification (Follow-Up) Code: 1			

MRS-400 (REPORT 9.9)

The Promotional Mix Efficiency Report compares the method of promotion by geographical area to an actual sales-correlation rating. This one-dimensional report calculates the net effect for each type of promotion and subsequently attaches a rating code for the actual effectiveness. The rating code is calculated using the sales trend. For example, a sales trend of +1.06[6] would produce a rating code of 1. The rating-code range values would reflect the degree of actual trend increase above 1.00. A rating code of 2 would reflect a larger trend value. A typical range would be:

Trend Range	Rating Code
1.00	0
+1.01 to 1.10	1
+1.11 to 1.20	2
+1.21 to 1.30	3
+1.31 to 1.40	4
−1.00 to .90	−1
− .89 to .80	−2
− .79 to .70	−3
− .69 to .60	−4

Product and promotion managers should look for a correlation between positive range values, geographical location, and promotional description.

The promotion manager may want to use a more finite geographical area (city, county, or territory) as a test vehicle. In addition, you may want to compare promotion costs to actual sales and produce a calculated value. This value would identify the payback potential of certain promotion programs used in the past.

Market Analysis Reports (500 Series)

Pure market analysis generally measures market profitability and potential. However, the enormous resource levels used to calculate market contribu-

6. Month-to-month territory-sales-total comparisons. For example, $800,000 divided by $750,000 = 1.06.

REPORT 9.9
Promotional Mix Efficiency

MRS-400

Frequency: Monthly
Quarterly
Yearly

PROMOTION DESCRIPTION	DATE	GEOGRAPHICAL AREA (REACH)	RATING CODE	SALES TREND
1. Newspaper				
2. Radio				
3. Television				
4. Direct mail				
5. Billboards				
6. Bench advertising				
7. Point of exchange				
8. Exhibits/shows				
9. Prize offerings				
10. Social-event sponsorship				
11. Parades/shows/events				
12. Contests				
13. Premiums				
14. Journal advertising				
15. Press releases				
16. Sport sponsorhip/identification				
17. Bumper stickers (window)				
18. Special sales/discounts/rebates				
19. Auctions				
20. Social/safety campaigns				
21. Educational campaigns				

tion and potential are far greater than small or medium-size organizations can manage. Many large firms, such as IBM, Exxon, and General Motors, would no doubt have little difficulty in locating such resource requirements. Market analyses are measured and calculated differently depending on the organization, and the methods used are usually unique to each organization.

Marketing managers often shy away from profit-and-loss reports. However, they would be inclined to listen if the analysis of profitability included market variables that influence this profitability. This section details two methods of revealing and calculating market analyses. The first shows how to identify territory (geographical) sales potential. The second shows how to project an area's net operating profit by product line.

MRS-500 (REPORT 9.10)

The Territory-Potential Index Report is similar to the 300 Series reports in that a ranking of geographical regions is used to calculate an overall potential. The market parameters used in this report could obviously include more or fewer parameters. The objective is to assign a territory rank for each market parameter. The sum of the rankings for each territory should produce an overall measure of potential. This overall ranking will be compared to the other territories and a potential index derived.

For example, territory 004 has the largest sales volume as well as the largest sales potential. However, a more elaborate model could be used. In this model (the optional rank model), the actual values for each market parameter for all territories are totaled. The mean value is found and then multiplied by a factor of 2. You can then divide by the number of range values (5 or more) to obtain an equal range distribution from which you can classify each parameter from excellent to poor. As in the straight ranking system, an overall rating is applied by totaling the number of "excellent" territory values to the number of "poor" ones.

In our example, we assign each parameter an equal weight. You can assign different weights depending on the actual parameters within your

REPORT 9.10
Hypo-Thetical Company
Territory-Potential Index Report
Period Ended 6/1/85
MRS-500 (Quarterly)
Region
District

Frequency: Monthly
Quarterly

DESCRIPTION	TERRITORY 001 R	TERRITORY 002 R	TERRITORY 003 R	TERRITORY 004 R
Gross Sales:				
Product A	$1,500,000	$2,000,000	$1,000,000	$3,000,00
Product B	400,000	500,000	600,000	700,000
Product C	200,000	100,000	50,000	600,000
Net Contribution (Dollars)	1,300,000	1,800,000	850,000	3,500,000
Efficiency Index YTD	.62	.64	.54	.66
Market Share	.10	.10	.09	.24
Population:				
Total	2,000,000	2,200,000	1,700,000	2,900,000
Over 65	100,000	250,000	75,000	400,000
Total Accounts	150	100	75	200
Total Inactive Accounts	35	50	25	50
Territory Average Annual Purchases	50	75	35	100
Employment Rate	.86	.90	.80	.91
Total Sales (Including Competitors)	20,000,000	25,000,000	18,000,000	18,000,000
Competitive Market Share (Leader)	.27	.16	.22	.24
Average Order Size	$450	$460	$425	$500
Geographical (Square Miles)	1,000,000	1,200,000	4,500,000	500,000
College-Level Education (Total)	2.3	2.7	.01	3.3
Sales Representative Experience (Months)	33	48	11	66
Total of Rankings*				

*Your totals will depend on how you decide to calculate these values.

REPORT 9.11
Hypo-Thetical Corporation
Capacity Correlation by Territory
Period Ended 12/31/85
MAA-505 (Quarterly)

Frequency: Quarterly
Yearly

TERRITORY	MARKET PARAMETER 1	WEIGHTED SCORE 1	MARKET PARAMETER 2	WEIGHTED SCORE 2	MARKET PARAMETER 3	WEIGHTED SCORE 3	SUM OF SCORES	RATING CLASSIFICATION
001	3.65	56	.98	33	51.9	51	140	M
⇕								
999								

marketplace. (Report 9.11 is an example of how to assign different weight factors for different parameters.) Four methods of ranking can be used in Report 9.10. The first is to assign equal weights for each market parameter and then rank the parameter according to the value. For example, College-Level Education would rank territory 004 first, territory 002 second, and so on. The second method of ranking assigns each market parameter a certain weight and then ranks each by territory. For instance, Employment Rate may be more important to sales potential than Total Population. In this case, each territory would have a rank, but the emphasis would be placed on the Employment Rate. The third method uses a preliminary scoring of each parameter and then assigns a ranking. The four territories in Report 9.10 have a range of College-Level Education between .01 and 3.3. Since the margin between .01 and 3.3 is quite large, we have to assign a scoring factor between 1 and 10 and then rank each territory. For example, a score of 10 would be given to territory 004, whereas territory 003 would be better reflected by assigning a score of 1. The fourth method is exactly the same as the third, except that different weights are assigned for each parameter. Again, your final potential would take into consideration the relative weights assigned to each market parameter.

The parameter Net Contribution of course is gross sales minus the total expense of each product (divided by the number of territories) by territory. For example, total expenses associated with products A, B, and C were $16,000,000. If the total number of territories were 20, then $800,000 would be applied per territory. Therefore, net contribution for territory 001 was $1,300,000 ($2,100,000 minus $800,000).

The Territory Potential Index Report can be calculated according to your final objectives. Marketing directors and field managers will use each territory's index value and sales volume to assess more accurately an area's performance. Over time it is possible to calculate each market parameter's correlation to sales. But you must use the optional rank system's final territory potential index. By using the final potential index value for each territory, you are in a position to see which of the market parameters you suspect are important, with respect to sales, are in fact important.

MAA-505 (REPORT 9.11)

The Capacity Correlation by Territory Report is an example of how statistical analyses can be interwoven with a standard MKIS report system. In our example, we constructed an application that uses a statistical program to predict the future potential of sales territories. The same type of report mechanisms can be applied to predicting product and/or marketing program success.

The steps to follow for implementing a statistical report link in your MKIS are highlighted by the ones we followed to produce Report MAA-505:

1. Determine which parameters are important. Hypo came up with dozens of market parameters, but analysis revealed that only three displayed a strong correlation to sales.
2. Determine how the inputs (parameters) will be scaled and weighted. Hypo divided each market parameter into a sales figure for the appropriate territory. Then, based upon how much Hypo wanted to weight a given parameter's impact, it assigned a score to that figure.
3. Determine how the scores will be evaluated. Hypo added the three individual scores to arrive at a sum of the scores. A rating classification or potential indicator was derived based upon the scores.

This simple illustration makes an important point: Too often, MKIS designers spend most of their time solving problems for routine applications, even though all MKIS users will be forced to go beyond the applications to analyze their own projects. The real benefit of an MKIS is its ability to take standard data and transform it into analytical information. Reports such as MAA-505 can help you to make this transformation.

MRA-510 (REPORT 9.12)

The Situational Analysis-Product Market History Report is similar to the sales-expansion report in Chapter 8. However, the market variables (numbers 9 and 10) are now factored into the profit-and-loss analysis. By

REPORT 9.12
Situational Analysis—Product Market History
Period Ended 6/30/85
MRA-510

Frequency: Monthly
Quarterly

Product A	1982	1983	1984
1. Total Market			
(Units)	1,000	1,500	2,000
(Dollars)	2,498,000	5,000,000	10,000,000
2. Company Sales (Units)	600	800	1,000
Gross (Units Shipped) (Dollars)	550	700	990
Product A	1,497,000	2,665,000	4,800,000
3. Price/Unit	2,750	3,800	4,850
4. Variable Cost/Unit	1,000	2,000	3,000
5. Contribution/Unit	1,750	1,800	1,850
6. Contribution/Dollars (5 × 2)	962,500	1,260,000	1,831,500
7. Overhead (Dollars)	200,000	300,000	400,000
8. Net Contribution (Dollar Margin)	762,500	960,000	1,431,500
9. Advertising Expense (Total)	100,000	300,000	150,000
10. Distribution and Logistics Expense (Including Direct and Indirect Selling Expense)	200,000	300,000	450,000
11. Net Operating Profit: Product A Market	462,500	360,000	831,500
12. Market-Share Percent	.60	.53	.50

factoring in these market variables, you can compute a net operating profit. However, net operating profit will be dependent on the marketing activities or programs designed to support each product.

This report is especially useful for product managers who want to keep abreast of each product's net contribution and life-cycle position and how different marketing programs affect the net operating profit. The report can also be used by directors and vice-presidents of marketing and/or sales as an analysis tool.

The interdepartmental-interface requirements discussed in Chapter 4 are particularly evident in Report 9.12. Numbers 4 through 9 in the report are usually accessed through the cost-accounting module interface (Figure 4.9). Numbers 3, 9, and 10 are entered from Marketing's Market Data Bank. This report can also be produced at the territory, district, or regional levels. The frequency cycle also can be varied.

Summary

Each organization's market is based in part on the relationship between total market demand and the demand that is available to the organization. Your objective is to bridge this gap to your advantage. The report examples here deal with two demand types: primary and selective. Primary demand reflects the total industry; selective demand is the potential available to your organization.

To bridge this gap, we looked at identifying market, demographic, and product segments. In Report 9.11, we identified a means of measuring our demand potential. And of course we evaluated the cost of communicating to certain markets and the effectiveness of the communication.

Action Plan

1. Describe the current state of your market and identify your total market-parameter requirements.

2. From Step 1, develop a Market Data Bank, using Table 3.5D in Chapter 3 as a guide, and a list of market reports (applications) you want to include as part of the MKIS.
3. Follow Steps 3 through 6 as outlined in the Action Plan for Chapter 6.

SECTION IV

ENHANCEMENT

Alternatives for Your MKIS

The Management Process

The MKIS Action Plan and Organizational Checklist

CHAPTER 10

Alternatives for Your MKIS

The first nine chapters of this book were directed toward developing an in-house Marketing Information System. Each of the alternatives—software packages, commercial timesharing, and microcomputers—that we discuss in this chapter offers excellent application possibilities for your MKIS. However, because of the constraints inherent in each one, they cannot be relied on exclusively to carry the burden of a unified MKIS.

Computer Software Guidelines

Most organizations acquire marketing system software to automate such applications as lead generation, sales analysis, and forecasting functions. Our purpose here is to outline several critical components of software selection. Table 10.1 is a directory of MKIS subsystems. Unfortunately, there seems to be no magical formula for success when dealing with software vendors.

Organizations with similar product lines and markets may have different opinions about how to use packaged software. Because the variety of applications from one marketing organization to the next is so immense, no single software package on the market today can be considered a comprehensive MKIS program. At best, the MKIS developer can install specific packages that address specific needs. Sales-order-entry, forecasting, and statistical-modeling packages are available, but they address only one function of the MKIS.

The search time that you and your organization can expend in locating usable software may produce insignificant results. Thus you should allot a fixed amount of time for your search, usually several weeks. Before you begin your search for a software package, you should have a general idea as to what you want, and you should be able to detail certain key features that you require. There is a control element in defining your information requirements. If you have no idea of your specifications, the vendor may give you what he thinks you need. But, if you are able to detail exact and quantifiable specifications, you will likely produce better results while

TABLE 10.1
MKIS Systems Directory

LTFS (LONG-TERM FORECASTING SYSTEM)

Bernard Giffler Associates
34 Linda Lane, Warrington, PA 18976
(215) 343-3345

Functions: Sales forecasting
Language: Assembly, COBOL
Hardware: Smallest mini- to large main-frame computers

SALES ANALYSIS SYSTEM

Marchbanks and Parker, Inc.
4538 Centerview Drive, San Antonio, TX 78228
(512) 736-1909

Functions: Sales analysis
Hardware: Burroughs: B 80/800/1700/1800
Language: COBOL, RPG II

MAS (MARKETING ANALYSIS SYSTEM)

Arthur Andersen & Co.
69 West Washington Street, Chicago, IL 60602
(312) 346-6262

Functions: Sales management (sales analysis, territory analysis, customer service, sales calls, sales budgeting)
Hardware: IBM 360/370, Amdahl: 470 V/6, Itel, Interdata: 7/32, 8/32
Language: COBOL

INSURNET MARKETING SYSTEM

American Information Development, Inc.
1902 Van Ness Avenue, San Francisco, CA 94109
(415) 441-4422

Functions: Marketing management: prospect profiles, letter printing, envelopes, mailing labels (hardware/software, turnkey system); also time-sharing service
Hardware: Microdata: Reality
Language: BASIC

TABLE 10.1, *continued*

SALES/1 THE SALESMAN'S MEMORY

Construction Information Systems, Inc.
P.O. Box 484, Mill Valley, CA 94941
(415) 332-5073
Functions: Sales-calls system for efficient follow-up of calls
Hardware: IBM 360/370, DOS, DOS/VS, OS, OS/VS, Data General, Datapoint, DEC
Language: COBOL

CMS MARKETING INFORMATION SYSTEM

Cincinnati Management Systems
P.O. Box 11111, Cincinnati, OH 45211
(513) 367-7356
Functions: Collects and analyzes transaction information for customers and prospects; customer profiles; account tracking
Hardware: IBM 360/370

STAMPS (SALES TERRITORY AND MARKETING PLANNING SYSTEM)

Decision Sciences Corporation
528 Fox Pavillion, Jenkintown, PA 19046
(215) 887-1970
Functions: Analyzes and evaluates optimum sales territory assignments, market potential, sales goals, budget goals, and constraints
Hardware: IBM 370, DOS, PRIME 400
Language: FORTRAN

SALES AND MARKETING ANALYSIS SYSTEM

Water Business Systems
47 New York Avenue, Framingham, MA 01701
(617) 879-2503
Functions: Sales and marketing data; customer profile, territory assignment, and evaluation; data collection, sales-call reports, sales tracking and service facilities; generalized report writer (also available on service-bureau basis)
Hardware: IBM System/34
Language: RPG II

TABLE 10.1, ***continued***

INQUIRY SYSTEMS AND ANALYSIS

1000 Washington Street
Suite 600
Boston, MA 02118
(617) 482-6256

Functions: A systems approach to inquiry follow-up; sales-lead processing/developing/tracking and management reporting service

LEAD CONVERSION SYSTEM

LCS Industries, Inc.
10 Pelham Parkway
Pelham Manor, NY 10803
(800) 431-1866 X200
(212) 931-2075 X200

Functions: Lead handling and analysis system available on service-bureau basis

interfacing your specifications with a central processing unit. Your goal is to match your requirements to an existing package. Table 10.2 lists some of the sources of software packages. Table 10.3, the Software Package Comparison Evaluation, is helpful for comparing each vendor's package. Even after you define your requirements and match them to available packages, you still have a great deal of work ahead of you. Most vendors

TABLE 10.2
Where to Find Software Packages

- Hardware vendors
- Hardware/software dealers
- Software developers
- Time-sharing companies
- DATAPRO, ICP directories
- Users
- Government agencies
- Trade associations
- Universities

TABLE 10.3
Software Packages Comparison—(Module) Evaluation

PACKAGE APPLICATION	VENDOR A	VENDOR B	VENDOR C
1. Maximum number of companies the system can handle			
2. Number of previous installations			
3. Number of service personnel assigned to each module support team			
4. System options:			
Forecasting			
Sales planning			
Product analysis			
5. Report options available?			
6. Does the system incorporate cross-reference reporting?			
7. Can the system support graphic displays?			
8. Is the following documentation provided:			
Input-output formats?			
Input preparation procedures?			
Control techniques?			
User manuals?			
Program run instructions?			
Keypunch procedures?			
Maintenance provisions?			

will negotiate prices, so you should ask each vendor to detail his delivery schedules, agreements, compromises, services, modifications, and support.

One extremely important aspect of software selection deals with system documentation. If the documentation seems difficult to understand, it will most certainly be difficult to maintain. A critical evaluation of the documentation is essential in order to avoid unnecessary modifications to the system. If over the long run you require system modification (growth), make certain that the package is adaptable to your hardware and file construction parameters. The ever-present system "bugs" usually are a result of an insufficient understanding of the package's capabilities. This is especially true as you add new hardware and program designs. You will want to know how the hardware affects the software and vice versa. If the acquisition of a particular piece of software requires major programming modifications, you may want to look elsewhere or design your own package or module.

When you select a software package, you are also selecting the vendor and its reputation. This reputation should be a very important part of your selection criteria. Ask the vendor for a client list and call several of the clients to check the vendor's support, modification, performance, and implementation record.

When planning each phase of your installation schedule, you should prepare a system similar to that in Table 10.4. By detailing who, when, where and how, you will enhance the control of your project. This schedule should also produce quantifiable benchmarks to measure actual versus planned progress. Never treat the selection of a software package as a temporary solution or compromise.

Each event description should identify who is responsible for a certain task of the MKIS implementation. Each estimated completion date should be adhered to as rigidly as possible. There are several positions on the schedule for where (contact and manager) the ultimate responsibility lies within each department that contributes to the MKIS development. The actual phases of implementation (the how) are outlined by the dates of education, generation, installation, and modification. Parallel operations represent the running of both the existing system and the system you are attempting to implement. For successful implementation, your new system data should match the data in the control portion of the old system.

Commercial Timesharing Applications

Computer timesharing vendors offer several application alternatives that you may want to consider in your MKIS development. The timesharing industry has grown at a tremendous rate in recent years because timesharing offers something that most in-house Data Processing departments

TABLE 10.4
Software Installation Planning Schedule

Date: __________

Vendor: __________
Address: __________

Telephone: __________

Contacts:
Accounting: __________
Data Processing: __________
Marketing: __________

Marketing Manager: __________

System Purchased: __________
Options and Modifications: __________

	IMPLE-MENTATION	FRONT-END EDUCATION	BACK-END EDUCATION	SOFTWARE GENERATION	SOFTWARE INSTALLATION	MODIFI-CATIONS	PARALLEL OPERATIONS
Original Dates							
Current Dates							

DATE	EVENT DESCRIPTION	RESPONSIBILITY OF	ESTIMATED COMPLETION DATE	COMPLETION DATE

cannot—immediate solutions to information processing. But, like software packages, timesharing can be used only as an adjunct to your system.

In-house Data Processing Departments are geared to handle transaction-level data, such as sales-order receipts and accounts payable, and routine reports that summarize the transaction data. Timesharing systems, on the other hand, are oriented toward special situations and planning analyses. Therefore, you might look to a timesharing vendor for forecasting or market-share analysis reports, but not for sales-order entry.

Timesharing can be an excellent vehicle for developing your applications before you bring them in-house. It is also a superb tool for those applications that are a subset of your MKIS but do not require a direct link. For example, you might have a sales-management report system with ten reports, all tied together through a flow of data. It would be a mistake to pull out three or four of the reports in the middle of the flow and turn them over to timesharing. It would not be a mistake, however, to produce the ten reports in-house and then, through data transfer (via telecommunications or data tape), do extra analyses on the timesharing system. A standard rule is that whenever data can be processed in-house *to your satisfaction and in a reasonable amount of time,* it should be, because once your MKIS is functional on more than one computer system, you will be forced to maintain duplicate data at certain levels. However, modern timesharing offers a variety of relatively painless ways to maintain marketing applications.

There are several characteristics of your applications that may make some of them appropriate for timesharing solutions. These characteristics include:

1. A need for external data bases:[1] Many timesharing vendors maintain updated economic, financial, demographic, and competitive data bases that may be useful on an ad hoc basis. You may not be able to justify maintaining these types of data in-house because of their infrequent use, yet you would like access to them for special analyses.

1. See Appendix B, the Business Research and Information Guide.

2. Undefined or changing analysis requirements: You may not know just how far your information will take you. Thus you are unable to commit to in-house DP on the specifics of the application. For those applications that you see evolving over time, timesharing systems offer an attractive solution.
3. A need for transmitting data to other geographical areas: What you need is a telecommunications network for data transmittal. Yet your DP department may not be able to provide it. If the application requires immediate information dispersal across the country or around the world, a timesharing system for its network may be your only alternative.
4. The desire to get the application up and running as soon as possible. Very few DP departments can provide the service or turnaround of a good timesharing vendor.

Once you have established a need for a timesharing solution, you will be faced with vendor selection. All major vendors offer a network, good documentation of their packages and services, and virtually unlimited computer resources. They do, however, vary to some degree with regard to:

1. The specialized types of software and data bases available
2. The amount of support provided for maintaining their own computer systems (some vendors tend to be down much more than others)
3. The amount of education provided to the user
4. The level of expertise of local sales and technical personnel

For specific applications, contact several vendors and present your ideas. Then select the vendor who can come closest to giving you exactly what you want. See Table 10.5 for a list of the major timesharing vendors.

To some extent, the companies listed in Table 10.5 provide business-related application software, including:

1. Data Base Management: The capability to create an on-line data base with complete inquiry and reporting functions.

TABLE 10.5
Top 10 Computer Time-Sharing Vendors

COMPANY	MAJOR SERVICES	NEW DIRECTIONS
1. Control Data Corp.	More than 2,000 applications for all phases of business	Data bases, e.g., Evans Economic Data Base
2. Automatic Data Processing Inc.	Geared primarily to accounting needs	Data bases
3. GE Information Services	Broad forecasting and general business offerings	Applications for the energy and retail store sectors
4. Tymshare, Inc.	Multifaceted services	Network expansion and bank-related services
5. United Information Systems, Inc.	Project management services	Business planning using interactive graphics
6. McDonnell Douglas Automation Co.	Doctors' office and hospital systems	Turnkey systems
7. Computer Sciences Corp.	General business applications	Small-business services
8. NCR Corp.	Financial and retail sector applications	Commercial banking
9. Bradford National Corp.	Security and trust accounting	Same as current offerings
10. National CSS, Inc.	DP development and end-user data-base management systems (DBMS)	Continued expansion of its DBMS line

Source: Marcia Blumenthal. "Processing Services Now a Whole New Ball Game," *Computerworld,* December 1, 1980, p. 11.

2. Statistical Analyses Capabilities: Standard types of statistical analyses including, but not limited to, correlation, regression, and variance analysis.
3. Forecasting: At all levels, from straightforward trend analysis to sophisticated packages such as the X11 and Box Jenkins.
4. Risk Analysis: Quantifying the risk in decision-making through use of such techniques as Monte Carlo Simulation.
5. Information Data Bases: Access to demographic, economic, industrial, competitive, and other data banks. Most often the data retrieval from these banks can be output via special reporting capabilities of the timesharing vendor.

6. Computer Graphics: Data output to time-series graphs, scatter plots, histograms, and bar and pie charts.
7. Planning and Financial Modeling: Planned vs. actual analyses.

Micro-Computer Applications

Most in-house computer systems and timesharing vendors have access to either large main-frame or high-powered mini-computers. Using these computers solely for your Marketing Department and its applications needs would be prohibitively expensive. However, inexpensive raw computing power is available even to the smallest marketing organization in the form of a micro-computer.

Today, a complete system of micro-computer hardware and software, including a 48K[2] processor, two disk drives, and monitor/CRT and printer, can be purchased for under $5,000. Relatively good micro-software is available for many applications and ranges in price from $50 to $500.

A micro-computer has several advantages. It is relatively inexpensive and can be installed and set up to run within just a few minutes. Because BASIC is the programming language of choice for most micro-computer manufacturers, micros also are very easy to program. In fact, most micro applications can be implemented even without BASIC by using selected pieces of inexpensive software that perform calculations and produce quality reports from simple English commands. Micro software packages are so improved now that their operation can be learned within three or four hours and mastered within a day or two. Micro-computers also offer a system that is completely under the control of the user. The user does not have to depend upon data-processing people for program development or system maintenance.

On the other hand, there are also distinct disadvantages in using micro-computers. Like commercial timesharing applications, if you are using an in-house computer as well as a micro, there is the possibility that

2. The 48K can control 48,000 characters of data in the central processing unit at any one time. Large computers have capabilities in the millions.

you will be duplicating data manipulation and storage. When you pull data from your in-house system to load into a micro, you create additional work for yourself. Also, because of the micro's overnight emergence, centralized software resources are limited. It is true that hundreds of micro-computer software packages are available, but you will have to search a great deal in order to find an application that suits your needs. You may also find it difficult to locate adequate service when you encounter hardware problems.

There are five general areas of use for a micro-computer in enhancing your MKIS:

1. Various types of list-oriented applications where you are required to maintain a record of items or activities that are a subset of one or most of the components of your MKIS.
   a. A sales-force or marketing roster that maintains active names and addresses of personnel for field distribution
   b. A new-product introduction checklist (similar to that in Report 7.1 in Chapter 7) for monitoring the development status of new products
   c. A competition file that maintains updated information on company and product data for all competitors, including those elements contained in Table 7.7 in Chapter 7
2. Ranking or trend information that provides executive-level analyses and "reporting by exception" (reports where only data values that fall above or below a pre-set standard are presented).
   a. Monthly sales-total tracking by sales representative, product, or customer that include only key sales totals (perhaps just a single gross amount) over several monthly or quarterly periods
   b. Commission-payment calculations that change on a frequent basis and are thus not appropriate for the main-frame system
3. Summary information that ties several MKIS subsystems together.
   a. Expense analyses (budget vs. actual comparisons and variances) of special marketing programs that would be hidden in a standard departmental accounting treatment
   b. Specialized customer analyses that would track sales results to such areas as "Key Account" or "New Account" programs

4. Word-processing capabilities linked to the micro-computer.
   a. Mailing-list maintenance and label preparation
   b. Preparation of standardized contract documents
   c. Preparation and distribution of promotional and sales follow-up letters
5. Special statistical routines.
   a. Forecasting
   b. New-product status and evaluation such as that contained in Report 7.2

In building your Marketing Information System, you will have to be creative. No successful system can be constructed based only on the applications obtained through an in-house system: There are simply too many constraints placed on typical data-processing operations for it to be at Marketing's individual disposal. Yet, to have an MKIS that answers all of your needs, you do need system tools that provide you with 100-percent responses. In order to achieve this goal, you must be willing to use software packages, commercial timesharing, and micro-computer applications to solve your marketing problems.

External Data and Information Sources

A prominent business research firm in Washington, D.C., proudly exclaims: "Virtually anything you need to know can be learned, if you know where to look!"[3] Finding information relative to marketing information systems is dependent upon the skills of each individual manager. Since not all information managers are created equal, the gathering of useful information for the purposes of market analyses or competitive profiling is an art unto itself.

To maintain system integrity is, in part, the ability to offer expanded information capacity beyond the scope of the MKIS. As we mentioned, it is not practical and, in many cases, not cost effective to store large quantities

3. Washington Researchers, 918 Sixteenth Street, N.W., Washington, D.C. 20006.

TABLE 10.6
Fee-Based Information Retrieval Services

COMPANY	DATA BASE	COVERAGE OR CATEGORIES OF COVERAGE
Lockheed Palo Alto, CA	Dialog	Dissertations Bibliographies Media publication Agriculture/food service Business/economics Contracts/grants/current research Energy/environment Government publications Humanities/art Law/current topics Medical Science Social Science Technology/engineering
New York Times Information Service New York, NY	AMI (Advertising and Marketing Intelligence Service)	Tracks key trade reports, research data, journal, reports, newspaper coverage
	MEDAB (Middle East Data Base)	Covers key issues from Middle East media tracking
PREDICASTS Cleveland, OH	Prompt (Others available)	Overview of market and technology data, containing technical and marketing coverage of: Acquisitions and mergers New products/technology Research & Development expenditures Government regulations Market statistics/trends Productions and capacity Shipments Sales Management procedure Competitive activity Capacities and expansion Price trends

TABLE 10.6, *continued*

COMPANY	DATA BASE	COVERAGE OR CATEGORIES OF COVERAGE
Aspen Systems Corporation Rockville, MD	ASPENET	On-line interactive retrieval of full text or biographical information with or without indexing, including: Litigation data Regulations and policy research Legislative drafting and publishing Regulatory research
CIS Congressional Information Service Washington, D.C.	CIS	Indexes of the largest organized information banks in the world, the U.S. Government, including: Public-interest data Social conditions Business conditions Economic conditions Natural resources Congressional committees Executive departments Social boards
Infosource, Inc. Pittsburgh, PA		Mergers and acquisitions Legal literature Regulations Market/marketing research Personnel/human resources New products/processes Industry overviews Company scans Distribution analysis Graphic displays of above
Duns Marketing Service Parsipanny, NJ		Operating ratios (190 lines of business) Financial statements (more than 800,000 of both private and public) Organizational profiles

TABLE 10.6, *continued*

COMPANY	DATA BASE	COVERAGE OR CATEGORIES OF COVERAGE
System Development Corporation (SDC) Santa Monica, CA	80 data bases available	Journal reprints Patents Books Theses Conference papers Annual reports Maps Contracts Grants Government legislation Hearings Newspaper articles Summary of research in progress Statistical and tabular data Voting records Reviews
The Information Store San Francisco, CA	DIALOG, The Source, ON-TYME, and SDC's Maildrop	Secondary market research Statistics, trends, economic factoring, industry news Current business news and trends Scientific and technical literature Engineering designs Medicine Pollution Food Physics Legal and legislative research
Dow Jones Princeton, NJ		News from *Wall Street Journal, Barron's,* Dow News Service Current quotes Historical quotes since 1978 Detailed financial statistics
Standard & Poor's New York, NY	DIALOG	Financial news for more than 10,000 leading companies

TABLE 10.6, *continued*

COMPANY	DATA BASE	COVERAGE OR CATEGORIES OF COVERAGE
		Financial statement changes Securities detail Bond ratings
PRESTEL LOGICA New York, NY	LOGICA, INC.	Public information Financial (exchange rates, money markets) Marketing (international and domestic trade) Statistics, commercial attaches, exhibitions, research papers, suppliers, and agents Travel (timetables, rates, hotels, restaurants, travelers' briefings, entertainment) Personnel (cost of living, expenses, statistics, living-abroad data, visa requirements) News (international news, weather, future events) Fun (demonstrations and games)
Information Access Corporation (IAC) Menlo Park, CA	DIALOG	Magazine index Legal index Business news index Newspaper index
Disclosure, Inc. Washington, D.C.	DISCLOSURE	Company profile using: 10k domestic financial 20k international financial 8k unscheduled material events Proxy statements Registration statements Prospectus 10Q quarterly financial
Mead Data Central New York, NY	NEXIS	Full text information and news-search system

of data that will be accessed only on very special occasions. To maintain system integrity, existing information, which is currently maintained within the MKIS, is integrated with special external secondary research and information. For example, the complete analysis of U.S. economic statistics that affect the construction industry by mobile-home classification requires additional informational support services. Because government statistical abstracts usually are not stored in an MKIS data bank, you would need external information supplements.

The secondary market research industry is fast becoming one of the most exciting industries today. Fee-based information retrieval services, information brokerage houses, information consulting firms, and specialized government research firms have begun to educate many business managers regarding not only the availability of information but also the perceived need for it.

Table 10.6 lists only a few of the many data-based (information) retrieval services available today. The categories listed are broad, and some may not be applicable to your organization. For example, not all organizations are concerned with patent activity. However, for high-technology firms, this type of information could show the need to advance the timing of certain product introductions, or to delay others. Government regulatory activity may be important to automotive and pharmaceutical manufacturers, but it would be less important to electronics manufacturers. The Middle East data base, MEDAB, would provide Exxon and other major oil companies with informational support, but it would provide little or nothing for manufacturers of recreation equipment.

The steps for using an external information service are outlined in Table 10.7. There are several key points to remember. Always outline your exact information requirements before you conduct your search or inquiry. Too many managers still contact an information broker with "give me all you've got on the fast-food industry." Typically you will either politely be told to reevaluate your needs, or you will receive an invoice for hundreds or possibly thousands of dollars for unnecessary search time. You also should do a preliminary search to determine if you can secure the information required without using an information service or broker. You

TABLE 10.7
Steps for Using an External Information Service

1. Define exactly your data or information needs
2. Find out whether the types of data you require are available
3. Determine whether these data are reliable
4. Determine whether the format of the data is acceptable to the user
5. Determine whether the information is important and relative to your organization's real needs
6. Describe the ultimate purpose of the information
7. Choose the appropriate means of presenting the data
8. Define the output format requirements
9. Determine the frequency for which you require the data

may not need the services of an information specialist in order to obtain the latest financial data for competitors. These data are available to everyone through the Securities and Exchange Commission under the Freedom of Information Act.

After determining where your information is located, determine the actual source of this information. Is the information contained in federal, state, or local files? If the data are available and reliable, are they or can they be formatted to your hardware specifications? Also, if data are to be forwarded, whether to you or to the original requestor of the information, be sure that they are in a format that can be easily interpreted. For example, graphical formats are typically a far more efficient means of presentation than data arranged in a column. Attempt to design your collection of information into final reportlike records that will serve as an integrated file system. Don't gather so much information that the collection becomes confused or misplaced.

Data brokers and data-base services are primarily a means for recognizing and solving areas of uncertainty. No one individual or group will know where or how to locate all levels of information. By knowing when and how to use secondary information retrieval services, you may actually minimize costs and failure. Usually external information, such as that presented in Table 10.6, should be used as a tool for planning and decision-making. Internal information (sales-representative compensation, product specifications, and so forth) is usually used for control. For a more elaborate list of information sources, see Appendix B, the Business Research and Information Guide.

Using Graphics with Your MKIS

Graphical presentation is one of the most effective means of translating data into information. Having the capability to present data in a "picture" format offers better understanding and a different perspective than "just numbers." Graphs, plots, and charts can help marketing managers understand their own information and gain greater insight into its significance before presenting it to the upper-management team. For presentation purposes, graphics help relate information with greater clarity and impact.

Columns and rows of statistical data and seemingly endless pages of computer printouts can be confusing and often misleading. Important trends and comparisons often become apparent only when information is presented in a graphic format. As the use of the computer in Marketing increases, unfortunately there will be a corresponding rise in the amount of data processed onto printouts. The intelligent information planner must be aware of this and attempt to replace tabular data with graphic information wherever possible.

In recent years, computer technology has reached a point where business applications of computer graphics are now economical and extremely professional. Four-color pen plotters can now be purchased for less than $4,000, and they can be attached to virtually every main-frame, timesharing, and micro-computer system. CRT color-graphics packages are available for even the least expensive micro-computers.

Whether done manually or with a computer, there are literally hundreds of graphic-display applications possible. With the combination of multiple colors, shading, and overlays, the number of application alternatives exceeds one thousand. Still, there are just five basic types of information graphics that are commonly found in most marketing organizations. You should use whatever computer technology and imagination you have in order to modify the following five basic types:

1. The time-series graph is one of the most popular means of presenting data. The graph displays a point-by-point record of a trend, over time, of a given variable. Report 10.1 provides an example of a time-series plot that contrasts forecasted sales to actual sales on a monthly basis for one year. The actual number of lines on the graph can be one, two, or twenty. However, once you exceed four or five lines, you may run the risk of presenting confusing data. Good applications for a time-series graph include:

   a. Sales tracking by product, territory, or geographical area in units and/or dollars

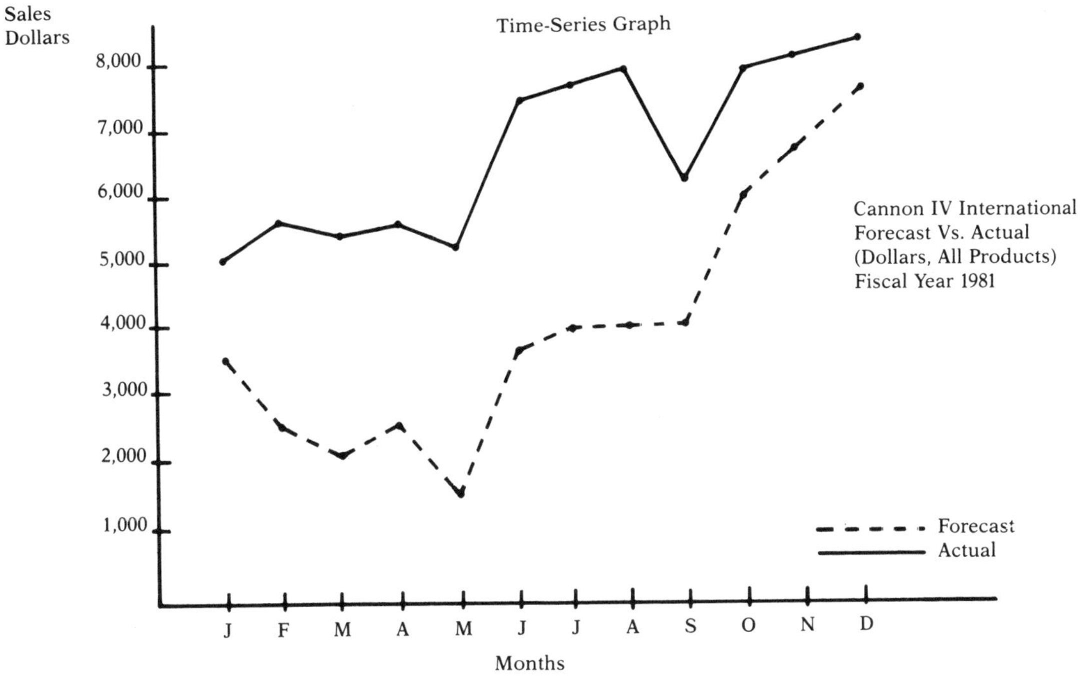

Report 10.1 Time-Series Graph

b. Comparative product sales tracking by product, territory, or geographical area in units and/or dollars

c. Forecasting by product, territory, or geographical area in units and/or dollars

d. Forecasting vs. actual comparisons by products, territory, or geographical area in units and/or dollars

e. Marketing expenses (actual, budget, or actual vs. budget) for any or all expense items

f. Market-segment comparisons (market segment A vs. market segment B)

g. Consumer-segment comparisons (consumer segment A vs. consumer segment B)

2. The scatter-plot presentation offers an X-Y comparison of two

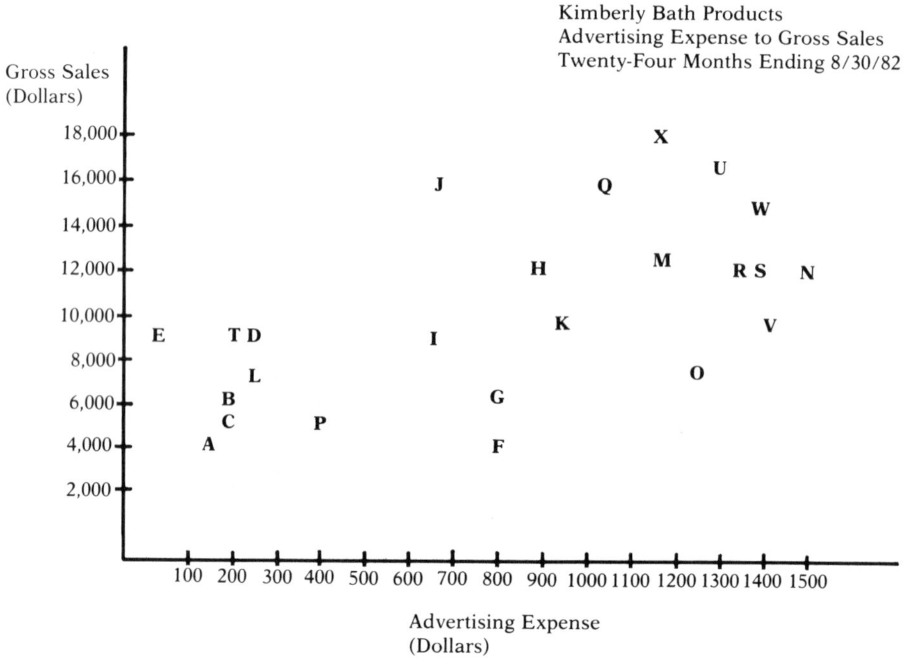

Report 10.2 Scatter Plot

distinct sets of data. The plotted points can represent either a time series or a single point in time. The graphic output represents a pictorial view of a data correlation. Report 10.2 shows the relationship between advertising expenses and gross sales dollars. The plotted points (A-X) represent a twenty-four-month sequence of this relationship. Good applications for scatter plots include:

a. Comparison of any expense item to any or all sales items
b. Comparison of any one product's sales to another

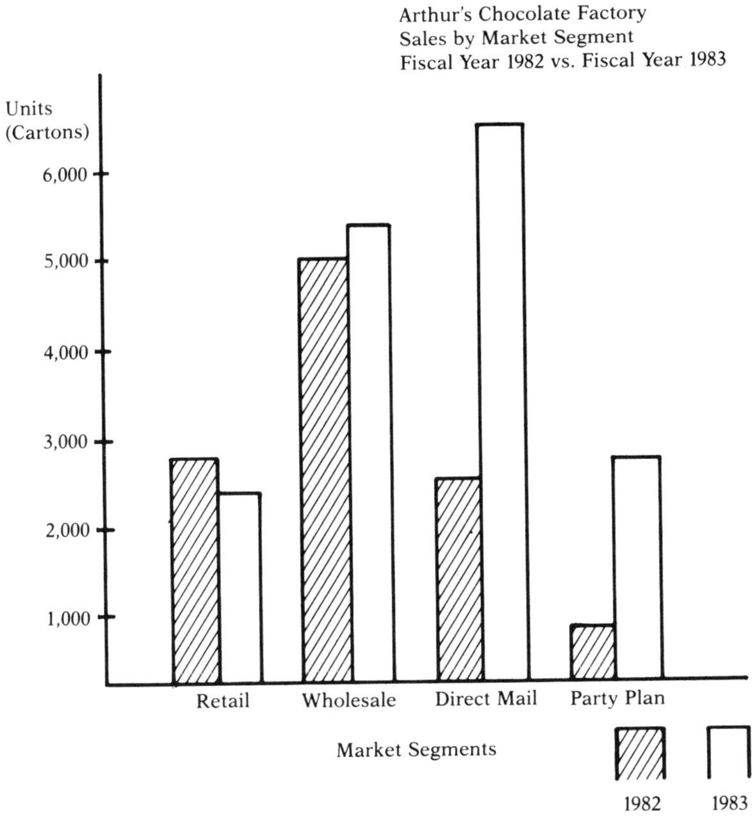

Report 10.3 Bar Chart

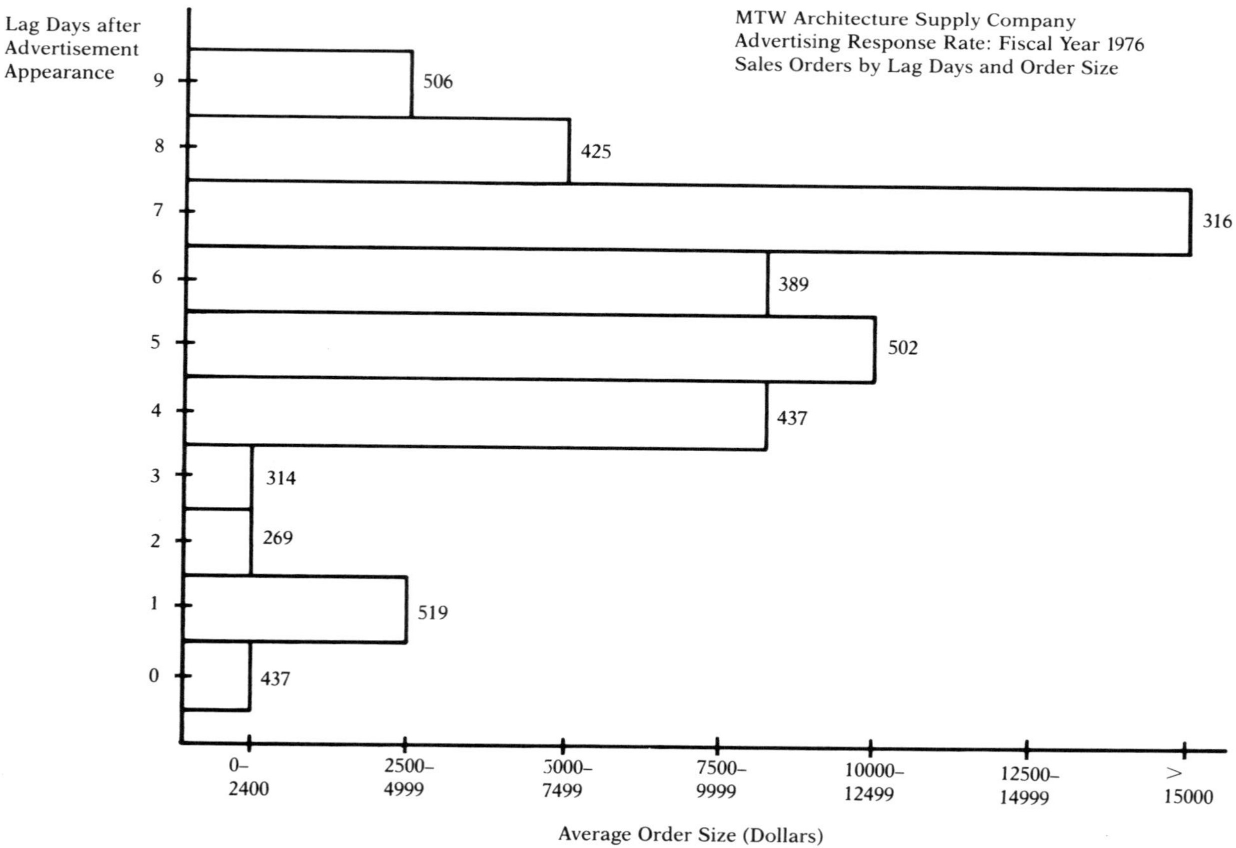

Report 10.4 Histogram

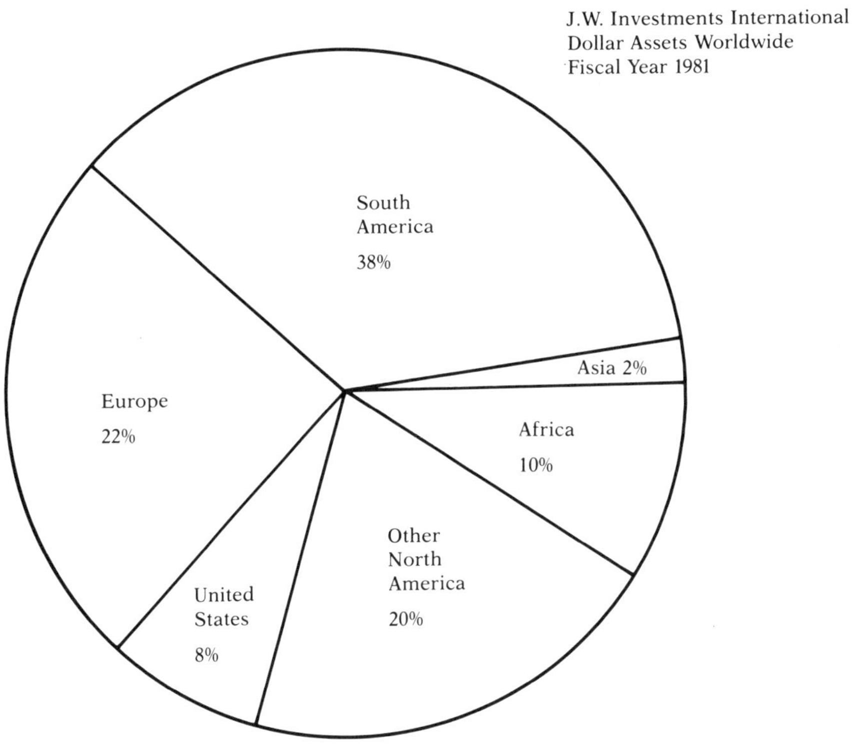

Report 10.5 Pie Chart

c. Comparison of market segment A to market segment B
d. Comparison of consumer segment A to consumer segment B

3. The bar chart presents a graphic view of data captured for one or several time periods. It is usually used to illustrate a change in one item over time or the difference between two related items. Variance bar charts can also be employed when the vertical axis is placed in the center of the horizontal axis. This allows the bars to be extended to both the right and left of the vertical line. Report 10.3 depicts unit sales for a two-year period in several different market segments. Good applications for bar charts include:
   a. Marketing P&Ls by line item

b. Sales by product
c. Sales by territory or geographical area

4. Histograms are much like bar charts in appearance, but their focus is geared more toward making a frequency count of a certain activity. For example, Report 10.4 compares an average order size with the number of days after a given advertisement that the order is received. The figures outside the bars indicate the actual number of orders received, regardless of size, on each day on or after the advertisement. Good applications for histograms include:
   a. Number of sales calls by hour of the day
   b. Number of responses by response time
   c. Number of sales orders by order size
5. The pie chart is one of the simplest but most effective examples of a graphic presentation. The pie usually illustrates the percentage that a given group of component items contributes to the whole. The pie chart in Report 10.5, for example, depicts dollar assets broken down by geographical area. Good applications of pie charts include contribution by:
   a. Market segment
   b. Consumer segment
   c. Product segment
   d. Expense type
   e. Sales by geographical region
   f. Leads by source
   g. Promotion rating by source

CHAPTER 11

The Management Process

An MBO Approach

Thus far, we have dealt primarily with the more technical aspects of designing, developing, and implementing your MKIS. Yet, much of the work to be done requires involvement from several people, both within Marketing and throughout the company. If you will review any Action Plan item from any chapter, you will see that in order to complete a specific task you will require some sort of people support. And when you are trying to coordinate up to fifty Action Plan steps over a relatively short period of time, the need for effective management in the MKIS building process becomes critical. Implementing the MKIS requires a large amount of time, resources, and human interaction. Your skill, experience, and creative abilities will be tested and retested throughout the process. We recommend that you control the events and outcomes by using a version of Management by Objectives (MBO). This MBO concept is the organization of specific measurable activities that can be quantified and reviewed over time. By defining beforehand what results should be achieved and what Action Plans are necessary to achieve them, day-to-day management problems become easier to handle. The logic is simple: Your direction will become clear as your plans become less general and more specific.

Figure 11.1, MKIS Implementation and the MBO Process, depicts the relationship between the organization and marketing philosophies and how they interact through this modified-MBO approach. The process of management involves planning, organizing, measuring, directing, and controlling. Thus, you should begin the MBO process by communicating with those involved in the implementation of the MKIS exactly what your final MKIS will contain, why it is necessary, and how it will benefit your organization. In order for this communication process to be effective, you may wish to follow a six-phase approach in managing your MKIS implementation plans.

To begin this process, you are required to have a specific set of MKIS design and development documents for your working review. These documents form the core of your MKIS planning system and are included

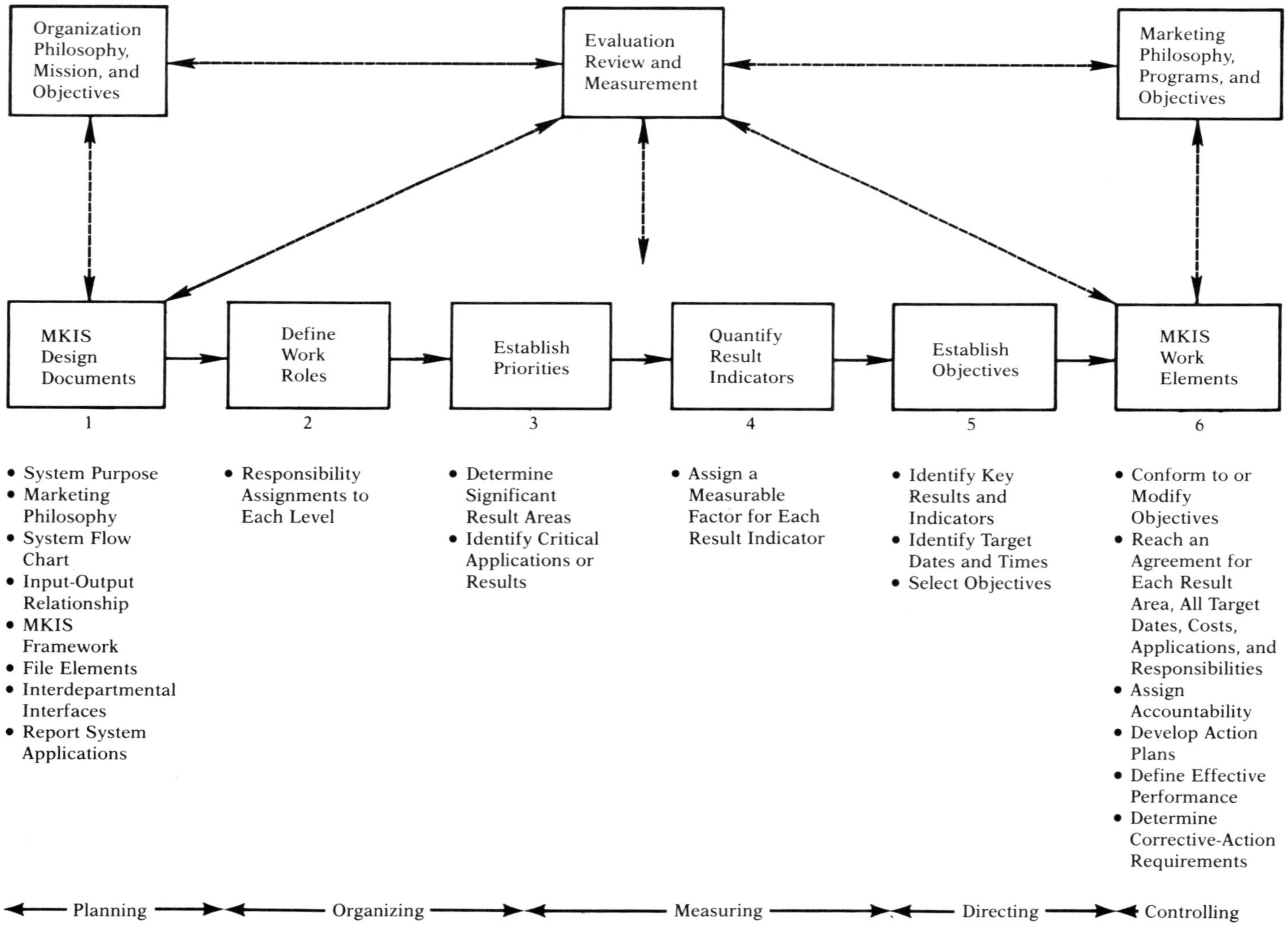

Figure 11.1 MKIS Implementation and the MBO Process

under Phase 1 of Figure 11.1 (if you have used the Action Plans in each chapter, the material is already at hand). Your communication with those involved in the implementation process will depend, in part, upon this documentation. By clearly delineating MKIS priorities and direction, and by communicating the MKIS priorities up, down, and across organizational lines, you will be able to motivate and control the MBO process.

To put the MKIS into action, the project leader must define each MKIS team member's role (Phase 2 of Figure 11.1). Top-management support is extremely important at this time. The project leader is responsible for both upper-management communication and supervision of individuals across departmental lines. This is not a matter of organizational position, but rather one of direction. As "supervisor," the project leader should meet individually and collectively with the MKIS team so that each team member understands what is expected of him, what role he will play in the overall effort, and how his role will interact with the roles of the other team members. For example, if the accounting manager is responsible for reviewing data-input provisions, the project leader or MKIS team should be prepared to explain to him how specific application reports depend upon accounting's data interface. Figure 11.2 provides an example of how the MKIS team can be organized.

After the design of the MKIS team's "organization chart" is complete, priorities can be set for the MKIS development (Phase 3 in Figure 11.1). Here you will need to differentiate between the "Blue Sky" elements of your MKIS framework and those elements which are of higher priority. You can do this by answering two basic questions:

1. Which applications in your Framework provide the greatest return on time spent?
2. Which tools are needed in order to support which types of applications?

In other words, what do you need most now, and which applications can take a lower priority? For example, you may have concluded that you will want your MKIS to track data relative to new markets your company wishes to enter. However, you will also want the MKIS to store data concerning

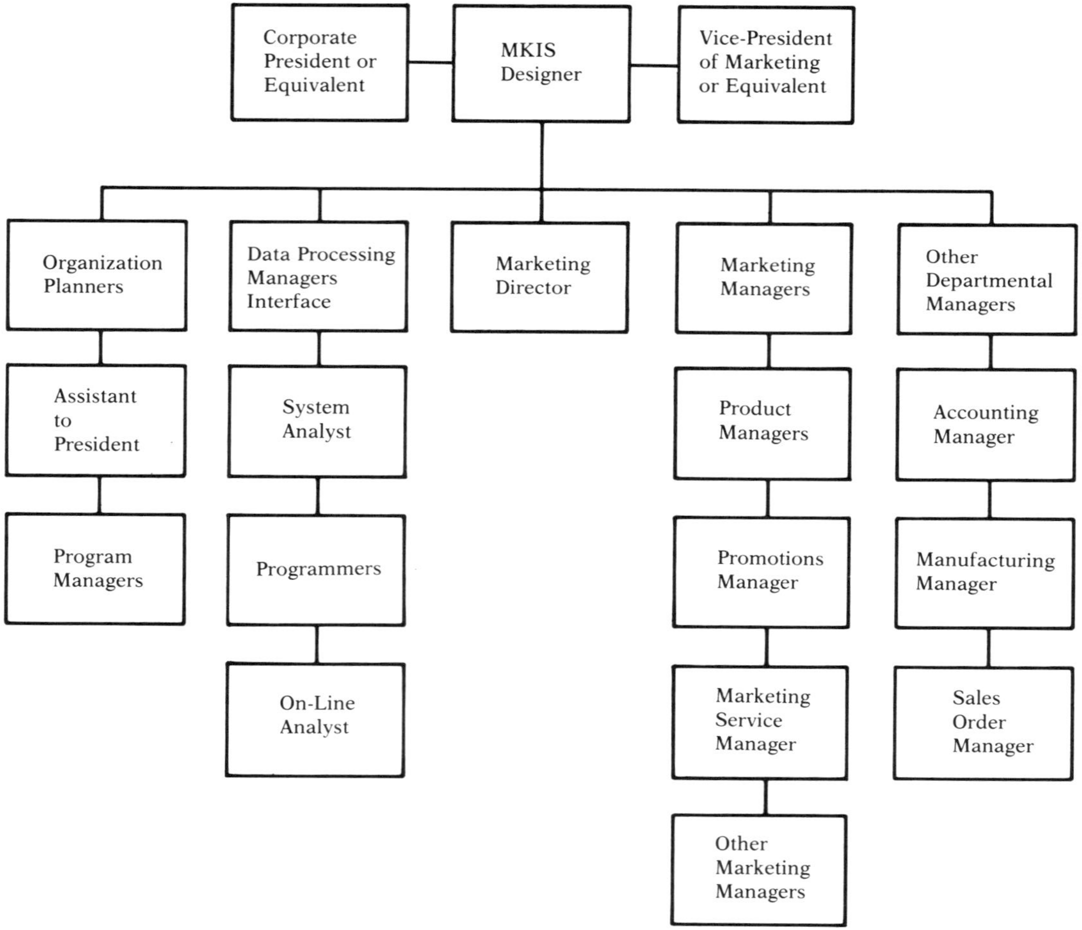

Figure 11.2 MKIS Implementation Team

your current market position with respect to both your products and those of your competitors. If you decide that it is more advantageous to have accurate information on current market positions, you should assign it a higher priority. In ranking your needs, you must distinguish what you need today for the basics of Marketing's operations and planning from that which can wait until the fundamental portions of the system have become operational. (To complete this type of comparison, you may wish to force rank all of your applications from "1 to n.")

The organization of resources is the most difficult component to quantify. The MKIS design and implementation require human, machine, and research-support resources. All must be keyed into a quantifiable-results program (Phase 4 in Figure 11.1). The human resource is, of course, subjective and therefore more difficult to measure. For machines such as on-line computer terminals, however, the quantification is simply a measure of the data accumulated and the ultimate applications of such data. You will be able to assess the payback of a machine by comparing its cost to its benefit in man-hours saved. But what is the value of using two analysts to evaluate and load competitive data into the system when one might do? The value could be found in better product positioning, product development ideas, or market identification. Each value might affect sales generation. But to what degree? The payback of this part of the system will never be black and white. The many intrinsic values and returns will be identified only through more efficient decision-making support, strategy formulation, and sales generation. These payback values with take several months, and perhaps years, to assess accurately.

The organization of results is the least difficult component to quantify. The MKIS designer will determine the functional MKIS areas for each team member or unit and assign priorities to all work assignments. For example, "the systems analyst will be responsible for the programming and testing of the MRA-300 report series by (date)." Table 11.1 offers an example of how to set up responsibilities, tasks, and objectives. The grade section should be used only by the designer for his reports to the senior-level officers and for his own reference.

TABLE 11.1
Management by Objectives Reference Guide

RESPONSIBILITY	TASK	OBJECTIVE	START	FINISH	GRADE
Designer	List interdepartmental-interface relationships	To meet with all interdepartmental managers to determine the extent of data exchange potential by (date).			
Developer	Identify informational levels within marketing	To detail the information flow within marketing by interviewing managers and flow charting their input by (date).			
Designer	Identify current stage of MKIS development	To review with Data Processing managers, system analysts, and marketing management the current state of marketing information as it pertains to decision-making support by (date).			

ESTABLISHING OBJECTIVES

The MKIS Checklist in Chapter 12 offers an excellent basis from which to prepare key result areas and indicators for the objectives which you ultimately establish. Of course, objectives need not be established for every planned result. Each objective should, however, have the following characteristics:

1. Contain a specific quantifiable component
2. Contain a target completion date

3. Outline, whenever possible, the costs involved
4. Be consistent with corporate and marketing goals
5. Be understood by everyone involved
6. Be realistic and attainable
7. Avoid duplication of effort and accountability
8. Be agreed to by everyone involved

The idea is to provide one or more manageable objectives for each MKIS task assignment (see the objectives sections in Table 11.1). By so doing, you will force a discipline upon the implementation of your MKIS. These objectives will aid the manager in formulating his direction and definition of the specific task. For example, one of the requirements of the MKIS designer is to identify the current stage of the MKIS development. The objective defines *what* is to be accomplished, *when* it should be completed, and *how* it should be accomplished. The important points to consider in setting objectives are:

1. Be specific in the direction of your work by stating precisely what you want to accomplish
2. Seek results that can be measured
3. Identify the criteria which signify completion of a task or of an objective to be met

Managerial Control: The MKIS Work Elements

Managing by reaction is based on a cause-and-effect relationship. Management by action establishes cause-and-effect relationships before the fact. Too often, ambiguous agreements lay the foundation for management by reaction. MKIS implementation, by its very nature, requires many action items and objectives. The goal is to order the Action Plan into a series of steps, with special emphasis given to the key steps. The task assignments to support each step should be established and agreed upon between those who will be expected to perform these tasks. As you begin to manage the implementation of the MKIS, you will find yourself in the midst of Phase 6 of the MKIS Implementation and MBO Process (Figure 11.1).

The final set of elements in the MKIS management process are the MKIS Work Elements. These six items represent the kind of things which you will have to do in order to accomplish all of the goals and objectives which you have set for the MKIS.

Step 1 will require you to conform to or modify your previously established objectives. Based on the development of certain key documents and system priorities,you will have created a given number, say ten, of objectives for your MKIS. As you delve deeper into the MKIS implementation, you may find that what was once Objective #7 should gain greater importance and be classified as Objective #3. This change may force you to revise certain elements of Phases 1-5 of your implementation plan (Figure 11.1). Likewise, you may discover that what was once a step (a work item that would lead to the accomplishment of a specific objective) may now become an objective in and of itself. For example, your Objective #1 may be to develop a system which compares territory sales performance over time. One of the steps needed to accomplish Objective #1 is that you will have to add a territory field indicator to all orders shipped. However, as you review all of your other objectives, you may find that many changes impact the way in which you receive and process orders. Consequently, you may wish to make "the creation of a new Sales Order Entry System" your new Objective #1.

Step 2 will require you to have all members of the MKIS team agree on specific result areas (the objectives), target dates, and costs. Being able to obtain this agreement will often be a function of how well prepared you are to define and defend your reasoning. Fortunately, your MKIS Framework, Benefits Package, and Marketing Philosophy will provide much of the documentation you will need for support. If you have followed our suggestions in the earlier chapters' Action Plans, then you will already have enlisted a great deal of assistance from others within the organization in the development of these MKIS documents.

Step 3, assigning accountability, relates to the individual's role as a part of the MKIS team. If you have established an organizational chart like that found in Figure 11.2, much of the accountability may already be assigned. The MKIS Designer will have overall control of the implementation process. Obtaining support from other team members will then be a function of how well the Designer is able to "sell" the project to the upper levels of corporate management.

Step 4, developing action plans, is related to Steps 2 and 3. (In practice all three steps may be integrated into one.) Developing action plans is an integral part of every manager's job. Having those plans accepted by management and staff requires preparation and the information to back them up. When dealing with line managers, you may need the support of upper management. This is why the positioning of upper-management personnel in the MKIS organization structure is so important.

Step 5, defining effective performance, is difficult to measure. It will vary, depending on the situation and the individual. Your selection of appropriate performance factors may be keyed to a basic understanding of each individual. In fact, establishing standards of this type may become motivational. The standard must be difficult to achieve, but it should be attainable and offer sufficient reason for exerting the effort. Standards such as error minimization, idea generation, turnaround time, accuracy and degree of thoroughness all reflect standards which could be used in conjunction with certain incentive graphs, charts, or other forms of recognition.

Corrective action (Step 6) should be supported by visual evidence of a significant variance. Time graphs to depict delays, performance charts, and report failures may all be used as support evidence. The purpose of corrective action is to maintain progression toward your objectives. Ideally, you have selected individuals capable of exerting self-correction when and where appropriate. Because we sometimes tend to over-manage in certain variance conditions, you should stress self-correction as the preferred method of corrective action. This may also produce a willingness on a responsible individual's part not to repeat past mistakes.

In addition, some variances will be the result of unreasonable objectives. Occasionally, one must re-evaluate the objective itself. The important point to remember here is to stay on target with your plan. You should also remember to provide an environment where everyone involved is aware of each other's progress and successes. Failures should be minimized and successes maximized. A high profile should also be maintained for the entire implementation team.

Action Plan

1. Review your organizational and marketing philosophies.
2. Draw up a list of those key MKIS documents (Framework, Input-Output Relationships, etc.) which you will use in order to guide the process of managing the MKIS implementation.
3. Decide who will comprise the MKIS team.
4. Identify specific tasks for the MKIS implementation process. Refer to the MKIS Checklist in Chapter 12 for a guide as to the types of tasks that might be included.
5. Identify the indicators of measurement for people, results, time, and objectives.
6. Assign objectives for each major task assignment (see Table 11.1).
7. Formulate your MKIS Work Elements (see Figure 11.1).

CHAPTER 12

The MKIS Action Plan and Organizational Checklist

The Checklist

The objective of this book has been to provide the manager with an easy-to-use reference guide for designing, developing, and implementing a Marketing Information System. This chapter provides an encapsulated review of Chapters 1 through 11. The MKIS Action Plan and Organizational Checklist summarizes the important ingredients for the successful design, development, and implementation of your MKIS. The Checklist is a working document that the MKIS manager can apply to each phase of the MKIS development process. Review the Checklist several times before proceeding with Step 1. This should provide you with an overall sense of direction and scope.

DESIGN (STEPS 1 THROUGH 15)

The checklist is divided into three major categories: Design, Development, and Implementation. The Design begins with an interdepartmental data examination (Step 1) and ends with the documentation of the MKIS framework (Step 15). This segment is the critical stage of any MKIS, since at this stage upper-management approval is necessary. During this stage, you lay the actual foundation of your MKIS. If your framework is inconsistent with your original MKIS objectives, you must find out at this stage.

DEVELOPMENT (STEPS 16 THROUGH 25)

During the development stage, the MKIS pieces begin to fall into place. Here is where the actual data banks or data-base elements are identified, formatted, and designed. The entire flow of your MKIS should be documented during the latter part of the development stage.

IMPLEMENTATION (STEPS 26 THROUGH 50)

The implementation stage is where your MKIS design and development become a reality. This stage is subdivided by data bank for ease of interpretation. Your marketing or data-processing analysts may want to proceed in this fashion or use a simultaneous data-bank implementation schedule.

TABLE 12.1
MKIS Checklist and Organizational Action Plan

Design

STEP 1

Examine your interdepartmental-interface requirements. Make a list of the departments or subdepartments in your organization that interrelate with Marketing. What kind of general data or information do they provide you? What kind do you provide them? How does the information exchange take place (meetings, file interface, written reports, computer printouts)? Diagram this information exchange process. (See Figure 3.1 in Chapter 3.)

STEP 2

Who is responsible in your organization for providing information to upper-level marketing management? (Review Figure 1.3 in Chapter 1.)

STEP 3

How would you categorize the stage of your MKIS development? Make a tentative schedule of how you would take the MKIS from its present stage to the level you view as optimal.

STEP 4

Begin to establish an ongoing relationship with your Data Processing and marketing-support departments. Perhaps develop a weekly or monthly work session to discuss your information needs. Make sure that you establish objectives for fulfilling your department's needs.

STEP 5

Identify specific marketing-management objectives in your organization that an MKIS would satisfy. (Review Table 3.2 in Chapter 3.)

STEP 6

Identify the specific tasks needed to achieve each objective. (Refer to Table 11.1 in Chapter 11.)

STEP 7

Establish firm operating control procedures that will influence the direction and timing of each task. (See Table 11.1 in Chapter 11.)

STEP 8

Organize your resource requirements. (See Table 3.2 in Chapter 3.)

STEP 9

Document your resource requirements to systematically influence the "need perception" of key decision-makers within your organization. (See Table 3.2 in Chapter 3.)

STEP 10

Relate your MKIS applications to a formal marketing-benefits package. (See Table 3.2 in Chapter 3.)

STEP 11

Determine your MKIS data-element requirements through the development of your Marketing Philosophy (See Table 3.3 in Chapter 3). Compare your existing data elements (Table 3.4) and your proposed elements (Table 3.5 A-D).

STEP 12

Define the purpose of your MKIS.

STEP 13

Provide a design overview of your MKIS. (See Chapter 4.)

STEP 14

Define your input-output relationships. (See Table 4.1 in Chapter 4.)

STEP 15

Design your MKIS framework. (See Figure 4.1 in Chapter 4.)

Development

STEP 16

Reevaluate your system structure and data linkages. (See Figure 4.2 in Chapter 4.)

STEP 17

Define your data-file elements. (See Table 3.5 A–D in Chapter 3.)

STEP 18

Evaluate your editing procedures, codes, and system-maintenance parameters.

STEP 19

Evaluate Steps 1 through 7 with your data-processing analysts.

STEP 20

Reexamine your interdepartmental-interface requirements. (See Figures 4.3 through 4.8 in Chapter 4.)

STEP 21

Establish department interface workshops.

STEP 22

Document common data utilization. (See Figures 4.9 through 4.14 in Chapter 4.)

STEP 23

Detail the design of your MKIS.

STEP 24

Document your preliminary-report capabilities. (Review Chapter 5.)

STEP 25

Document your MKIS progress to date.

Implementation

Sales-Management Data Base

STEP 26

Obtain or devise the following, and put these items in a common file: A sales-management structure (organization chart) for your organization, a product price list for all products, and a distribution list of all sales reports used in your company.

STEP 27

Develop a list of sales-management reports that you want to include in this module of your MKIS. Include whatever is appropriate from those you are already using. Also use the Marketing Information Questionnaire and your organizational-interface data elements where appropriate.

STEP 28

With your new list, interview all users of the existing or proposed reports and include their comments and recommendations in your list.

STEP 29

Applying the principles described in Chapter 5, design your preliminary sales report specifications.

STEP 30

Review your preliminary report specifications with the appropriate users and obtain whatever form of approval is required.

STEP 31

Armed with your specifications, meet with your Data Processing Department to discuss implementation of the module. Make sure that you, the users, and DP understand each step of the implementation process. Document it in writing with a work schedule.

Product Data Base

STEP 32

Obtain or devise the following, and use the Marketing Information Questionnaire and organizational-interface data elements where applicable:

Product specifications data, product introduction schedules, sales history (minimum 3 years), market segmentation of your products and your competitors', standard costs of production, overhead and variable costs, new production schedules, and product-line forecasts.

STEP 33

Arrange your data in a common file.

STEP 34

Establish product-type report formats that reflect the information in Step 32. (Use whatever is appropriate from existing reports, and add your data elements defined in previous steps.)

STEP 35

Interview all users of existing or proposed reports. (See Step 28.)

STEP 36

Detail your report specifications. (See Step 30.)

STEP 37

Obtain approvals (approval cycle).

Consumer Data Base

STEP 38

Obtain or devise the following, and use the Marketing Information Questionnaire and organizational-interface data elements where appropriate:

Your existing consumer master list or file and your consumer base per geographic segment. Specify consumer profiles, characteristics, product interest, sales history, and service history by geographical location, including demographic data. Structure data in a common file. (See Table 3.5C in Chapter 3.)

STEP 39

Develop a list of consumer reports that reflect the information in Step 38 but which is not currently reflected in your existing consumer reports. (Use whatever is appropriate from existing reports, and add your data elements defined in previous steps.)

STEP 40

Interview all users of existing or proposed reports and include their comments and changes. (See Step 28.)

STEP 41

Design system specifications for your consumer market reports and detail exactly what you want each report to accomplish.

STEP 42

Obtain report approvals where necessary. (See Step 20.)

Market Data Base

STEP 43

Obtain or devise the following, and use the Marketing Information Questionnaire and organizational-interface data elements where appropriate: Geographical (segmentation) demographics, index potential parameters, market-segmentation parameters, competitive data, industry data, and government data.

STEP 44

Arrange these data in a common file. (See Table 3.5D in Chapter 3.)

STEP 45

Develop initial market/marketing reports. (Use existing report data wherever appropriate, and add your data elements defined in previous steps.)

STEP 46

Interview users. (See Step 28.)

STEP 47

Design your final system (report) specifications. (See Step 41.)

STEP 48

Obtain report approvals. (See Step 30.)

STEP 49

Develop and document a work plan for each system (report) specification module (sales, product, consumer, and market).

STEP 50

Electronic data processing (EDP)/Marketing implementation. (See Step 31 and Chapter 11.)

APPENDIX A

Marketing Information Systems Glossary

Italicized terms are defined within the glossary.

BATCH SYSTEM A *system* that accumulates transactions for an application for perhaps a day or a week and then processes them as a group.

COMMUNICATIONS TERMINAL See *Terminal.*

COMPUTER SYSTEM A collective term for the computer *hardware,* the programs of instructions, and the data files to be processed. (A computer system can contain more than one computer, and at the same time, a computer may be a part of more than one computer system.) See *EDP system.*

CONSUMER PROFILE An organized set of buying preferences and characteristics of a buyer or buyer group as applied to a specific product or service.

CONSUMER TARGET The potential customer (or group of potential customers) to which a specific marketing or sales effort is directed.

CPU See *Processor.*

DATA BASE The data files used by a *computer system* that make up a body of information describing company operations.

DATA-BASE MANAGEMENT SYSTEM A set of *programs* and manual procedures by which a body of information is organized into machine-readable *files* of uniform and compatible structure, from which reports and interactive inquiry/responses can be prepared.

DATA ELEMENT A specific piece of information contained within a *data record.*

DATA RECORD A group of *data elements* stored together, which pertain to a common source or group.

DEMOGRAPHICS The characteristics of the market, including such variables as age, sex, family size, income, occupation, education, family, religion, nationality, and social class.

DIRECT MAIL A communications program to transmit messages using a mail service to research-selected individuals (letters, surveys, technical memos, product flyers).

DISK STORAGE A form of *random-access storage* where the *storage medium* consists of one or more disks (like phonograph records) magnetically coated.

DRUM STORAGE A form of *random-access storage* where the storage is magnetically contained on the cylindrical surface of a drum.

EDP (ELECTRONIC DATA PROCESSING) The use of electronic computers for the automatic manipulation of data. Also the data-processing group in an organization.

EDP SYSTEM A synonym for *computer system*. The computer *hardware* plus *programs* and *data bases*.

FILE Any collection of records holding similar data or transactions that are stored together to permit systematic access and modification.

FILE LAYOUT The manner in which the *data elements* are organized in a *file*.

FLOPPY DISK Also called a diskette. A small disk of thin, plastic-based magnetic oxide, sealed in a plastic envelope, used in key-entry equipment and as *mass storage* for most mini- and micro-computers.

FORECASTING A *system* for predicting the sales of a product or service in a future time period(s).

GEOGRAPHICS The characteristics of the market that relate to the location (nation, state, city) of the consumer.

GRAPHICS The visual presentation of data or information in chart or table format, often multicolor.

HARDWARE Collective term for all the equipment in a *computer system:* the *processor,* main memory core, tape units, *disks* and *drums,* and all input-output devices.

INTERFACE The relationship between two or more groups (people, data, systems, or machines).

LIFE CYCLE The stages of a product/service life, including development, introduction, growth, maturity, and decline.

MANAGEMENT INFORMATION SYSTEM (MIS) A *computer system* designed primarily to produce analyses of the data files to support managerial decision-making rather than simply to undertake file-updating functions and transaction reporting.

MARKETING CONCEPT The orientation that the primary goal of the organization is to understand consumer needs and values and to develop products/services for those specific markets.

MARKETING MIX The design of explicit variables (price, promotion, packaging) to alter or affect the ultimate consumer's purchase response.

MARKET POTENTIAL The maximum *market share* (service or product, in dollars or units) of a specific consumer group, market area, or industry.

MARKET SEGMENTATION An identified position of the external environment consisting of consumers who maintain different needs, purchasing practices, perceptions, values, and responses.

MARKET SHARE A company's actual unit or dollar sales divided by the total market estimate (units or dollars).

MASS STORAGE A general term for all external *random-access storage* devices: disk, drum and disk-pack equipment, or data cells.

MEMORY A general term for the various methods of storing data in a form accessible to the *processor.* Memory includes (1) the very limited memory within the *processor* itself, (2) the memory section of the computer, which holds the program and those data currently being processed, and (3) the *storage devices* (tapes or *random-access storage*) that provide relatively long-term memory for the *system.*

MERGE To combine two or more *files* that are organized the same way into a single file using the same sequence as the original files.

MICRO-COMPUTER Any of a class of small, low-cost *computer systems,* primarily of interest to the business manager who wants to control his own data analyses.

MINI-COMPUTER Any of a class of small, low-cost *computer systems* originally developed for the small scientific user but now finding important applications in small business and branch offices of larger firms, suitable for many forms of low-volume business *EDP.*

MIS Management Information System.

MKIS Marketing Information System.

MODULE A section of an overall *data base;* i.e., consumer analysis module.

MODEL A representation of a real-world situation developed from the raw data processed by the computer. Management decisions are tried on the model to see what effects they have on operations before they are implemented in the company itself.

ON LINE A device attached to or under control of the computer itself that allows the user to interact directly with the computer. A *system* that involves one or more on-line devices.

PERIPHERAL DEVICE Any piece of *hardware* that is part of the *computer system* but is not directly connected to the central *processor.*

PROCESSOR (CPU OR CENTRAL PROCESSING UNIT) That part of the computer containing the electronic circuitry, by means of which the computer's arithmetic and logical functions are performed.

PRODUCT CONSISTENCY The manner in which products relate to one another.

PRODUCT DEPTH The average number of items offered by a company or organization within each product line.

PRODUCT POSITIONING The placement of a product in the marketplace with respect to competitive products and consumer preferences.

PRODUCT SEGMENTATION The classification of products by their characteristics (size, price, utility).

PRODUCT WIDTH The number of product lines within a company or organization.

PROGRAM A detailed sequence of commands or instructions that the computer obeys in performing any data-processing operation.

RANDOM-ACCESS STORAGE Any *storage medium* from which the computer can extract data in any desired sequence, usually *disk* or *drum storage*.

REAL TIME A *computer system* that processes transactions as they occur (as opposed to processing a batch at a time).

RECORD See *Data Record*.

SOFTWARE All programs and operating instructions for the *EDP system*.

SORT Organizing the records of a *file* in the sequential order specified by a sort key associated with each record. Also the operation of dividing a file into two or more ordered or partially ordered files before merging (called a partial or initial sort).

STORAGE DEVICE The piece of *hardware* that holds the *storage medium;* for example, a tape handler.

STORAGE MEDIUM The actual material (such as magnetic tape or disk) on which data are recorded and from which they are read by a *storage device*.

SYSTEM An organized effort to reach a goal, made up of procedures and tools (and usually people), each of which has an assigned task or job. Through the system flow raw materials to which the procedures and tools are applied. For example, in an *EDP system:*

Procedure = Program
Raw materials = Data
Tools = Computer hardware

SYSTEM ANALYSIS AND DESIGN The study of the inputs, outputs, operations, and purposes of existing systems to find an equivalent way to do the same thing using more efficient methods, equipment, and the like. Also the analysis of unsolved problems to develop methods for solving them.

TAPE STORAGE A form of serial-access *mass storage* in which the *storage medium* is magnetic material on plastic tape.

TERMINAL A typewriter-like device that permits a computer and a user to communicate interactively. A teletype or similar device.

TEST MARKETING A program for introducing a specific product/service to a control group of consumers.

TIME SHARING A technique that permits a number of users to perform on-line transactions with individual programs in a single large machine simultaneously.

UPDATE An operation combining merging and selecting that results in new records being added to a *file* and existing records replaced or deleted as necessary, without disturbing the overall file structure.

APPENDIX B

Business Research and Information Guide

State Agencies

Most organizations within a state's jurisdiction must file a vast amount of business information, such as financial statements, annual report statistics, and inspection reports. Most states will comply with the public's request to analyze such data or statistics. The following state agency titles are located in every state capital. The best sources for business information have an asterisk after the agency title.

STATE INFORMATION AGENCIES

1. *Division of Banking*
   Data and/or statistics from state-chartered banks. Semi-annual and quarterly reports, corporate change notices, new branch locations, total assets and deposits, fiduciary statements and relocations are available upon request.

2. *Department of Commerce**
   State, county, city and SMSA market demographics, psychographics and statistics. This department will also provide directories of manufacturers in the state, listed by product and SIC code.

3. *Department of Consumer Services*
   Data on the records of complaints concerning products, services or companies. Litigation records are available upon settlement closings.

4. *Department/Division of Economic Development**
   An extension of the Commerce Department; provides state and market statistics in the hope of enticing industrial development. State and county demographics and market statistics.

5. *Department of Environmental Regulation*
   Data and/or statistics regarding state air pollution standard violations, development and control of toxic substances, test protocols for chemical handling, and water, air, and food inspection reports.

6. *Department of Food and Drugs*
Regulates and documents information regarding pharmaceuticals, cosmetics, food production, processing, packing, labeling and distribution procedures. Inspection and investigation reports are available. Product registration forms are available but product trade secrets are confidential.

7. *Department of Insurance*
Insurance company financial reports. Statements include both the balance sheet and profit and loss data. Detail includes policy and rate classifications, investigation records and articles of incorporation.

8. *Division of Labor/Industrial Relations*
Data on employment and unemployment levels by occupation, wage and safety violations records, labor statistics and trends by industry; decisions on arbitration regarding labor laws.

9. *Department of Occupational Regulations*
Data recording the education levels and other qualifications of members of professions and certain business persons. Information relative to doctors, pharmacists, insurance agents and real estate brokers is available. Each department should maintain a complaint file concerning licensed professionals in the state.

10. *Division of Purchasing*
Reveals records of state and local contracts: bids, specifications and service requirements. Contractor applications and information are also available.

11. *Secretary of State—Division of Corporations*
Details of each organization's articles of incorporation. Such detail as merger notices, officers, consolidation notices, and capitalization data are available. Annual reports are generally required by each state and are the source of each corporation's capitalization data.

12. *Division of Securities**
An excellent source for corporate information regarding stock offering prospectuses made within the state.

13. *Bureau/Division of Workman's Compensation*
Data on organizational inspections, injury and accident violations and health and safety penalties.

For Further Information:

State Information Book
Potomac Books, Inc.
P.O. Box 40604
Palisades Station
Washington, D.C. 20016

The Book of the States
Council of State Governments
Iron Works Pike
Lexington, KY 40511

Federal Agencies

The federal agencies listed are only a small portion of the number of information offices, but they constitute a large part of the available data and statistical offerings.

1. Securities and Exchange Commission
Washington, D.C. 20549
(202) 523-5360

Form 8-A	Securities register
Form 8-B	Securities successor issue register
Form N8-A	Investment company register
Form X17-A-5	Securities brokers financial and operating data
Form N-8B-1	Management investment company register
Form BD	Securities broker registration
Schedule 13D	Register of any individual or company with greater than five percent of any company's securities
Schedule 14D-1	Register of tender offerings

Schedule 14D	Register of tender offerings
Form 6K	Foreign company securities register
Form 8K	Organizational change register as it pertains to each company
Form 10K	Annual report filings
Form N5	Small business management register
Form N-5R	Small business management annual report filings
Form N-1R	Management investment companies annual report
Form 10Q	Quarterly report filings
Form N-1Q	Quarterly report filings by management investment companies

2. Department of Commerce
   Bureau of Economic Analysis
   Washington, D.C. 20230
   Consumer demographics, economic indicators.
3. Department of Commerce
   Bureau of the Census
   Washington, D.C. 20233
   State, county, SMSA (Standard Metropolitan Statistical Area) data and demographics, housing data.
4. Superintendent of Documents
   U.S. Department of Commerce
   Bureau of the Census
   U.S. Government Printing Office
   Washington, D.C. 20402
   Market statistics at both state and federal levels.
5. Department of Commerce
   Information Service Division
   Bureau of Economic Analysis

Washington, D.C. 20230
Census data relative to consumer segmentation; statistics.

6. Market Share Reports
Department of Commerce
Industry and Trade Administration
Bureau of Trade Regulation
Washington, D.C. 20230
Product comparisons.
7. Internal Revenue Service
Freedom of Information Room
111 Constitution Avenue
Washington, D.C. 20224
(202) 566-3770
Tax-return profiles.
8. Department of Agriculture
Economic Statistics and Cooperative Service
14th and Independence Avenue, S.W.
Room 1419S
Washington, D.C. 20250
(202) 447-4611
Agriculture statistics.
9. Civil Aeronautics Board
1825 Connecticut Avenue, N.W.
Room 719
Washington, D.C. 20415
(202) 632-4431
Carrier statistics.
10. Patent and Trademark Office
Department of Commerce
Room 11C12, CP3 Crystal Plaza
Arlington, Virginia
Washington, D.C. 20231
(703) 557-3525
Complete trademark and patent information.

11. Consumer Product Safety Commission
111 18th Street, N.W.
Suite 300
Washington, D.C. 20207
(202) 634-7700
Regulatory activity data, including recalls.
12. Federal Home Loan Bank Board
1700 G. Street, N.W.
Washington, D.C. 20552
(202) 377-6463
Bank and savings and loan statistics.
13. Federal Reserve System
20th Street and Constitution Avenue, N.W.
Room B1122
Washington, D.C. 20551
Bank and savings and loan statistics.
14. Department of Health, Education, and Welfare
Hubert H. Humphrey Building
200 Independence Avenue, S.W.
Room 1187
Washington, D.C. 20201
(202) 472-7453
From education statistics to social-security statistics.
15. Department of Labor
200 Constitution Avenue, N.W.
Room S2002
Washington, D.C. 20210
(202) 523-7675
Labor statistics.
16. National Center for Health Statistics
Department of Health, Education, and Welfare
3700 East-West Highway
Hyattsville, MD 20782
(301) 436-8500

General health and vital statistics concerning hospitals, births, nursing homes.

17. Food and Drug Administration
    Department of Health, Education, and Welfare
    5600 Fishers Lane
    Room 4-65
    Rockville, MD 20857
    (301) 443-1753
    Food and drug contents, litigation records.
18. Department of Commerce
    Bureau of the Census
    Federal Office Building No. 3
    Room 2089
    Suitland, MD 20233
    (301) 763-7273
    Industry statistics.

Information Services

For directories of the total information services with quick research capabilities available today, consult:

1. Gale Research Company
   Encyclopedia of Information
   Systems and Services
   Book Tower
   Detroit, MI 48226
   (313) 961-2242
2. Information Alternative
   The Directory of Fee-Based Information Services
   Post Office Box 657
   Woodstock, NY 12498

Some of the more well-known information services are:

1. Chase World Information Corporation
   One World Trade Center
   Suite 4627
   New York, NY 10048
   (212) 552-3378
2. Cordura Publications, Inc.
   1200 Prospect Street
   Suite 460
   La Jolla, CA 92037
   (714) 459-9751
3. Cuadra Associates, Inc.
   1523 Sixth Street, Suite 12
   Santa Monica, CA 90401
   (213) 451-0644
4. Economic Information Systems, Inc.
   9 East 41st Street
   New York, NY 10017
   (212) 697-6080
5. FIND/SVP
   500 Fifth Avenue
   New York, NY 10036
   (212) 354-2424
6. FOI Services, Inc.
   12315 Wilkens Avenue
   Rockville, MD 20853
   (301) 881-0410
7. Frost and Sullivan, Inc.
   106 Fulton Street
   New York, NY 10038
   (212) 233-1080
8. INFORM
   Minneapolis Public Library and Information Center
   300 Nicollet Mall

Minneapolis, MN 55401
(612) 372-6636

9. Information for Business
8 West 40th Street
New York, NY 10018
(212) 840-1220
10. Packaged Facts, Inc.
274 Madison Avenue
New York, NY 10016
(212) 532-5523
11. Washington Researchers
918 16th Street, N.W.
Washington, D.C. 20006
(202) 828-4800
12. World Trade Library and Business Information
Center of Golden Gate University
One Embarcadero Center
Suite 216
San Francisco, CA 94111
(415) 391-7800

Data-Base Services

For a more detailed directory of on-line data-base service organizations, contact:

Cuadra Associates, Inc.
1523 Sixth Street
Suite 12
Santa Monica, CA 90401
(213) 451-0644

One-year subscription: $60.00.

Also refer to Table 11.6, Fee-Based Information Retrieval Services.

Miscellaneous Data Sources

The following are miscellaneous external data sources of information for system enhancement and marketing application and analysis.

1. Marketing Development 402 Border Road Concord, MA 01742	New Product Introductions on New York Stock Exchange.
2. Marketing Economics Institute 441 Lexington Avenue New York, NY 10017	*Marketing Statistics and Strategy* (book), $15.50. *Industrial Market Directory*, $80.00
3. Marketing Science Institute 14 Story Street Cambridge, MA 02138	*Research Activities Newsletter*, free.
4. Market Chronicle W. B. Dana Company 25 Park Place New York, NY 10017	Newspaper (stock analysis), $20.00
5. Marketing for Sales Executives Research Institute of America, Inc. 589 Fifth Avenue New York, NY 10017	Newsletter for high-level management, $36.00/year.
6. Marketing Information Guide Hoke Communications, Inc. 224 Seventh Street Garden City, New York 11535	Book listings, article references, marketing information (index by subject/geographical area), $12.00/year.
7. Marketing Letter Alexander Hamilton Institute 605 Third Avenue New York, NY 10016	Marketing trends, $45.00/year.
8. American Marketing Association 222 South Riverside Plaza Chicago, IL 60606	*Marketing News*, $5.00/year.

9. Marketing Times
Sales and Marketing Executives International, Inc.
380 Lexington Avenue
New York, NY 10017

New Product Research Products Performance and Evaluation, $10.00/year.

10. Standard Rate & Data Service, Inc.
5201 Old Orchard Road
Skokie, IL 60076

Media Rates, SMSA Distribution, $13.00/year.

11. New York Stock Exchange (N.Y.S.E.) Fact Book
New York Stock Exchange
11 Wall Street, New York, NY 10005

Statistics, market activity, shares, other data on all N.Y.S.E. members.

12. Potentials in Marketing
Lakewood Publication, Inc.
732 Hennepin Avenue
Minneapolis, MN 55403

New Product Introductions and Services, $10.00/year.

13. Predi-Briefs
Predicasts, Inc.
200 University Circle
Research Center
11001 Cedar Avenue
Cleveland, OH 44106
(on-line information service is available)

Abstract data of products, markets. Information is culled from journals, papers, government statistics, reports, $770.00/year.

14. Sales and Marketing Management, Inc.
633 Third Avenue
New York, NY 10017

Articles on marketing, selling, and distribution, $22.00/year.

15. Sales and Marketing Management
Survey of Buying Power
Ken Reiss Publishing
633 Third Avenue
New York, NY 10017

Demographics, sales, household data breakouts, $30.00.

16. Standard Corporation Records
Standard & Poor Corp.
345 Hudson Street
New York, NY 10014

Financial data for 5,600 corporations, $512.00/year.

17. Statistics—America Gale Research Company Book Tower Detroit, MI 48226	Market Research Sources, Business Information Sources, Special Library Services
18. Weekly Government Abstracts Computers, Control and Information (also: library and information sciences) U.S. Department of Commerce National Technical Information Service 5285 Port Royal Road Springfield, VA 22161	Newsletter on computers, system information, information research on hardware and software, $45.00/year. Reports on systems and marketing, $30.00/year.
19. Business International (BI) Data Business International Corporation 1 Dag Hammarskjold Plaza New York, NY 10017	On-line computer information service of economic, demographic, and labor data for more than 70 countries, $480.00/year.
20. American Market Research Reports Frost and Sullivan, Inc. 106 Fulton Street New York, NY 10038	Market research trends for market segments analysis for all industries, $600.00-$1,000.00/each.
21. University of Florida College of Business Administration Bureau of Economics and Business Research 221 Matherly Hall Gainesville, FL 32611	Statistical abstracts (also available through most other state universities).
22. U.S. Department of Commerce Bureau of Economic Analysis Washington, D.C. 20230	Consumer-type demographics, government indicators.
23. United Nations Publications Room LX 2300 New York, NY 10017	Statistics for international comparisons and study.

24. Where to Find Business Information
The Hudson Group, Inc.
Pleasantville, NY 10570

25. Business Services and Information
Guide to the Federal Government
Management Information Exchange, Inc.
Philadelphia, PA 19144

26. County and City Data Book — Approximately $75.00.
U.S. Department of Commerce
Bureau of the Census
File Reference No. CCDB-809
Washington, D.C. 20233
Attn: Data Services Division

BIBLIOGRAPHY

Articles

Assmus, Gert. "Evaluating Changes in the Marketing Information System." *European Journal of Marketing,* vol. 11, no. 4. 1977.

Axelrod, Joel N. "14 Rules for Building an MIS." *Journal of Advertising Research.* June 1970.

Berenson, Conrad. "Marketing Information Systems." *Journal of Marketing.* October 1969.

Blumenthal, Marcia. "Processing Services Now a Whole New Ball Game." *Computerworld.* December 1, 1980. Pp. 1, 10–11.

Boone, Louis. "A Proposed Cure for the Information Explosion." *Business Horizons.* December 1972.

Borts, Maurice. "How to Prepare a Sales Statistics Report." *Canadian Business.* January 1975.

Brandes, Ove. "Management Processes in Industrial Marketing, Current Empirical Studies." *Management International Review,* vol. 12, nos. 4–5. 1972.

Cox, D. F., and R. E. Good. "How to Build an MIS." *Harvard Business Review.* May-June 1967.

Derman, Irwin H. "Do You 'Mis' Understand?" *Business Horizons.* October 1972.

Dickson, W., and J. K. Simmons. "The Behavioral Side of MIS." *Business Horizons.* August 1970.

Doppett, Neil. "Down-to-Earth Marketing Information Systems." *Management Advisor.* September/October 1971.

——. "Marketing Info Systems' Use Shows Progress." *Marketing News.* March 23, 1979.

Feder, Richard A. "How to Measure Marketing Performance." *Harvard Business Review.* May-June 1965.

Ferguson, David M. "What Information Does Marketing Need?" *Canadian Chartered Accountant.* June 1966.

Gibson, Lawrence D., and Charles S. Mayer. "An Evolutionary Approach to Marketing Information Systems." *Journal of Marketing.* April 1973.

Harpole, George P. "A Marketing Information System for the Wood-Products Manufacturer." *Forest Products Journal.* November 1973.

Herson, Richard M. "How to Make Your MIS Work." *Marketing Communications.* December 1971.

Kallina, Carl. "Data Base Approach Solves Informational Problem." *Marketing Plan.* March 23, 1979.

Kotler, Philip. "The Future of the Computer in Marketing." *Journal of Marketing.* January 1970.

_____. "From Sales Obsession to Marketing Effectiveness." *Harvard Business Review.* November-December 1977.

Little, John D. "The Marvelous Marketing Machine." *The Wharton Magazine.* Fall 1979.

McDermott, Dennis R. "A Service Organization's Marketing Information System." *Industrial Marketing Management.* June 1978.

Montgomery, David B. "The Outlook for MIS." *Journal of Marketing Research.* June 1973.

_____, and Glenn L. Urban. "Marketing Decision-Information Systems: An Emerging View." *Journal of Marketing Research.* May 1970.

Piercy, Nigel. "Behavioral Constraints on Marketing Information Systems." *European Journal of Marketing,* vol. 13, no. 8. 1979.

Ranard, Elliot D. "Use of Input-Output Concepts in Forecasting." *Journal of Marketing Research.* February 1972.

Rayburn, L. Gayle. "Accounting Tools in the Analysis and Control of Marketing Performance." *Industrial Marketing Management,* vol. 6, no. 3. 1977.

Robertson, Dan H. "Sales Force Feedback on Competitors' Activities." *Journal of Marketing.* April 1974.

Schewe, Charles D. "Management Information Systems in Marketing: A Promise Not Yet Realized." *Management Informatics,* vol. 3, no. 5. Published by the International Federation for Information Processing. 1974.

_____. "Traditional Marketing Techniques Can Improve Acceptance of MIS." *Marketing News.* November 16, 1979.

——, and William R. Dillion."Marketing Information System Utilizations: An Application of Self-Concept Theory." *Journal of Business Research.* January 1978.

Sparks, Jack D. "Taming of the 'Paper Elephant' in Marketing Information Systems." *Journal of Marketing.* July 1976.

Stephens, H. Virgil. "A Profit-Oriented Marketing Information System." *Management Accounting.* August 1974.

Tipgos, Manuel A. "Structuring a Management Information System for Strategic Planning." *Managerial Planning.* January-February 1975.

Zani, William M. "A Blueprint for MIS." *Harvard Business Review.* November-December 1970.

Books

Bellenger, Danny N., and Barnett A. Greenberg. *Marketing Research: A Management Information Approach.* Homewood, Ill.: Richard D. Irwin, 1978.

Buzzell, Robert D., Donald Cox, and Rex V. Brown. *Marketing Research and Information Systems: Text and Cases.* New York: McGraw Hill, 1969.

Chase, Cochrane, and Kenneth L. Barasch. *Marketing Problem Solver,* 2nd ed. Radnor, Pa.: Chilton Book Company, 1977.

Dearden, John. *Computers in Business Management.* Chicago: Dow Jones-Irwin, 1966.

Hugo, I. St. J. *Marketing and the Computer.* Oxford: Pergamon Press, 1967.

Jackson, Donald W., Lonnie Ostrom, and Charles H. Smith. *Marketing Profitability Analysis: An Annotated Bibliography.* Chicago: American Marketing Association, 1977.

King, William R. *Marketing Management Information Systems.* New York: Van Nostrand Reinhold, 1977.

——. *Quantitative Analysis for Marketing Management.* New York: McGraw Hill, 1967.

Kotler, Philip. *Marketing Management: Analysis, Planning, and Control,* 3rd ed. Englewood Cliffs, N.J.: Prentice-Hall, 1976.

Lewis, Richard. *A Logistical Information System for Marketing Analysis.* Cincinnati: Southwestern Publishing, 1970.

Maslow, Abraham H. *Motivation and Personality*. New York: Harper & Row, 1954.

Morrisey, George L. *Management by Objectives and Results for Business and Industry*. Reading, Mass.: Addison-Wesley, 1977.

Pokempner, Stanley J. *Information Systems for Sales and Marketing Management*. New York: Conference Board, 1973.

Sevin, Charles H. *Marketing and the Computer*. Englewood Cliffs, N.J.: Prentice-Hall, 1963.

Schoner, Bertram, and Kenneth P. Uhl. *Marketing Research: Information Systems and Decision Making*, 2nd ed. New York: John Wiley and Sons, 1975.

Simon, Sanford R. *Managing Marketing Profitability*. New York: American Management Association, 1969.

Staudt, Thomas A., D. A. Taylor, and D. J. Bowersox. *A Managerial Introduction to Marketing*, 3rd ed. Englewood Cliffs, N.J.: Prentice-Hall, 1976.

INDEX